IF I'M A CHRISTIAN,
WHY
AM I DEPRESSED?

Finding Meaning and Hope in the Dark Valley
One Man's Journey

ROBERT B. SOMERVILLE

Edited by Xulon Press
Cover Design by: CMC Design-Carlyle M. Crawford, Santa Clarita, CA.

Printed in the United States of America

ISBN 9781498407779

www.xulonpress.com

S ome people say that Christians should never be depressed. I take issue with that, being a quadriplegic who has battled cancer and struggles daily with pain. I love my Savior, am passionate about His Gospel, and enjoy the ministry He has given me. But that does not exclude me from occasionally stumbling into the miry pit of dark emotions. This is why I heartily support the message in this exceptional book. My friend Robert Somerville speaks not only as a seasoned and authoritative Bible scholar, but out of the depths of his own experience. Mark my words—the book you hold in your hands will provide comfort and compassionate insight, as well as practical steps to help you rise above the dark, grim cloud of depression. I enthusiastically endorse *If I'm A Christian, Why Am I Depressed?* and recommend it to pastors, families, leaders, and Christian counselors!

Joni Eareckson Tada, Director of Joni and Friends International Disability Center, speaker and author of many books to guide and comfort the sufferer

There is no better guide for a depressed person than someone who has been through that darkness, someone who is very wise, who is fighting for you, and who speaks with love. With this in mind, Bob is the ideal guide. And then to hear from his wife Mary—who loved him while he was barely recognizable as the man she married—is an added gift.

Dr. Ed Welch, Faculty at CCEF and author of the books, *Depression: Looking Up from the Stubborn Darkness* and *Depression: The Way Up When You Are Down* (Resources for Changing Lives) and many other counseling books

My friend, Bob Somerville, has written an insightful and important book on depression. This isn't simply a book that addresses the topic with biblical or clinical precision (although it does that), it is a book written from the inside out ... a book birthed out of personal suffering and through that darkness finding himself being met by the Savior who understands suffering and pain better than any of us. His wife (and my good friend), Mary's contribution is invaluable. I heartily recommend it.

Elyse Fitzpatrick, counselor, speaker and author of many Gospel centered books

Bob's real-life approach to depression sets it apart and makes this book especially valuable and timely. I have seen a lot of people dealing with depression in my many years of counseling with enormous consequences. This book will greatly benefit those going through this dark valley as it comes at it from a first-person vantage point. The suggested Response (homework) with each chapter is excellent in helping to apply the valuable biblically based instruction. Carol and I also appreciate the way that we see how Mary was such a helper during this very difficult time. Thanks for being vulnerable and writing this book!

Dr. Wayne Mack, pastor, professor, lecturer and author of *Out of the Blues* and *It's Not Fair* that are also books on depression and a host of other books on Biblical counseling

No one living in today's world is untouched by the subject of depression—someone, somewhere. This book helps the sufferer and those who walk beside them by never sidestepping the reality of our humanness and despair as we live in a fallen world. Dr. Somerville knows the subject from the objective, helping side of a counselor. He also shares the reality of living through his own "dark night of the soul." Truthful, unvarnished, experiential, always practical, he circles around back to the everlasting, living Word of God which is our only real help. In our common suffering, God *is faithful ... to provide a way of escape, that you may be able to bear it* (1 Cor. 10:13).

Dr. Luis Palau, international evangelist and author

I have read several books on depression, some of which have been helpful. What makes this book stand out from all of the others is that the author transparently, humbly, and helpfully shares his own story of battling deep depression on every page. He offers practical, compassionate, gospel-centered, and biblically based counsel for those who battle with depression. He deals wisely with both spiritual and physical issues, including the choice to take medications. He gleans some of the best insights both from Scripture and interacts with many of the most important Christian books on this topic. One of the most effective chapters is written by his wife who speaks to those trying to care for a depressed person. He also includes testimonies from others who have, by God's grace, endured their own seasons of depression. He and I reach a common conclusion. Perhaps the Lord allowed him and his wife to go through this so that the rest of us can benefit from their story (Romans 8:28). They remind us, through their experience and study, that our trials can be used of God to teach us to treasure Christ all the more, as He leads us through the valley of the shadow of death.

> Dr. Jim Newheiser, pastor, counselor, author, Director of the Institute for Biblical Counseling and Discipleship of San Diego, CA.

I have a new, favorite book to give to people struggling with depression, and you are holding it in your hands. My friend, Bob Somerville, knows what it is to depend on the grace of Jesus when sorrow overwhelms your body and soul. His personal experience with depression combined with his profound knowledge of Scripture makes him a uniquely gifted guide for hurting people. In his book he helps those struggling with depression to move towards hope and joy using the resources in God's Word. If you or someone you love is dealing with the bitter pain of despair then I am praying for you to read this book.

> Dr. Heath Lambert, Executive Director Association of Certified Biblical Counselors

I can't wait to see how God will use this book in many lives, just as He has already used the author greatly in my life and the life of my family and church. Everyone that learns to endure depression in this kind of God-centered, Scripture-saturated way will join me in giving thanks for Bob's faithful example and legacy.

Dr. Timothy W. Cantrell, missionary pastor/teacher in South Africa

Misery loves company, but something infinitely better is real, biblical encouragement coming from someone who has endured a similar trial and emerged intact. The apostle Paul says God "comforts us in all our affliction, so that we may be able to comfort those who are in any affliction, with the comfort with which we ourselves are comforted by God" (2 Corinthians 1:4).

Bob Somerville has withstood the horrible agonies of profound depression, and he testifies that God's healing comfort is the only sure and effectual anchor for anyone adrift in those troubled waters. Bob is better qualified than anyone I know to deal with this difficult yet crucial subject. He writes with both keen biblical insight and tender empathy. I'm certain this volume will be helpful--not only for those who struggle with depression, but also for anyone trying to help a disconsolate friend or loved one.

Dr. John MacArthur, pastor/teacher Grace Community Church,
President The Master's College and Seminary,
bible teacher on Grace to You

Contents

Thank You!

My heart is full to overflowing with gratitude for all those who were the means that the Lord used to help see me through the dark valley that I will describe in this book. Heartfelt thanks to my colleagues at the college who stood with me and gave me needed counsel and support along with all the friends who prayed including my wonderful students.

My gratitude to my caring pastor Steve Jackson, elders, and church family who came alongside us with many expressions of their love. A special thanks to one elder, David Gabriel, who was there time and again with the special counsel needed at that time.

So much appreciation to my family for their gracious help in countless ways in seeing me through. Thanks to my brother Jim and sister Mary Lou who came across the country to be with me. Thanks to our children who stood with me when they hardly knew me, with many expressions of their love—Dan and Tiffany locally and Michelle from South Africa with the encouragement of her husband Tim and their church family.

Many thanks to our daughter, Michelle Cantrell for putting her editing skills to work in helping me write this book along with my wife Mary. I'm so very grateful.

How can I say thanks enough to my Heavenly Father for the gift of my beloved wife? Her steadfast love and patience has been there for me throughout all of our marriage but in this deep valley of the despair of my soul she was there with love, patience and wise counsel, moment by moment, day in and day out. I rise up and bless her as a woman who fears our Lord, walks in His love, and demonstrates it to all around her. Thank you, my love!

And with my whole heart, I thank God, whose faithful and steadfast love saw me through this dark place and brought me back into the sunshine of seeing His face!

Introduction

I am endeavoring in this book to write about what I experienced and what I learned in the one foray into deep depression through which I journeyed. I pray that I will never have to pass that way again! It was a dreadful experience, some of which is hard to remember because I was so far out of it so as not to have a clear recollection of it. Many other parts are hard to remember because it is humbling to think of the wildness and incoherence of my thoughts and doubts. The chapter titles are the questions that I wrestled with.

When C.S. Lewis set out to write his autobiography *Surprised by Joy* he said "I have been emboldened to write of it because I notice that a man seldom mentions what he had supposed to be his own most idiosyncratic sensations without receiving from at least one (often more) of those present the reply, 'What! Have *you* felt that too? I always thought I was the only one.'"[1] How encouraging it is for those struggling with faith to read how Lewis was dragged by God over the threshold of faith, kicking and screaming and went on to inspire faith in millions! Likewise, each time I speak on the subject of depression and share some of my most humbling and even reviling thoughts that went through my mind in the depths of the depression, I have at least one (often more) come to me following the session and state "I have had those same thoughts! I know how you felt because I have been there! I have never shared my thoughts with anyone else because I didn't think anyone would understand, and I believed I would be condemned!"

Remember that you are not alone in your struggle against depression. Statistics indicate that this year alone, millions of Americans will suffer mild to severe depression. With that in mind I have shared the stories of others whom God has brought across our path, who have come out on the other side or who are still in the battle with depression. Read their stories and be encouraged! They are warriors who have also learned to put their hope in our faithful God. May their stories give you courage to take heart and fight on!

I trust that these subjective thoughts on the subject of my depression and the objective teachings from the Word of God which are presented will encourage you to trust in the God who is there and who can truly surprise us by the joy of the Gospel. In the midst of depression, we may not have the feelings of joy, but it is there in seed form because of the knowledge that He loves us and will never leave us or forsake us. That is one objective fact of the universe.

In seeking to write this account I have become convinced that my words are very feeble in their ability to express the anguish that my soul experienced and really inadequate to express the complete satisfaction for the soul that can be found in Jesus. It is my hope that you will continue to read and that God the Holy Spirit would take this account of what my wife and I went through in our dark valley of depression and encourage you in your faith in our altogether faithful God and His sufficient Word. It is here that we will find hope!

Robert B. Somerville

The Valley of Vision

Lord, High and Holy, Meek and Lowly,
Thou hast brought me to the valley of vision,
 Where I live in the depths but see thee in the heights;
 Hemmed in by mountains of sin, I behold thy glory.

Let me learn by paradox
 That the way down is the way up,
 That to be low is to be high,
 That the broken heart is the healed heart,
 That the contrite spirit is the rejoicing spirit,
 That the repenting soul is the victorious soul,
 That to have nothing is to possess all,
 That to bear the cross is to wear the crown,
 That to give is to receive,
 That the valley is the place of vision.
Lord in the daytime, stars can be seen from deepest wells,
 And the deeper the wells the brighter thy stars shine;
Let me find thy light in my darkness,
  Thy life in my death,
  Thy joy in my sorrow,
  Thy grace in my sin,
  Thy riches in my poverty,
  Thy glory in my valley.

—— ❧ CHAPTER 1 ❧ ——

The Story of My Depression

Peace has been stripped away, and I have forgotten what
prosperity is. I cry out, "My splendor is gone! Everything I
had hoped for from the Lord is lost!"
The thought of my suffering and homelessness is bitter
beyond words.
I will never forget this awful time, as I grieve over my loss.
Yet I still dare to hope when I remember this: The faithful
love of the Lord never ends!
His mercies never cease. Great is his faithfulness; his mercies begin afresh each morning. I say to myself, "The Lord
is my inheritance; therefore, I will hope in him!
(Lamentations 3:17-24 NLT)

*I*f you have picked up this book it is very probable that you, one
of your family members, or a friend of yours is going through
the stubborn darkness of the soul known as depression. My heart
goes out to you. I have experienced those horrors up close. The pain
of a major depression may be as great a malady as we are called to
go through in this life.

How well I remember sitting in the emergency room on the
morning of August 12, 2009, wondering if I would be committed
to a psychiatric ward. It seemed that morning that I had literally
lost my mind. I was thinking wild, bizarre, and crazy thoughts,
including those of suicide, and I could not sit still. I had experienced

yet another sleepless night. But how did I get here? Allow me to tell you my story.

In my role as pastor-teacher, for thirty-five years I had been able to bring hope to those in distress through the sustaining power of God's Word. Now, as a teacher of biblical counseling in a Christian college, I understood and taught that God's Word, and specifically, God the Father and the *Incarnate Word, Jesus,* are sufficient to sustain and guide individuals through *every* hardship they might face— including depression. But *all* of that was being put to the test through the crucible of experience when I awoke one morning to be confronted by my wife.

It was Mary's birthday when she said to me, "I think you're in depression." I thought, *I couldn't be in depression! I'm a counselor who has helped dozens of people in depression! No, that's not something I'll ever deal with.* But I realized that I needed to check it out, so I began reading the book *Depression: A Stubborn Darkness* written by Dr. Edward Welch. When I got to chapter 2, I said, "This is me and I'm depressed! How did I get here?" Of course I read every word of the book (which we had on our shelf and had read before), but now with new interest and with the desire to apply it to *myself*; very thankful that one of my colleagues in biblical counseling understood what I was going through so thoroughly and offered hope and practical ideas as to what I could do. I wanted to learn what God had for me in the midst of it. But things did not get better immediately. In fact for the next two months my feelings got progressively worse, culminating in that morning in the emergency room.

Allow me to give some further background. The summer before my depression, my wife and I had gone on a speaking assignment in Russia instead of catching up on much-needed rest. Upon beginning the school year I experienced back pain from a herniated disc. During the following nine-month period I could no longer stand to teach. Sometimes the pain was so severe that I could hardly walk. This led to surgery and strong pain medications. Not free from pain after the surgery, we discovered through another MRI that the disc had re-herniated. I was advised to maintain complete bed rest for two months so my nerves could heal. During that time I lost fifty pounds and most of my muscle mass. Besides these physical factors, I was maxed out in my teaching load, seeking to serve in our church, and giving counsel in an extremely emotional situation. Subsequently I found myself in severe depression—the dark night of the soul.

When the fall semester came I couldn't teach. The counseling professor was in depression! How humbling is that! But my colleagues and the administration at the college couldn't have been more supportive. I thought that I would never teach or preach again. I thought my life was over and my usefulness for God's kingdom was finished. When you're in the pit, there isn't any hope. Jeremiah described it so well when he said, "Peace has been stripped away, and I have forgotten what prosperity is. I cry out, 'My splendor is gone! Everything I had hoped for from the Lord is lost! The thought of my suffering is bitter beyond words. I will never forget this awful time, as I grieve over my loss'" (Lam. 3:17-20 NLT).

Before the severity of all of this broke, we had made what we thought was a temporary move into a very small apartment in a senior complex because we could no longer navigate the three levels and thirty-two stairs of our townhouse. So we were in a tiny apartment with a parking lot view during this whole ordeal. Our journey at this apartment lasted a year and a half. God had seen fit to take away our health and comfort, beautiful home, profession, and church ministries. He had stripped me of my self-sufficiency and the record of a depression-free life. He was teaching, softening, and molding me. He was allowing me to see that all I need is Him and His body, the church—that His love is enough! I learned that it's not about me and what I can do for Him; it's all about knowing Him!

Just what are the symptoms of deep depression, what the Puritans called melancholy and what the medical community calls *clinical* or *major* depression? If you are extremely sad and anxious, or you are feeling hopeless most of the day for at least two weeks or longer, you probably don't need anyone to tell you that you are in depression. Everyone feels sad and blue at times, but typically these feelings pass in a few days. However, if you are in *major* depression, your mood is severely depressed and your activity level is as minimal as possible over an extended period. This greatly interferes with your daily functioning and impacts all of those around you.

You may have lost the joy of your salvation. You may not even feel like a believer. I did not believe that I was saved. How could anyone be a genuine Christian and be thinking the thoughts of despair and suicide that I was thinking? Worship songs and messages that had moved my heart seemed meaningless and hopeless. I could no longer believe they really applied to me.

With depression, there is a numbness and complete lack of positive feelings about anything. Guilt and feelings of worthlessness consume you. Your conscience works overtime in convicting you. Everything is negative. A minor problem becomes major as you imagine the worst possible outcome. Your mind is drawn to your saddest memories, the record of your own sins, failures, and disappointments. Negative thoughts crowd out all happy ones.

There is nothing in the future that appeals to you. In the negative grid of the despair, you believe that everything will turn out wrong. I remember thinking *I will never be able to work again. Our income will be so very small that we will be required to live out our days in my brother-in-law's basement apartment.*

You have lost interest or pleasure in what used to interest you. I had no interest or pleasure in historical reading, mystery novels, and playing games with my wife or the family. I no longer thrilled to the competition of a sports event. A comedy was no longer funny. All of these things had been sources of fun and recreation, but nothing was fun or interesting anymore. Life was blah to the max!

You have trouble concentrating and find it hard or impossible to make decisions. In my case, it took twenty minutes for me to look in my closet to decide what t-shirt to wear for the day. Then half of the time I would just wear what I had worn the day before.

Your thoughts and movements have been slowed down. You feel like your brain is fuzzy and in slow motion. During my depression, an exam that previously took me three hours to grade ended up taking me three days to grade. I knew an answer was wrong and that I should grade it wrong, but that would mean the student would need to revise it and I would have to deal with it again, and I did not want that. I would agonize for an hour or two over questions that would normally be graded in ten minutes. I was thoroughly indecisive.

Often I would just stare at the computer, pretending to be doing something when in reality I was just attempting to look busy.

You may feel like a child. You just can't decide what to do, and you want someone else to decide for you. You don't want to be alone, yet you don't want to be around people or talk.

All of this negative thinking can easily produce thoughts of death or suicide. I prayed for God to take my life. I thought of ways I could take my own life. I could step off the curb in front of a car. However, I knew that was a murderous solution and confessed my wrong thoughts to my counselor and my wife so that they could be vigilant in keeping me safe. If this is you, you need to let someone know: someone who lives with you or is close by who can lend support when you feel desperate. You need to seek counsel and be honest about this issue. It is humbling, but when we humble ourselves, in due time God will lift us up (1 Pet. 5:5b-11).

You are constantly fatigued. You are restless and irritable. Sleep escapes you or you may just feel like sleeping all the time. I found it hard to get to sleep, and my sleep was restless as I tossed and turned all night long. When I woke up in the morning I was just as tired as when I went to bed. My worst nightmares hounded me in the night, bombarding me with guilt.

To some people, food becomes tasteless and they lose their appetites. Others try to comfort themselves by eating all the time and end up gaining weight. I lost fifty pounds and all muscle mass because nothing really appealed to me. My wife is a great cook and I have always loved her cooking, but in my depression I could barely force myself to eat.

You may even have unaccounted-for pain. My back pain, strong medications and subsequent physical deterioration brought on the depression. But you may have had the depression first and with it, resulting headaches, neck aches, and other aches and pains that may come from increased levels of inflammation.

There are no words to adequately describe the anguish you feel. You don't know where to turn. It seems hopeless. How can you go on? I wondered if my feelings would ever become normal and natural again.

This is only a partial description of the despair that consumed me. You believe that God has cut you off completely, and you have no peace and are without hope. David also described the agony of this desperate state when he said, "My bones wasted away through my groaning all day long" (Ps. 32:3). The mental pain is excruciating, and there seems to be no way of escape—not even in your sleep. When combined with physical pain and exhaustion, it can be an incomprehensible horror.

You Are Not Alone

You may have wondered, *Am I the only one who has ever experienced this kind of thinking?* While you might feel alone, the fact is that depression is a common problem. All of society tells us that it is a common problem.

According to *The Depression Answer Book,*

> … well over 18 million people, 6 percent of the total population of the United States (are depressed). Counting spouses, significant others, parents, children, grandparents, doctors, nurses, psychotherapists, and friends, depression touches the lives of about 200 million people in the United States right now.[1]

In 2007, *Newsweek* carried a cover story, indicating that millions of American men would be diagnosed with depression that year. But millions more suffer silently, unaware that their problem has a name or unwilling to seek treatment. In her article "Men and Depression," Julie Scelfo writes,

> Although depression is emotionally crippling and has numerous medical implications—some of them deadly—many men fail to recognize the symptoms. Instead of talking about their feelings, men may mask them with alcohol, drug abuse, gambling, anger or by becoming workaholics. *And even when they do realize they have a problem, men often view asking for help as an admission of weakness, a betrayal*

of their male identities. The result is a hidden epidemic of despair (italics mine).[2]

These statistics on depression are actually quite "depressing" and certainly reveal that depression is a common problem. But if we have been studying our Bibles, we already know that truth. In depression we feel as if our problem is unique and no one else can really understand our utter despair of life, our lack of joy, or our complete sadness of heart. But God, in His Word through the apostle Paul, states very clearly that there is "no temptation (trial or test) that has overtaken you but such as is common to man" (1 Cor. 10:13). Depression is one of the common temptations of man. If this is a common problem, then there can also be a common solution.

It is somehow comforting to know that one is not alone in this malady. It became very clear to me that many men and women go through depression but never share their struggles with anyone. One man who came to sit with me so that Mary could have an afternoon out shared that he had gone through a serious period of depression. He would cry for no explainable reason. He kept an old sweatshirt in the car and on the way home from work he would soak it with his tears. He could not explain the feelings of despair, but they were real, and so were the tears. I asked him, "Who did you tell?" His answer was, "No one, not even my friends at church. I figured they didn't want to hear about it, and besides, I didn't think there was anything they could say that would help."

I asked, "What did you do?" He answered, "I just endured. I gritted my teeth and went to work. After soaking the sweatshirt with my tears on the way home, I would pull to the side of the road before reaching my home and say to myself, *I can't discourage my wife and children with this behavior. Now put on a good face in front of the wife and kids.* After about six months it just gradually lifted."

As I have shared my experiences with depression, many have come to tell me of their own trials with depression. They have stated they have never told anyone else because they felt guilty about their feelings or they felt they would be judged. It can be a subject that is hard to talk about in the Christian community. That is one of the main reasons why I am writing this book. We need to know that it is a common problem—even among believers.

We also need to know the rest of the verse: "God is faithful." God watches over every temptation and trial that you will ever face in your life and He will never "allow you to be tempted beyond what you are able." He will measure each trial to what you are able to endure. You may feel overwhelmed and be physically at the end of your rope. But the truth is that God never allows any believer to be tested or tried beyond what the Lord will enable him to endure. Just as Satan had to have permission to test Job, so God measures each trial to what you are able to bear.

But there is still more! The God who is faithful will "provide the way of escape also, so that you will be able to endure it" through the victory you have in Christ. He never gives you a trial or a test, a period of depression, without providing the way of escape—whether it be through faithful counselors or the ministry of His body to you. Look for that way through. Seek Him, and He will be there for you.

Those who are suffering gain much comfort from those who are willing to share their experiences freely. It gives great hope to hear how our faithful God has enabled others to endure and even triumph in their sufferings. A pastor of a large church called and told me of his experience with severe depression that took him off of work for five months. In the midst of my hopelessness, it was encouraging to know that another pastor had faced these same struggles and to hear of the victory the Lord had given him. Even if I didn't have the confidence to believe that I would be delivered, I could hear that our God was able to deliver. Ken and Joni Eareckson Tada, in their book about their marriage, frankly share about their own periods of depression. They give God all the glory for granting them hope.

I have read of many godly men in the past who went through bouts of depression, including Martin Luther, the great reformer; David Brainerd, the missionary to the American Indians; William Cowper, the prolific hymn writer; and Charles Spurgeon, the prince of preachers. But they all endured to the end and left lasting works for Christ behind them. They found "the way of escape" through the trial. Now they are all enjoying the land of eternal sunshine.

David Brainerd wrote of his melancholy damps and his successive deliverance:

> My spiritual conflicts were unspeakably dreadful, heavier than the mountains and the overflowing floods. I seemed enclosed in hell itself; I was deprived of all sense of God, even of his being; and that was my misery.... My soul was in such anguish that I could not eat, but felt as I supposed a poor wretch would, that is just going to the place of execution.[3]
> My mind was remarkably free from melancholy damps and animated in my work. I found such fresh vigor and resolution in the service of God that the mountains seemed to become a plain before me. Oh, blessed be God, for an interval of refreshment, and fervent resolution in my Lord's work![4]

Charles Haddon Spurgeon, possibly the most prolific of reformed preachers, wrote in his *Lectures to My Students*:

> Knowing by most painful experience what deep depression of spirit means, being visited therewith at seasons by no means few or far between, I thought it might be consolatory to some of my brethren if I gave my thoughts thereon, that younger men might not fancy that some strange thing had happened to them when they became for a season possessed by melancholy; and that sadder men might know that one upon whom the sun has shone right joyously did not always walk in the light.

> It is not necessary by quotations from the biographies of eminent ministers to prove that seasons of fearful prostration have fallen to the lot of most, if not all, of them. The life of Luther might suffice to give a thousand instances, and he was by no means of the weaker sort. His great spirit was often in the seventh heaven of exultation, and as frequently on the borders of despair. His very deathbed was not free from tempests, and he sobbed himself into his last sleep like a greatly wearied child.[5]

We understand that depression is a snare that has been trapping men and women throughout history and into our present age. It appears that women are more likely than men to experience a major depression probably because of the hormone fluctuations they experience at various stages in life.

Depression comes to Christians and non-Christians alike, the weak and the strong. We are not only spiritual beings; God has made us of clay—vulnerable to weakness, sin, disease, and yes, depression.

Is There Any Escape?

Where do you turn for help when depression overwhelms you? What do you do when the counselor wakes up depressed and that counselor is you? Through the years, I have counseled many people in all levels of depression, but I never expected it to be an issue in *my* life—after all, shouldn't the biblical counselor somehow be exempt?! I found I was not exempt! After all, it is a common problem.

The hope is right where Jeremiah found it: "I still dare to hope when I remember this: The faithful love of the Lord never ends! His mercies never cease. Great is his faithfulness; his mercies begin afresh each morning. I say to myself, 'The Lord is my inheritance; therefore, I will hope in him'" (Lam. 3:17-24 ESV)!

We must turn to the Lord and seek Him for help. We live in a fallen world, but in Christ we have hope for this world and the next and can cry out with Paul,

> In all these things we are more than conquerors through him who loved us. For I am sure that neither death nor life, nor angels nor rulers, nor things present nor things to come, nor powers, nor height nor depth, nor anything else in all creation, [or feelings of depression] will be able to separate us from the love of God in Christ Jesus our Lord. (Rom. 8:37-39)

Response

We all desperately need hope every day of our lives! I encourage you to seek your hope in the Lord through His Word. It helps to journal what we're going through and learning. Why not get a journal and begin with this first response?

- Journal a paragraph or two describing the anguish you feel.
- Write a paragraph telling how my experience has given you hope, if it has.
- Write out 1 Corinthians 10:13 in your journal and on a 3x5 card.
  - o Seek to memorize it.
  - o On the back of the card write out a prayer, paraphrasing the verse as a prayer back to God. It might look like this: "Father, I thank You that You are faithful and that all our problems are common to man. I thank You that You never give us a temptation, test, or trial that is greater than we can handle. I thank You that You always provide a way through the problem so that we can handle it. Lord, as I face my depression today help me to look for the way out that You have provided so that I might be able to endure."
  - o Review the card and pray it back to God several times each day.
- Read 1 Corinthians 10:13, Hebrews 4:14-16, and 1 John 1:9 and answer the following questions on each verse:
  - o What has God promised you?
  - o What hope and encouragement do you get from these three passages?
  - o How will you respond to God's promises in your situation?
- Make a date to get together with a biblical counselor or someone who you respect that can point you to the scriptures for direction and encouragement.

Valley of Vision Prayers

During the time of my depression I found that it was very difficult to pray. It was so helpful and encouraging to rely on the prayers of others. I found the prayers in the book *Valley of Vision* to be of great comfort and encouragement. I hope these prayers at the beginning of each chapter will comfort your heart as they did mine.

A College Student's Story of Despair and Praise

*E*dward T. Welch puts it very well when he describes depression as a "stubborn darkness" because that's exactly what it is. It's stubborn because as hard as you try, it doesn't go away on your terms and only gets worse before it can get better. It is darkness because you really feel like you're the only person in the world who feels this way and that nobody else understands. It feels as if there is no hope—that this is *it*!

For me, it seemed to last for ages. I thought I had always felt this way and that I always would. I went from being a happy, bubbly person who loved serving the Lord and ministering to people, to someone who hated even the thought of living another day.

There really aren't any events that I can think of that contributed to my depression. Nothing had happened to me…. school was going fine, volleyball was going well, and life at home was as it always had been. Everything was normal. At least, that's what I thought and this made me feel even more frustrated and guilty.

I still remember the day that I first knew something was wrong. It was the Monday before Halloween and I realized that I was thinking illogically. My thoughts were repetitive, condemning and all-consuming. I literally questioned everything that I did and concluded that it was all sin. I thought I was losing my mind. For me, the mental symptoms were the most miserable and most frustrating. All the racing and obsessive thoughts that never gave me a break, the anxiety, the lack of concentration or ability to think straight, and those times when I felt like I was losing touch with reality! Was I going crazy?

In the back of my mind I knew this kind of thinking was wrong, but that didn't change anything. In the matter of a day, my whole life seemed to have taken a 180 degree flip in the wrong direction. I remember being so angry with myself for not being able to get it together. Why couldn't I just stop thinking this way?

I no longer had a desire to do anything. Just getting out of bed in the morning seemed like the hardest task in the world. I couldn't even smile at someone when walking on my way to class. I remember all the crying.... so much crying! Crying became an everyday ritual. It was the only way I felt I could let out the way I was feeling without hurting anyone.

The physical symptoms were miserable as well. I had fatigue and weakness, where it was a struggle to even hold my head up or walk from class to class. I had insomnia that woke me up every other hour during the night while I was trying to sleep. I also had a loss of appetite, loss of interest in all activities and friends/ family. I had problems with my digestive system (probably from a lack of food and sleep.) Headaches, brain fog, blurred vision; I had it all.

During this time, I contemplated suicide for the first time ever. I was never actually close to attempting this, praise the Lord, but I remember thinking that I would rather be dead than have to live the rest of my life feeling this way.

After about a week and a half in this dark and confusing pit, God led me to Dr. Somerville. I came to him crying and desperate for help. I was certain that this was all my fault and that I was caught in some big sin that I couldn't get a grasp on. I was discouraged, defeated, and out of options. But God, who is always faithful to His children, would never let me go from His hand and He had a plan.

After desperately spilling out all these things that had been haunting me for the past week, Dr. Somerville first asked me about past medical conditions, how much I had been sleeping, and what my stress level was like. This caught me by such surprise! I hadn't even once considered that this could be health related. That was the day that I discovered I was suffering from depression.

At first, this was hard for me to grasp. I thought that Christians should never be depressed. They're supposed to find their joy in the Lord! But I quickly had to learn that as spiritual and physical beings, depression is more than just sadness, it can become a debilitating state that comes as a result of spiritual or physical infirmities. Many Christians have experienced depression since the beginning of time. It has to be combated with care for the soul and body.

Well, this episode of depression lasted for about 3-4 weeks but got significantly better over winter break. I had a recurring episode in February after I had come back to school. This finally forced me to start looking into what could medically be causing this. Through our searching we found that I had a hormonal imbalance. I was majorly lacking in some necessary hormones. We began addressing this issue, but I still struggled through fighting this depression all semester. Although it was progressively getting better, it still was something I had to work through with every waking moment.

Looking back to my episodes, I can honestly say that those were the darkest times in my entire life. I felt like I had even been deserted by the One Person who I had always turned to during trials. It felt like my Savior had left me. I no longer felt like I had a relationship with Jesus Christ and that I really was all alone to suffer this way for the rest of my life.

But, no matter how much I felt that way, I had to constantly remind myself that it wasn't true! I had to learn that no matter how much my body and mind seemed to be changing, God was never-changing! God is constant and loves me just as much through those times as He does any other time.

Once I became His child, I was "stuck." Nothing could separate me from the love of Jesus Christ as Romans 8:38-39 says. I had to depend and lean on God every minute of every day. My whole life I had really been confident of my relationship with God. But once my depression hit, I became more dependent than I had ever been on Him. I had to learn to trust that God would keep His promises no matter what.

Every Christian should have to learn that lesson! I learned to look not at my present fleshly estate, but instead to look to eternity with Him where I would have a perfect, flawless body, where I would forever spend eternity enjoying my Savior. That became my hope! Even if I would spend the rest of my life depressed here on this earth, it would be okay because God would give me the strength to press on. One day I would be rid of it in heaven. God gave me this hope and constantly reminded me of it daily. I can't ever say that I've "walked through depression," because God carried me through it! He carried me the whole way!

Three months after my depression, I still continually deal with wrong thoughts, anxieties, and feelings. Those times have left a huge scar that I may need to deal with for the rest of my life. But God is gracious and so good! He continues to give me strength daily and courage to face those things. With every day, I sense healing and moving on. I have learned to pray through all things— every concern, question, or anxiety. This has given me a closer relationship with my Savior that I do not regret! I am still in the midst of discovering health contributors and working through my sleep patterns, exercise and eating habits. It's a slow process that requires a lot of trial and error, but God uses it to continue to teach me patience and reliance upon Him alone.

The three most important things I would recommend to someone facing depression stem from the things that I had to learn as well through my trial.

1. Seek answers from a medical standpoint first. I really had to humble myself in this area because I'm a young college volleyball player. I should be just fine! I had to accept that I might need to take care of myself physically before continuing to live my "normal" life again. Sometimes we need to fix the physical side of things before blaming it all on spiritual matters.

2. Speak truth to your heart daily. Learn to start talking to yourself instead of listening to yourself. I wish I had learned this earlier on during my trial. Depression has a way of making your mind feel like it is on repeat mode. It is always playing those thoughts that condemn us the most. I had to learn to stop listening to those constant and obsessive thoughts and start filling my mind with the truth. Dr. Somerville taught me how to take every thought captive and fill my mind instead with what the Bible says is true. Philippians 4:4-9 helped me with that.

3. Remember Romans 8:28. This was probably the most beneficial verse for me through my depression. I

constantly questioned why God was allowing me to go through something like this and how it could ever be good. I had to remember that God only does that which is most glorifying to Him and that which is the very best for His children! I had to look not at my current state, but towards eternity and realize that He was using this for my good and ultimately for His glory. I now can say that I have encouraged multiple people through my testimony, learned what dependence upon God really looks like, and most importantly, God has strengthened my relationship with my Savior even more! It is because of this that I can say, "Praise Him!"

Morgan Fay

God All-Sufficient

O Lord of Grace,
> The world is before me this day,
>> And I am weak and fearful,
>> But I look to thee for strength;
> If I venture forth alone I stumble and fall,
>> But on the beloved's arms I am firm as the eternal hills;
> If left to the treachery of my heart I shall shame thy name,
>> But if enlightened, guided, upheld by thy spirit,
> I shall bring thee glory.
> Be thou my arm to support,
>> My strength to stand, my light to see,
>> My feet to run, my shield to protect,
>> My sword to repel, my sun to warm.
> To enrich me will not diminish thy fullness;
> All thy lovingkindness is in thy Son,
> I bring him to thee in the arms of faith,
> I urge his saving name as the one who died for me.
> I plead his blood to pay my debts of wrong.
> Accept his worthiness for my unworthiness,
>> His sinlessness for my transgressions,
>> His purity for my uncleanness,
>> His sincerity for my guile,
>> His truth for my deceits,
>> His meekness for my pride,
>> His constancy for my backslidings,
>> His love for my enmity,
>> His fullness for my emptiness,
>> His faithfulness for my treachery,
>> His obedience for my lawlessness,
>> His glory for my shame,
>> His devotedness for my waywardness,
>> His holy life for my unchaste ways,
>> His righteousness for my dead works,
>> His death for my life.

Where's the Hope?

And now, Lord, for what do I wait? My hope is in You.
(Psalm 39:7)

*Y*ou feel hopeless. Your problem is too big, too unique. You are desperate and scared. What is missing? Hope! Everything is bleak, gray, and forlorn. You see everything through the dismal grid of your depression. You're looking for something you can do to get you out of this pit of despair. You can put up with a lot if you have hope.

What I am going to tell you about in this chapter is not something you can do, but about a *Person* whom you can trust. Hope is found in the Person *Jesus Christ*, not in a pill or a prescription and not in just knowing facts or changing your circumstances.

Please read carefully what follows, for it is most important in gaining hope. You may be saying to yourself, *Oh I already know that, so I will just skip on to the next chapter.* It's like reviewing the directions to a place that you have never been before. You think that you know the way so you don't bother to read the directions, and you end up getting lost. After you have wandered around and lost a lot of time you realize, *I should have taken the time to read and follow those directions because now I'm really lost and I have to start all over.* Please read on!

Despite your state of hopelessness, you have a God who is there and who wants to help you; there are answers in His Word that address your situation. "This *hope* we have as an anchor of the soul, a *hope* both sure and steadfast" (Heb. 6:19a, emphasis added). This hope is based on the great mercy of our Father and the resurrection of Jesus from the dead (1 Pet. 1:3).

Hope is the firm belief in God's ability and His promise to bring goodness out of chaos, just as He did when Jesus arose from the grave. Abraham believed in the God "who gives life to the dead and calls into being that which does not exist. In *hope against hope* he believed, so that he might become a father of many nations" (Rom. 4:17-18).

Sufferer, if it truly seems like your life is in chaos, you need an anchor: the God of the impossible. You need to have hope against hope and put your trust in God just as David did when he penned these words, "And now Lord, for what do I wait? My hope is in You" (Ps. 39:7). When you suffer, your faith is put to the test. Questions are raised when you face a personal tragedy. Why would God allow this to happen to me? If God is good, why doesn't He do something? Is something wrong with my personal belief system? There has to be some meaning to what I'm going through!

I want to encourage you to suspend judgment for now and trust the One who does understand. Tell Him that even though you don't understand, you trust Him anyway and will let God be God.

So what are you to do when it seems hopeless? It is helpful to recall what drew you to God in the first place—the hope He is able to offer you. Where does that hope come from and how can it help you in your present circumstances?

Hope in God's Character

Hope is found as you get to know the Father. Don't be afraid to get close to Him. He's an amazing, awesome God, deserving our trust and worship! In your weakness rely on His grace and power every moment of every day. Every one of His attributes relate to your life right now. Why not get a journal and look up these references, write out the things you learn while in the valley, and fill your mind with the goodness and greatness of your God?

He is everlasting and the one and only God (Dan. 4:34-35). He is love, sacrificial love (1 John 4:16). He is good and only decrees what is good (Ps. 25:8; 86:15). He is holy and perfect (Isa. 6:1-2). He is patient with us although we rightfully deserve His judgment (Ps. 86:15). He is gracious (John 1:16-17). Being joined to Christ means that we have new life that begins to look like His—a life of love and holiness. We are free to say yes to our new Master, God.

He is omnipotent and has all power to create the universe and orchestrate the affairs of all of His creation (Gen. 1; Col. 1:16-19). He is omnipresent; everywhere at once, so He can hear our prayers and work in answer to them (Ps. 139:7-9; Jer. 23:23-24). He is omniscient; there is not one thing that He is unaware of. He knows the past, the present, and the future. He knows you and me completely and is with us (Ps. 139:1-6). He is unchanging in all His being (James 1:17). He is all-wise and His ways are unfathomable (Rom. 11:33-36). He is the blessed controller of all things, who works all things after the counsel of His will (Eph. 1:11). You can know that your difficulties haven't come upon you without His superintending over the events of your life.

This mighty God is faithful. As we have already considered, in the midst of it you can cling to His promise that "No temptation has overtaken you but such as is common to man; and *God is faithful*, who will not allow you to be tempted beyond what you are able, but with the temptation will provide the way of escape also, so that you will be able to endure it" (1 Cor. 10:13). I can testify to His abundant faithfulness. I thought my depression was more than I could handle, but God knew I could endure more through His strength, and He proved faithful and right.

Hope in the Gospel of Jesus Christ

The gospel of Jesus Christ gives you hope! There is hope for you because there is hope in Christ—for the past, present, and future. The answers to all of our questions are found in Jesus Christ, including the question of God's goodness. As Jesus' incarnation and ultimately His substitutionary death and resurrection show us that God is for us, how can we doubt that He will see us through whatever suffering He calls us to endure?

If you have placed your faith in Jesus' death for you on the cross and have been born again into His family, this glorious plan to save you had been established from eternity past. The Father chose you before He made the universe so you can know that your salvation is in no way dependent on any merit of your own (Eph. 1:3-6a)! Through His lavish grace, He decided to love you with such a fierce love that he would pour out his wrath on his Son in your place (Eph. 1:7). The Son, Jesus Christ, would love you so much that He would take on flesh, bear your sin in his own body on the cross, be raised from the dead, and ascend to heaven where He is now interceding for you, to the praise of His glorious grace (Eph. 1:5, 6; 2 Tim. 1:9, 10; Heb. 7:25)!

So that you stay focused on hope, you need to preach the gospel to yourself every day. It's a story of hope from beginning to end. The death of the perfect Lamb of God was for *you*. In Revelation we read that there is a book of life of the Lamb that was slain and that if you are in Christ, your name has been written in that book since before the foundation of the world (Rev. 13:8). Your greatest need has been met—peace with God. You need not fear His wrath; rather, you can rest and rejoice in His marvelous grace. That will produce in you a grateful love and a desire to obey and bring Him glory.

That is the good news that I sought to focus on with the help of my wife. We read the Gospel accounts in Matthew, Mark, Luke, and John and book after book about the gospel including the marvelous letter to the Ephesians. I saturated my numb mind with the wonderful truths of the gospel. We placed gospel promises on three by five cards and covered the walls of our tiny apartment with them so that no matter where I looked I saw a gospel promise. We posted them on the bathroom mirrors and on the door so I saw them as I left the apartment. My mind was working so slow that I could not remember promises myself, but my wife Mary would quote them to me. I would think, *Why can't I remember those verses? I know them! I memorized them!* Now I needed to trust in those promises even against the coldness of my heart toward them.

Could God be refocusing my attention on His performance for me instead of my performance for Him? What an exchange: "He made Him who knew no sin to be sin on our behalf, that we might become the righteousness of God in Him" (2 Cor. 5:21). (See the response at the end of this chapter for a practical way to focus on the gospel on a daily basis.)

Hope through God's Provisions

You can also take hope because of the wonderful resources God has given us. The secular solution for depression is psychotherapy, behavioral modification, and/or medication. Drugs are being advertised as the solution to depressive feelings. Commercials tell you to talk to your doctor about this or that medication. "Talk therapy" is another recommended treatment that through God's common grace can help some people sort things out. However, it can only offer humanity's perspectives and has no power to effect real change on the heart level—the kind of change that pleases God. Our hope and comfort is not found in the world. In the end it's not about me, but about the Lord of heaven and earth whom I must seek to worship with all my heart. I must lose my life in Him, His gospel, and His kingdom in order to find my life.

You Have the Word of God

How would my wife and I have survived this trial without God's wisdom and perspective found in His Word? Thankfully, God gives us everything we need for life and godliness in His Word, and it is sufficient to enable us to respond in a godly manner to any situation and to overcome any test (2 Pet. 1:2-3). The Bible became my solace and my compass.

Pastor John Piper says, "The stresses of life, the interruptions, the disappointments, the conflicts, the physical ailments, the losses—all of these may well be the very lens through which we see the meaning of God's Word as never before. Paradoxically, the pain of life may open us to the Word that becomes the pathway to joy."[1]

In Psalm 19, David wrote a hymn of praise for God's glory in natural revelation—the universe, and in special revelation—His Word. He proclaimed, "The law of the Lord is perfect, *restoring the soul*" (Ps. 19:7a). Our souls need restoring, and the Word of God is able to do just that. The Word restores our broken souls by building our faith in God. The psalmist David put words in my mouth with which to trust and praise God: "O God, You are my God; I shall seek You earnestly; My soul thirsts for You, my flesh yearns for You, In a dry and weary land where there is no water" (Ps. 63:1-2).

God's Word is my plumb line. It reveals my sin. Because God is the ultimate authority, His words are our authority. His words are true. We can count on them! Because Scripture is God's very words breathed out through man, it holds ultimate authority, and is therefore infallible and inerrant as well. It has the authority to tell us when we have sinned and gotten off the path that pleases God, and it can tell us how to get back on the path and be trained in righteousness (2 Tim. 3:16-17). If sin has precipitated this depression, the Word will help me deal with it and get back on the path of obedience as an act of my love and worship.

You Have the Holy Spirit

You can have hope because the Holy Spirit dwells in you. Do you need help and comfort? He is the Helper, the Comforter (John 14:16-17). The apostle Paul wrote from prison, "We exult in hope of the glory of God" (Rom. 5:2b). Why did he say this? Because suffering produces good results in our lives, by the power of the Spirit—not our own strength. "Hope does not disappoint, because the love of God has been poured out within our hearts through the *Holy Spirit* who was given to us" (Rom. 5:5). The Holy Spirit wants to assure us of God's love for us when we're in the pit. Allow Him to do His work.

Don't doubt in the dark what God has revealed to you in the light. You are kept through His power, not your own. He teaches you about Jesus Christ and brings that teaching to your remembrance (John 14:26). He sanctifies you to obey Jesus Christ (1 Pet. 1:2). The Spirit is also interceding for you with groaning too deep for words (Rom. 8:26). In your depression when you can't even form words, He is praying for you.

You Have Prayer

You also can have hope because God hears and answers your prayers. As you pray you demonstrate your dependence on Christ.

If you don't pray, you are denying your need for Him and saying in effect that you can handle your problems and spiritual life on our own. You need God to teach you and to work in your heart to give you love for Him and a heart that desires to worship and obey Him in your best times and especially when you are experiencing depression.

Go to your merciful Father in prayer. Lay all of your desires before Him with a willingness to accept His answer. We must relinquish this depression and the future to God. An unknown author expressed it this way:

Lord, I am willing to receive what You give;
To lack what You withhold;
To relinquish what You take;
To suffer what You inflict;
To be what You require;
And to do what you send me to do.

During my bout with depression I did not even feel worthy to pray. There was no feeling in my prayers. All was emptiness and despair, and yet I prayed simply because God says to pray and He tells us, "You do not have because you do not ask" (James 4:2b). We are told to be like the persistent widow and keep asking, so when I did not have faith to believe God would answer me, I just continued to pray. So I encourage you to keep praying even when there is no feeling in it. Just tell Him the truth: *Lord, you know I have no faith to believe that You hear me or care. But I ask because You have said to ask* ... and then pray!

Another resource you must avail yourself of is the prayers of God's people. In a letter written in 1527, Martin Luther gave credit to the prayers of the faithful for bringing him out of the depths of depression:

For more than a week I have been thrown back and forth in death and Hell; my whole body feels beaten, my limbs are still trembling. I almost lost Christ completely, driven about on the waves and storms of despair and blasphemy against God. But because of the intercession of the faithful,

God began to take mercy on me and tore my soul from the depths of Hell.[2]

You Have the Body of Christ

There is hope because you are part of the Body of Christ—the church. You don't have to endure this alone. The church has many important roles: to practice Christ-centered worship, to train Christians to do the work of the ministry, to reach out with the good news about Jesus Christ to the community and the world, and to minister to one another through love. God shows up in our lives through the body of Christ when fellow believers go into action and help us in our suffering. They are His hands and feet. They help bear our burdens. When I was struggling, our church family ministered to us in many practical, wonderful ways that I will never forget. All praise to Him!

Paul wrote to the Corinthian believers, "God, who comforts the *depressed*, comforted us by the coming of Titus; and not only by his coming, but also by the comfort with which he was comforted in you" (2 Cor. 7:6-7). We must allow others in the Body of Christ to encourage us as long as it is still called "Today" (Heb. 3:13a). They won't be able to unless we are willing to make ourselves vulnerable and admit that we are in depression and need help.

As hard as it is, we need to seek fellowship with other believers both at church and in our daily lives. Although we feel like withdrawing, we need to not forsake the meeting together with other believers. It is when we come together with others that we can draw strength from them. Allow those who have been through this valley to tell you their stories to enlighten your way. God will bring you comfort as others share with you comfort that they have received (2 Cor. 1:4).

Again, you will have to fight a battle with your feelings. I had served as a pastor-teacher for thirty-five years of my life but now I found myself not wanting to attend church. It had been six weeks since the surgery and I was strong enough to go to church, but I did not want to face people. Mary challenged me with the truth of God's Word. We need encouragement day after day. We are not to forsake the gathering of ourselves together (Heb. 10:25). We should be speaking to one another in psalms, hymns, and spiritual songs and giving thanks together with one another (Col. 3:16). I knew I should go.

I just wanted to get in and get out. I tried to avoid people. I wanted to go in after the first song had started and leave before the last song had ended so that people couldn't ask, "How are you doing, Bob?"

I would think, *I feel like dirt! I have no feelings! I just heard a message on the gospel that should encourage me and yet I feel condemned, unworthy, unsaved, and guilty for even having the thoughts I am having right now. They don't really want to hear this! What can I say?* All the time I was thinking this, I was conscious that I had that "deer in the headlights look." Then I would say something like, "Okay, I guess." Or "Somewhat better, I think." Awkward silence would usually follow, and I just wanted out of there. It was right for me to go to church in obedience to Scripture even though all of my feelings cried out against going. I am glad now that I went. I know that my soul was fed even though I could not sense it at the time.

When it came to answering people about how I felt, a counselor helped me to learn to answer this way: "Well, the truth is that my feelings are often despairing but God is good, and by faith (weak though it is) I am trusting He will bring me through this." This would let others know the truth and yet not overwhelm them, and I could say this even though I knew my faith was very weak at that point.

You Have Biblical Counselors

I am so grateful for the man in our church and for my colleagues at the college who were equipped and available to help me during my painful journey through depression. They counseled from the Scriptures and through prayer, always pointing me to Christ. Having been a counselor myself, I knew the value of this. Biblical counseling is just discipleship centered on an issue that needs addressing. It brings hope because it has the power and authority of the Word of God and it is life-on-life. It is one believer encouraging, exhorting, helping, and restoring another in his or her relationship with Jesus Christ.

I needed people to do these things with me weekly; people to challenge me to memorize and meditate on the Scripture passages that applied to my situation and to seek to apply them to my life.

They would help me to do what I had been doing before but now thought I couldn't. These counselors agonized in prayer with me and tried to encourage me with all they had in Christ. What dear brothers in the Lord, to whom I will be forever grateful!

Their goal was to help me get my eyes off myself and become a dedicated follower, a worshipper of Jesus Christ once again. They approached me as a saint—a blood-bought child of God who needed reassurance and comfort. They approached me as a sufferer—one who was feeling the effects of our sin-cursed earth in the dysfunction of my body and who needed encouragement. They approached me as a sinner who needed to repent of any known sin and receive cleansing and peace in my soul. They were speaking with authority as they pointed me to Scripture—an authentic and authoritative truth. (See Appendix 7—Resources for Biblical Counseling)

Hope through a Purpose

When you're depressed to the point of inability to function, you have to deal with what gives your life meaning and purpose. If life is all about you and what you can accomplish—that is, your success and comfort, then there isn't much hope. But if there is purpose beyond you, found in the gospel and who God is, then there is hope. The most important factor in life is your relationship with Christ and your oneness with Him! It's not about being loved, respected, and admired by others. It's not even about meeting your own perceived needs. It's all about God and His plan for your life.

There is hope only in living for God's glory. The chief end of man is to glorify God and enjoy Him forever. Living for money, great friendships, possessions, success in one's career, and a life of self-indulgence is dissatisfying and cannot bring real joy.

Our hope for joy and peace come through seeking first God's kingdom, not our own. Life does not consist in the abundance of our possessions or our pleasures, but in seeking to glorify our great God and Savior as we are motivated to obedience because of His great love and sacrifice for us.

We need a purpose in depression, and God's purpose is that you love Him first of all and then that you love your neighbor as yourself

(Matt. 22:37-39). You may have to battle to do that. I certainly did. I found myself very self-focused. But life is not all about you, but about God and others. You need to align yourself to His purpose day by day. Your greatest goal in your suffering is to magnify Jesus and to bring Him glory in the midst of your pain. This may be done in the simplest ways by reaching out to someone else. For example, I mentioned earlier that I wanted to go in to church during the first song and leave on the last song. I didn't want to talk to people. However, Mary needed additional fellowship, and she did want to talk with others. So I could say to her, "Let me go out to the car, and I will wait there. Take as much time as you need." It was a very small thing, but at least I was thinking outside of myself.

Hope in the Father's Loving Discipline

At the height of my depression I read the passage of Scripture which tells about God's discipline or training of His children. *"Whom the Lord loves he disciplines and he scourges every son whom he receives"* (Heb. 12:6). This scripture may sound like a strange place to find hope: in the Father's loving discipline. And yet the hope was there for me. It was actually a breakthrough text. Remember that at the height of my depression I did not think that I could possibly be saved because of the doubts and fears that hounded me and the black thoughts of despair I experienced. I knew that Christians cannot lose their salvation, so I figured that I must have been deceived that I was ever saved. I did, however, have a strong feeling that I was under discipline. The depression was like a mental scourging.

Then I came across this passage. There it was! I was God's child. God only disciplines those who are his children—those He loves! This passage is not speaking of the discipline for sin, but rather the discipline or training that strengthens you in righteousness, discipline that enables you to grow in Christlikeness. God only disciplines and scourges every child whom He receives. If this is an emotional scourging then it is the loving discipline of the Father and if He is disciplining me then I must be His. *Thank you, Lord. This scourging proves I am yours.*

But there was yet another assuring truth in this passage. How could I have forgotten it? But I had. Of course it is not joyful to go through depression. No discipline is joyful at the time. *"All discipline for the moment seems not to be joyful, but sorrowful;* yet to those who have been trained by it, *afterwards it yields the peaceful fruit of righteousness"* (emphasis mine) (Heb. 12:11). The joy would come, but only after I had been trained by the discipline of the loving heavenly Father. This was a comfort to my soul. The scourging of the Father meant I was a son, and of course it would not be joyful at the time, but I had assurance the peaceful fruit of righteousness would come. I had found hope in a most unusual place. And, it's all as the result of His grace. Jerry Bridges makes this clear:

> Paul said, though, that it is the very same grace, God's unmerited favor, that brought salvation to us in the first place — that disciplines us. This means that all our responses to God's dealings with us and all our practice of the spiritual disciplines must be based on the knowledge that God is dealing with us in grace. And it means that all our effort to teach godly living and spiritual maturity to others must be grounded in grace. If we fail to teach that discipline is by grace, people will assume, as I did, that it is by performance.[3]

When we go through suffering as believers, God is treating us as a father who diligently disciplines His dearly loved children (Heb. 12:7). He is up to something good that can be grasped only by faith.

If Joseph had kept his mind on the evil done to him by others instead of trusting the Lord in the midst of those evils, things would have turned out differently. There would have been no reconciliation with his brothers. What trust he demonstrated when he was able to say, "As for you, you meant evil against me, but God meant it for good" (Gen. 50:20)! Without his unrelenting trust there would have been no type of Christ in the Old Testament who saved Israel through the famine and thus preserved the line of Christ.

If Job had not recognized that all the sorrow that came upon him was permitted by the God in whom he trusted, he would have been filled with bitterness. We would never have had his example to follow in suffering. Instead, he put his trust in God's providence and said, "Naked I came from my mother's womb, and naked I shall return there, The Lord gave and the Lord has taken away, blessed be the name of the Lord" (Job 1:21).

We see that through our trials, God is pressing us closer to Himself. He becomes all our hope. You don't see it now, but you take it by faith. You can trust Him because He can do far more than you could ask or think, according to the power that works within you (Eph.3:20). William Cowper, who suffered much of his life with fearful depression, wrote, "Ye fearful saints, fresh courage take; the clouds ye so much dread are big with mercy and shall break in blessings on your head."[4]

Conclusion

So my dear, despairing friend, by now you may be thinking, "I asked for a drink of water and you just blasted me with a fire hose. I thought there was no hope, and you have given me so much that I can't even take it in. Yes, this chapter is just to whet your appetite, to show you that there is an abundant supply of hope. There is enough water to quench your deepest thirst. Come and drink. There is hope in the character of God. Study Him. Know Him. Trust Him. There is hope in the Gospel. Preach it to yourself daily. There is hope in the Word of God. Dive in. There is hope in the Holy Spirit. Let Him comfort and convict you. There is hope in prayer. Ask. Seek. Knock. There is hope from biblical counselors and the Body of Christ. Surround yourself. There is hope as you see God's purposes and rejoice in His loving discipline. Lift your eyes. The goal of the rest of this book is to help you avail yourself of this hope, step by step.

Response

Every day each of us needs to find a way to focus on the hope we have in the gospel. "And now, Lord, for what do I wait? My hope is in You" (Ps. 39:7). As the psalmist has said, our hope is found in Christ. Our circumstances can serve as a window for helping us to see Jesus more clearly and then to love Him more dearly. How does that happen? How do we find Him in the hard places we are going through? May I suggest a way that might help you?

- Journal the main points in this chapter to reinforce them in your mind. Underline what stands out to you in the book as you go along.
- Each day, read a passage from the Gospel of Mark (or another Gospel), asking yourself the following questions:
  o Who is Jesus?
  o What does He say and do?
  o And how can He help *me*?
  o What can He do or be for me in my struggle?
  o Ask the Holy Spirit to give you "eyes" to see Him.
- In your journal, record your findings from the verses you read.
- Particularly note Jesus' character qualities (His patience, kindness, and compassion), how He interacts with people, how He treats them, what He does for them, who He claims to be. After you record your findings, write out how this glimpse of Jesus helps or strengthens you in your situation. What can He be or do for you in your struggle? What has He already done for you that you can appropriate for yourself?
- Write out a prayer. Thank the Lord for revealing Himself to you. Confess how you have forgotten Him and ask for the faith to believe He is who He is even within your situation. As your circumstance becomes a "window to God," you will find your faith in Him strengthened. The Spirit will use these precious truths to begin to lift the "fog" of your own thinking. That, in turn, will bring you to repentance and to a stronger faith because it is rooted in your personal knowledge of Christ, who is your only hope!
- Each of us needs to find a way to focus on the hope we have in the gospel every day. Jerry Bridges encourages us to preach the gospel to ourselves daily. Mary and I developed a means of doing just that. I would encourage you to practice this every day for a month and see if the Lord uses it to encourage your heart in Him. See "Focus on the Gospel," Appendix 1.
- If you need to examine your heart to see what it means to trust Christ as your personal Lord and Savior, see Appendix 5.

A Story of a Hopeless Life Transformed

*F*or the praise of His glorious grace it is my pleasure to testify about God's work in freeing me from my long struggle with depression. My first attempted suicide took place in 1975, when I took an overdose. At the time I was hospitalized and under psychiatric treatment.

The life I lived before conversion was self-centered, revengeful, with an emptiness that I tried to fill in the flesh, looking for fulfillment in all the wrong places. I was hopeless. According to Scripture, I was spiritually dead (Eph. 2:1-3; Titus 3:3). "But when the goodness and loving kindness of God my Savior appeared, He saved me, not because of works done by me in righteousness, but according to His own mercy, by the washing of regeneration and renewal of the Holy Spirit" (John 4:1-30; Titus 3:4-5; Eph. 2:8-9).

By God's grace I was saved in 1986 through faith in the finished work of Christ on Calvary's cross (Eph. 2:8-9). This came when I heard the Gospel from 1 Corinthians 15:1-11. Here, in this grace of God, *hope* was born..... *A living hope!*

Sin always has consequences, though. The life I lived before my conversion brought with it serious life-long, painful consequences. Unbiblical counsel only confused me more and more! Uncontrolled destructive emotions, negative thoughts and feelings; and sinful anger, resentment, unforgiveness, and bitterness remained undealt with. I used to confess these sins to God but had not learned how to biblically put off those sinful attitudes and how to put on Christ. Therefore, I was still in bondage. Thoughts of suicide drove me to seek help at my church by going for long-term counseling. But the counseling did not help me deal with my sin, so the problems carried on. My second attempted suicide took place in 1992, after which I was hospitalized for two weeks and put on sleep-therapy. From there I was moved to a mental institution. While in that institution I received electroconvulsive therapy (shock-therapy) for eight individual treatments. This therapy was administered under full anesthetic every second day. In that year I was under anesthetic eleven times altogether, having undergone surgery as well. During the in-between day I had to sleep off the terrible migraines that this shock-therapy caused. The treatment was supposed to "rectify the chemical imbalance" in the brain with which I was diagnosed. I was also on several psychiatric drugs at this stage. The side effects of these medications resulted in needing other medications like tranquilizers, and so forth, to counteract those side effects.

When I came out of the institution I was on several antidepressants and still under the consultation of a psychologist and psychiatrist. I was very dependent on my family. I couldn't walk without assistance. Eventually, I was diagnosed with bipolar disorder. Lithium and monoamine oxidase inhibitors were added to the other medications. These drugs are used less often today because they have been associated with troublesome side effects like elevated blood pressure and strokes, especially with the intake of certain foods.

At the time our pastor was in the hospital with depression and the counselor at church said that I needed professional help. We heard about a pastoral counselor who regularly appeared on television and made an appointment to see him. He, in turn, referred us to a psychiatrist in the same building! We were going around in circles!

Four years later, in 1996, I was hospitalized for the last time with depression. In the hospital I had suicidal thoughts. But God always protected me from my own self-destruction and eventually led me to the place where I could find answers and healing.

Discouragement and despair eventually brought me to a Christian homeopathic doctor through a friend. This homeopath prayed with me during every appointment and had a gift of encouragement. She slowly weaned me off the psychotropic drugs.

At last I started going for biblical counseling with a counselor who believed in the sufficiency of God's Word. God granted me repentance from my sinful anger, resentment, bitterness, and unforgiving spirit that I came to realize was the root cause of this terrible bondage. As I received wise counsel over a period of eighteen months, I learned how to walk in the Spirit and not fulfill the deeds of the flesh.

I attended a "Know Your Bible" course in Christian doctrine. Through studying the character of God—His attributes—His greatness, His goodness, His sovereignty, and His supremacy over all things, I was able to let go of all my anxiety and depression. He created in me a desire to know Him more (Phil. 3:10), and to grow in grace and the knowledge of Him (2 Pet. 3:18).

This desire led us to find a church where the Bible is taught faithfully and in depth. I now have a solid foundation so I can face the trials of life with joy and counsel others with the comfort that I have received. By God's grace I am no longer dependent on any medication for depression or bipolar disorder! I have been freed from that bondage ever since and I am so thankful to Him for what He has done.

I thank God for my husband's love and support throughout all these difficult years. God's grace enabling him to love me amazes me as I look back, with so much gratitude. We will be married forty years at our next anniversary!

God's grace is sufficient for me. His power is made perfect in my weakness (2 Cor. 12:9). O, the power of the cross! Jesus said, "If you abide in My Word, then you are truly disciples of Mine: and you will know the truth, and the truth will make you free" (John 8:32). I am free indeed! It is because of His truth that I am in my right mind today. He is the "lifter of my head" (Ps. 3:3), the help of my countenance and my *living hope* (Ps. 42, 43)!

All Glory to God!

Francis Waddell

Voyage

O Lord of the Oceans
 My little bark sails on a restless sea,
 Grant that Jesus may sit at the helm and steer me safely;
 Suffer no adverse currents to divert my heavenward course;
 Let not my faith be wrecked amid storms and shoals;
 Bring me to harbor with flying pennants,
  Hull unbreached, cargo unspoiled.
I ask great things,
Expect great things,
Shall receive great things.
I venture on thee wholly, fully,
 My wind, sunshine, anchor, defense.
The voyage is long, the waves high, the storms pitiless,
 But my helm is held steady,
 Thy word secures safe passage,
 Thy grace wafts me onward,
 My haven is guaranteed.
This day will bring me nearer home,
Grant me holy consistency in every transaction,
 My peace flowing as a running tide,
 My righteousness as every chasing wave.
Help me to live circumspectly,
 With skill to convert every care into prayer,
Halo my path with gentleness and love,
 Smooth every asperity of temper;
 Let me not forget how easy it is to occasion grief;
 May I strive to bind up every wound,
 And pour oil on all troubled waters.
May the world this day be happier and better because I live.
Let my mast before me be the savior's cross,
 And every oncoming wave the fountain in his side.
Help me; protect me in the moving sea
 Until I reach the shore of unceasing praise.

—⁂ CHAPTER 3 ⁂—

Lessons from the Life of Elijah

For whatever was written in earlier times was written
for our instruction, so that through perseverance and the
encouragement of the Scriptures we might have hope.
(Romans 15:4)

"*H*ow does Elijah fit into *Gospel*-centered advice for depression?" you might ask. That is a good question! That is just what we will see. I actually gave this message over thirty years ago before I had experienced any depression. I was able to teach people how to counsel the depressed by studying how God counseled his suicidal prophet Elijah. I did not know at that time how much I would personally need this message, but as I came out of my depression, I realized how invaluable these insights were. Now I pass them on to you—unchanged, only with more personal conviction. God's Word is so relevant and so full of hope!

Elijah was a man with a nature just like ours (James 5:17). Read his story in 1 Kings 17-19 and then let's walk through it together to see God's cure for depression.

Identify Contributing Factors

When we are depressed, we want to know where these negative feelings come from. Is it an incurable disease that has come out of nowhere? What has happened to change a confident, capable man into a helpless child? What happened to change the fearless prophet

Elijah who defeated 450 prophets of Baal on the mountaintop to the groveling refugee begging God to take his life? What were the contributing factors that led to Elijah's breakdown and depression?

Conflict and Confrontation

Because of Elijah's faithfulness to God's Word, he lived a life of confrontation. King Ahab was the most wicked king who had ever ruled over Israel (1 Kings 16:33). He provoked God! God called Elijah to stand against him. He had to confront him face to face by predicting the drought. He had to hide from him for three and a half years while Queen Jezebel killed every true prophet she could find. Then he had to come out of hiding and confront the king again. The king of course reversed the charges and labeled Elijah as the troubler of Israel.

When his brook hideout dried up, Elijah even had to confront the widow who would be his lifeline. He had to call her to trust the words of a stranger. He asked her to give up her very last meal, trusting God's promise to provide. Then he had to face her wrath and grief when her son died and she blamed him for it.

Nobody wanted to help Elijah. He had to swear with an oath before he could convince Obadiah to risk his life for him.

The confrontations climaxed on Mt. Carmel when Elijah invited the whole nation to watch him in a battle with 450 prophets of Baal and 400 prophets of the Asherah. The prayer contest was 450 to one, to see which God would answer by fire and prove himself to be true. The false prophets were in a frenzy, calling on their god from morning until evening, leaping about the altar, and cutting themselves with swords until their blood gushed out on them. How this must have brought sorrow and anger to Elijah—seeing God's people mixing worship of Yahweh with Baal worship! He was calling them to decide who they would follow. Feel the tension!

Imagine the physical and emotional exertion! Think about the effort of building a stone altar with twelve heavy stones, digging a deep trench around it, slaying and flaying the animal, pouring on water and then pouring out your heart in your last ditch effort to see a nation rescued from self-destruction. Then there is the emotional tension of waiting to see if God will answer your outrageous request with fire. If God doesn't answer, your life is over.

Fire falls and consumes the offering, the wood and the stones and the water and even licks up the dust. You are overwhelmed with joy and relief. What elation you feel as revival breaks out and the people declare, "The Lord He is God!"

But your job is not done. Now you must oversee the capture and execution of the 450 prophets of Baal by the river in the valley. You cannot let one escape. At last, it is time to pray for rain to bless the nation as they return to the true God. You tell King Ahab to enjoy a meal while you climb the mountain again to wait for God's answer. You don't take time to stop and eat. Persevering prayer is hard work.

Just to prove that you have won the contest, you give Ahab a head-start in his chariot, then you gird up your loins and with the hand of the Lord upon you, you race the rain storm and outrun the horses in a twenty-mile marathon to Jezreel.

But instead of enjoying a victory celebration, Elijah plunges into fear and despair. Even in our times of greatest usefulness, victory, and success, we may be just a step away from falling into the darkest depression. The emotional and physical strain of continuous *conflict and confrontation* can bring a sudden collapse to even the strongest of God's servants.

Response of Fear

Elijah may have beaten Ahab and all the false prophets, but he hadn't beaten Jezebel. Now all her fury was directed at him. The people may have turned back to God for a moment, but Elijah knew they wouldn't stand by his side when it would cost.

We would expect God's man of steel, His super-prophet to respond to a woman's threats with words of thunder, but this time Elijah turns tail and runs for his life. Elijah hadn't been afraid when he was hiding from the king during the years of famine. He hadn't been afraid when the widow's son had died. He hadn't been afraid when he was outnumbered on the mountain top. But 1 Kings 19:3 says, "And he was afraid and arose and ran for his life ..." It wasn't the circumstances that had changed. Elijah had lived with death threats for a long time. But it was his heart that had changed. Now he was afraid and *fear* lead to depression.

Response of Self-Reliance, Self-Focus, Failure to Trust the Power of God

Instead of asking God to strengthen him for the next battle and instead of remembering the power of God, Elijah trusted his own two legs to get him out of trouble. This is the man who prayed for drought and got it! This is the man who had seen God provide by sending ravens with food and widows with bottomless jars of oil! This is the man who brought down fire from heaven with his prayer! This is the man who asked God for rain and within hours the parched ground was drinking in its first shower in two-and-a-half years! This man, this same man, forgot to pray and just ran! *Self-reliance, self-focus, and failure to trust* the power of God leads to depression. It can happen to any of us. Reliance on God is a moment by moment, day by day choice.

Fatigue and Response of Isolation and Despair

Elijah was not only running *for* his life, now he was running *from* his life. He was tired of being the lone voice for truth. He was tired of the death threats. He was tired of the faithless people. He just wanted to be alone. He traveled about 80–120 miles to Beersheba in Judah but that wasn't far enough. He left his servant there and went a day's journey into the wilderness by himself, sat down under a juniper tree, and "requested for himself that he might die, and said, 'It is enough; now, O Lord, take my life, for I am not better than my fathers'" (1 Kings 19:3-4).

Here Elijah is—physically and emotionally spent, all by himself in the wilderness, forgetting his recent victory, and in utter despair. He now thinks of himself as useless, a failure. He prays according to his feelings instead of praying according to God's promises or power as he had before. He begs God to take his life.

When you are depressed, you seek to isolate yourself. You filter all positive information through a negative grid, and nothing is encouraging, happy or good. If it is good, it just doesn't apply to you anymore. You doubt your salvation. You center your thoughts and actions on yourself. It is all "Woe is me."

I don't know how many times I prayed and wished for God just to take me home, to take me out! I didn't believe I would ever have normal emotions again. I felt like I had literally lost my mind! Solomon knew it and wrote, "The spirit of a man can endure his sickness, but as for a broken spirit who can bear it" (Prov. 18:14)?

So what led to Elijah's broken spirit? What was the pattern of Elijah's life up to this point? When the word of the Lord said something to him he went and obeyed. Was Elijah directly in the center of God's will? The answer is absolutely and unequivocally, "Yes!" That obedience led him into conflict and confrontation. It led him into a place of physical and emotional exhaustion. The contributing factors to Elijah's depression were God-ordained and unavoidable. But then, in a moment of weakness, his response to his God-given circumstances showed a lack of faith. Instead of seeking refuge in God or God's people, He resorted to isolation. He wanted a desolate place where he could die without anyone to question him. "A man who separates himself seeks his own desire" (Prov. 18:1).

Like Jesus, after forty days of fasting in the wilderness, Elijah could have resisted every temptation; he could have continued to trust God instead of fearing his enemy, but in his frailty he succumbed to self-reliance and despair. He let his fatigue drive him to isolation and despair.

God the Counselor

How did God handle His servant's depression? Can you imagine God saying, "Okay, if that's what you really want!" Then ZAP! He takes Elijah home! God could have done this with no problem! Remember, He had just sent down fire from heaven to do the job on Mount Carmel. But what does God do now for His despairing prophet?

Rest and Physical Nourishment: Tokens of His Grace

God gave His servant physical rest. The scripture says that Elijah lay down and slept. It doesn't say that God judged him for his depression and asking to die. In fact, God made sure that Elijah was one of the two men who never died! God is longsuffering and remembers that we are but dust (Ps. 103:14). God gave sleep first. Sleep refreshes the mind and body and is definitely a gift. Sometimes the physical factors need urgent attention before the inner causes of the depression can be addressed.

God gave His servant physical nourishment. An angel woke him up twice by touching him and telling him to get up and eat, and there at his head was a freshly baked cake, not just a piece of bread but a real special nourishing meal for him along with water to drink. The sleep, the angel, and the food were all proofs of God's love for Elijah. He went in the strength of that food forty days and forty nights.

Here we see that God, the great counselor, addressed Elijah's physical needs first. There is a definite connection between the mind and body. John Piper points this out when he says, "What we should be clear about ... is that the condition of our bodies makes a difference in the capacity of our minds to think clearly and of our souls to see the beauty of hope-giving truth."[1]

The Diagnosis: Gathering Data

While the body is being cared for, we need to care for the soul. God starts by gathering data. He asks Elijah, "What are you doing here?" (1 Kings 19:9, 13). It is almost the same question he had asked the very first despairing sinners, "Adam, where are you" (Gen. 3:9)? God pursues us. He doesn't allow us to stay alone in our depression. He also doesn't give the solution until He has an explanation of the problem. Elijah confesses his fear and despair, while asserting his devotion to God and complaining of everyone else's failures. God knows all things, but He still asks. He gets Elijah to verbalize his view of the situation. How much more do we as counselors need to ask questions to understand the sufferer? And the sufferer needs to acknowledge the problem and explain his perspective on the situation.

The Cure: Knowing God

What was God's cure for Elijah's depression? Did Elijah need a better self-image? Did he need a more positive outlook? Did he need more faith? Did he need a rebuke? Did he need a better support system and more success? God's loving solution was to just show

Himself to Elijah, and that was enough. God called him to come out of the cave and stand on the mountain, the same mountain where the same God had revealed Himself to Moses and where He had given the Law. Then God passed by with a wind so strong that it rent the mountain and shattered the rocks, but the Lord was not in the wind, nor the earthquake, nor the fire. He came and spoke to Elijah in a gentle whisper. Elijah faced the thundering elements with awe, but he covered his face in the presence of that quiet voice. He covered his face even as the angels do (Isa. 6:2), for no one can see God and live (Exod. 33:20).

We too must know God. We must know the God who gave the law with trumpet blast and earthquake and smoke; the God who is a consuming fire; the God who we can never please in our own strength because even our best efforts are tainted (Isa. 64:6); the God who doesn't wait for us to come to Him. He comes to us. He clothes Adam and Eve. He provides the ram in the thicket so Abraham doesn't have to slay his son. He reveals Himself to Moses as the God who is compassionate and gracious, slow to anger and abounding in loving-kindness (Ps.103:8). He gives His only Son to be the perfect sacrifice to take away sin (Rom 5:8-9). Do you know and love Him? Do you fear Him? Do you trust Him?

Often depression can come from a sense of failure, which we will always have if we are trusting in ourselves. We must trust in Jesus who was the only perfect man. He will take our sin and give us His righteousness. He will give us the peace *of* God which comes from peace *with* God. When I was thirteen, my father died suddenly of a heart attack. My mother took my sister in one arm and me in the other arm and smiled through her tears and said with amazing peace, "We know where Daddy is, and we know we'll see him again." But I didn't know I would see him again. I decided then and there that I needed to make that transfer from trusting in myself to trusting in Christ as my Lord and Savior. We have to humble ourselves, admit we are sinners in need of a Savior, and fall on God's mercy and grace. When we do, God receives us with open arms and forgives us, and we become His blood-bought children with all of His resources available to us. His love motivates us to trust Him through the dark times. His Holy Spirit empowers us to live a life that pleases Him (Rom. 5:5).

The Cure: God's Voice and Awareness of His Presence

God spoke to His servant. He was not in the wind, earthquake, or fire; but He revealed Himself in a *still, small voice*. Faith comes by hearing and hearing by the Word of God (Rom. 10:17); miracles and signs only prepare the way. God asked him what he was doing there neglecting his duties, deserting his people, and hiding from an impotent queen when such a God of power was on his side. From behind his cloak, Elijah poured out his fear and frustration before the Lord. It was not for lack of zeal that he had run away, but because he had lost all hope of success. Scared and alone, he felt it was useless to try any longer. God condescended to answer Elijah's every complaint with his next commission.

When you're in depression you don't feel God's presence. You are in the trough and you can't see out. You feel alone and forsaken by God. You long for the voice of God to tell you what He wants of you. It comes, dear sufferer, *in the still, small voice of His Word* just as clearly as it did for Elijah.

I went to the Word of God for my comfort and direction. The Psalms and other scriptures can become an oasis in the desert that can soothe and calm the soul. I lived in the Psalms where David, who often experienced depression, pours out his soul to God. David confessed that he could not see his God at times and laid bare his doubts, anxieties and anguish of soul. (See chapter 8 on Psalms of Lament.) Yet God always pulled him out of the miry pit and set his feet upon a rock and put in his heart a song of praise to his God (Ps. 40).

God's Word is sufficient and speaks to us of hope because of the Father's favor and our Savior's unquenchable love for us. We need to have this drummed into us over and over again. Scripture assures us that "His divine power has granted to us *everything* pertaining to life and godliness, through the true knowledge of Him who called us by His own glory and excellence." This is through the agency of "His precious and magnificent promises" found in His Word (2 Pet. 1:3-4).

Don't think you are being hypocritical if you read the Bible when you don't feel like it. You wonder why you should read if your brain will not engage. Why should you read if you will just forget it an hour later? You must read out of faith and obedience. God's Word will restore your soul. It will revive you and strengthen you and enlarge your heart (Ps. 119:25-32). Keep listening to that still, small voice!

The Cure: A Proper Perspective

God gave His servant a proper perspective of the facts. Is he really the only one left? God told him that he was not; there were 7,000 who haven't bowed the knee to Baal (1 Kings 19:18). Elijah had chosen to forget about faithful Obadiah and the one-hundred prophets he had kept hidden in caves. He had chosen to forget about his own faithful servant whom he left before his final journey into the wilderness. And there were more on his side that he didn't even know about. God gave him hope by reminding him of His remnant. We also choose to forget our blessings. God gives us hope as our counselors help us think on what is true, honorable, right, pure, and lovely (Phil. 4:8).

I needed the proper perspective—to be encouraged over and over again with the truths of the Gospel. Yes, I am more sinful and flawed than I dared believe but also more welcomed, loved, and forgiven than I dared hope because I have placed my faith in Jesus' substitutionary death for me on the cross. He wasn't through with me yet!

The Cure: A Task to Accomplish

God gave His servant an assignment. He had more for Elijah to do. God wanted him to go in the strength of that sleep and food for forty days and forty nights to the mountain of God where he would be prepared for a new commission. His next assignment was to anoint new kings in Aram and Israel and his own successor. These powerful leaders would destroy Baal worshipers. Elijah's work would not be in vain; others would carry it on. He had to get moving. Out of Elijah's trust and love for his God, he got up and did what God commanded him to do with the strength that God provided. God also has work for you to do. Find your duties and fulfill them. As you get up and do the next thing, you will find healing.

Conclusion

Can God restore people today like he restored Elijah? I can say yes as a counselor who has seen countless people restored. I can say yes from experience! I can say yes, based on the promises of God's Word. God does work all things together for good (Rom. 8:28-29) even depression.

What happened in my case? My body was restored with rest and nutrition, careful use of medication, detox, physical therapy, and exercise. Gradually my spirits were lifted as I drew close to God through His Word, prayer, and godly counsel. I got a new perspective. I had a task to accomplish, and I went back to teaching even before I was fully myself again. The depression eventually lifted completely.

I had to learn that I had a new normal, and I needed to take precautions against relapse. I now have to set limits for myself in order to care for my health. I have manageable discomfort with my back but continue to do the physical therapy that is needed. But I am fully restored and I thank God every day for the privilege of serving him and sharing with others how God's grace got us through. I have been able to preach again at churches, camps, and conferences and give them an account of God's faithfulness to us and see God use the comfort He gave to us to strengthen others. What a joy to be able to pass the mantle on to others who will carry on the work! God has given us a lovely home again in which to live and minister in the years ahead as God allows.

In the chapters that follow, I want to take what we have learned from God's counsel to Elijah and expand on it with more scriptures and practical advice. We will look at the contributing factors that cause depression. We can find hope in the fact that our sovereign God controls these factors for our good. If our own sin is a contributing factor we can learn how to deal with that guilt. We will learn how to avoid the sinful responses of self-reliance, fear, worry, and anxiety. We will then explore the cures that God offers us. First we will look at care for the physical body. Then we will explore the hope we can have as God reveals Himself to us through His Word. We will see how we can express our grief to God and commune with Him through the Psalms. We will see how He can restore our joy and give us new work to do!

Response

If you haven't read this powerful account in 1 Kings, chapters 17-19 I encourage you to stop and do so now. We are going to apply these lessons from Elijah's life to your situation in chapter 4.

A Story of Spiritual Despair Leading to Hope in Christ Alone

I was blessed with the incredible privilege of being born to Christian parents who knew and loved the truth of God's Word and who were committed to raising me in the knowledge of that truth. I grew up attending a church where our pastor is one of the foremost living evangelical expositors of God's Word, and I sat under his preaching since I was in the nursery. I was always the kid in Sunday school or in Bible class that knew all the answers. I loved asking my dad theological questions and having spiritual discussions. I took pride in all my theological knowledge and my memorization of Bible verses, but I had very little love for the Lord.

This spiritual pride continued relatively unchecked in my life until I attended The Master's College. Because of friendships I developed there, as well as the in-depth Bible teaching I was receiving nearly every day from class and chapel, I began to ask myself the hard questions of exactly *why* I enjoyed theological discussions and doctrinal knowledge — was it because I loved God, or was it because I took pride in others thinking I was spiritually astute? I began to fear that it was the latter.

Then, in the fall of my senior year of college, I participated in a semester-long study-abroad in Israel, where I was able to study the Bible in the Holy Land. It was a fantastic experience, and I had a great time learning even more about the Scriptures. However, while we were there, one of our professors lectured on the tragic life of King Joash from 2 Chronicles 23. Joash followed the Lord all the days of Jehoiada the Priest, but once Jehoiada died, Joash forsook his external façade of righteousness. Jehoiada had been a spiritual "crutch" for Joash; once he died, Joash's faith proved to be false. Our professor challenged us then and there and asked us if once our spiritual crutches of studying in Israel and even being at The Master's College were taken away, if we would be faithful to the Lord. This question began to gnaw incredibly on my thoughts.

By this time, I had already committed to leading a summer missions trip to Uganda, Africa, for the following summer. For this mission trip, we were assigned to read John Piper's excellent book *God is the Gospel*. In that book, Piper points out that the message of the Gospel is not just that you get to escape Hell, but that you gain a relationship with the living God. Piper poignantly asks his readers: "If you were to die and go to heaven and all the joys of heaven were there, but Jesus wasn't there, would you be happy?" That piercing question only increased my concerns about the validity of my own spirituality.

Fast forward eighteen months to January, 2009, when everything that had been weighing on my mind suddenly coalesced into a drastic downward spiral of depression. I feared that I was like the people who are warned in the book of Hebrews—that I had had a knowledge of the truth but not a genuine saving faith and that I was in danger of being in a position from which it is impossible to repent (Hebrews 6) and in which there no longer remained a sacrifice for sins (Hebrews 10). I was even afraid that I was secretly so hard-hearted that I was like the Pharisees who had committed the unpardonable sin and that there was absolutely no hope for me. This was the start of a very dark year in which depression weighed on my mind nearly every day.

The extent of this depression was pretty terrible. I knew enough truth and doctrine to know that if you are a genuine Christian, although horrible things can happen to you in this life, you have the perfect assurance of eternal joy with Christ waiting for you. However, I had no assurance of salvation, but rather seemed personally guaranteed of my eternal damnation—and therefore was terrified. I was depressed every morning I woke up, and even grew to be afraid of anything that could kill me. I feared that my life was simply in some sort of holding pattern until death finally found me and I entered Hell forever. I feared that by my pride and self-righteousness, I had sinned away any and all chances for true repentance and now God was permanently angry with me.

Charles Spurgeon, writing on David's lament in Psalm 3, wrote in his *Treasury of David* that "It is the most bitter of all afflictions to be led to fear that there is no help for us in God." This certainly was the case with me. I knew that only God can save from sin, but if I had made God my permanent enemy, then I had no hope whatsoever. This thoroughly depressed me to the extent that I saw no point in living, yet it was my fear of Hell that kept me from suicide.

By God's grace, so many people rallied around me during this time. My parents prayed for me constantly, and my dad spent many long hours talking me through my fears. A wonderful couple was an incredible support through this time. My boss at the time, who was a believer, was very understanding and prayed for me. Most of all, my wonderful girlfriend (who is now my precious wife) stood by me and encouraged me with the truth of God's grace and forgiveness every day. In fact, I clearly remember her telling me one evening, "Steve, forgiveness was *God's* idea in the first place!"

Also during this time, I discovered the writings of J.C. Ryle, an Anglican Bishop who ministered during the 1800s. Ryle's writings were so doctrinally sound, and yet so kind and comforting and full of so much hope that was founded on the person and work of Jesus Christ, they ministered to my soul in an incredibly special way. Second only to the Word, Ryle's writings were the one thing that filled me with hope.

On top of all this, that same professor who warned us about the tragedy of Joash moved back from Israel to California at this time. He found out about my struggles, and he kindly reached out to me and offered to meet with me every week. Week after week, he devoted time to me out of his busy schedule and helped me recalibrate my thinking according to biblical standards. He kept reminding me of truth, and he continually encouraged me to actively fight doubt and to actively place my faith and trust on Jesus Christ. He reminded me that God, by nature, is a forgiving God (Psalm 86:5) made possible by Jesus' substitutionary death. He challenged me to pursue the spiritual disciplines of Bible reading and prayer, even if I felt like I was damned. He encouraged me to repent of sin wherever I saw it in my life, to replace sin with righteousness, and to actively trust the grace of Christ.

It's not easy. It's been a struggle. At first, it was a day-to-day battle to remind myself of God's grace and forgiveness. After some time, it began to be a week-to-week struggle. Now, five years later, it's more of a month-to-month struggle. Sometimes there are good days. Sometimes there are bad days. A good day is when I let the truth of God's Word rule my mind and when I actively keep my eyes fixed on Christ and His glory. A bad day is when I let subjective feelings of fear and condemnation overrule what I know to be true. Bad days happen when I begin to base my acceptance with God upon what I have done (or, conversely, my *lack* of acceptance with God on what I've failed to do) and when I forget about Christ and the grace He offers me in Christ.

Often, I just need to return to "the basics" in my thinking. I remind myself of the free offer of the Gospel (Isaiah 45:22; Matthew 11:28-29; John 6:37), of God's forgiving nature (Psalm 86:5), and that He rejoices over forgiving lost sinners (Luke 15). I sing to myself old hymns that relay deep doctrine—hymns that remind me of truths like: *"The vilest offender who truly believes, that moment from Jesus a pardon receives"* and also *"Enough for me that Jesus saves, this ends my fear and doubt! A simple soul I come to Him, He'll never cast me out!"* When I remind myself of what is true and I stay my mind on that, my emotions often soon follow.

Time in the Word is absolutely crucial. I know that if I go about three days without reading God's Word, I'm setting myself up for another relapse into depression. My mind won't be saturated with the truth, which leads to me feeling far off from God, which leads to me fearing that I've sinned too much to have a relationship with Him, which leads me to dread condemnation, which leads me to despair. Time after time, this is the spiral of depression that trips me up if I stray from renewing my mind with the Word.

What also helps is fellowship with other believers. We attend an excellent church (the same one I grew up in) and a weekly

Bible study. The believers at church and Bible study are a continual encouragement to me.

When speaking to anyone in a similar state of despair, I would encourage the person to:

1. "Take and read"—to pick up the Bible and read about the grace and hope that God offers sinners who are at the end of their rope. This is what freed many men who struggled with depression and despair throughout church history: St. Augustine, Martin Luther, and John Bunyan. All of them found peace from their depression and despair by turning to God's written Word. In fact, the hymn writer Isaac Watts put it best when he wrote: *"Laden with guilt and full of fears, I fly to Thee, my Lord; and not a glimpse of hope appears, but in Thy written Word. The volume of my Father's grace does all my grief assuage; Here I behold my Savior's face almost in every page."*

2. Seek out fellow Christians and ask them to pray for you and to invite them to speak truth into your life. We are not meant to function on our own (1 Cor. 12), and we need fellow believers to help us through dark times like this.

3. Just keep going. Don't give up. Our God is a God of hope who delights in the salvation of sinners. I would encourage you to trust His saving nature and to place your faith completely upon Jesus Christ and what He did by dying on the cross and rising from the grave on behalf of sinners.

A Man who Continues to Hope in Christ

Love Lusters At Calvary

My Father,
> Enlarge my heart, warm my affections, open my lips,
>> Supply words that proclaim 'Love lusters at Calvary.'
>
> There grace removes my burdens and heaps them on thy Son,
>> Made a transgressor, a curse, and sin for me;
>
> There the sword of thy justice smote the man, thy fellow;
> There thy infinite attributes were magnified,
>> And infinite atonement was made;
>
> There infinite punishment was due,
>> And infinite punishment was endured.
>
> Christ was all anguished that I might be all joy,
>> Cast off that I might be brought in,
>> Trodden down as an enemy
>> That I might be welcomed as a friend,
>> Surrendered to hell's worst
>> That I might attain heaven's best,
>> Stripped that I might be clothed,
>> Wounded that I might be healed,
>> Athirst that I might drink,
>> Tormented that I might be comforted,
>> Made a shame that I might inherit glory.
>> Entered darkness that I might have eternal light,
>
> My savior wept that all tears might be wiped from my eyes,
>> Groaned that I might have endless song,
>> Endured all pain that I might have unfading health,
>
> Bore a thorned crown that I might have a glory—diadem,
> Bowed his head that I might uplift mine,
> Experienced reproach that I might receive welcome,
> Closed his eyes in death that I might gaze on unclouded
> Brightness,
> Expired that I might forever live.
> O Father, who spared not thine only Son that thou mightiest spare me,
> All this transfer thy love designed and accomplished;
> Help me to adore thee by lips and life.
> O that my every breath might be ecstatic praise,
>> My every step buoyant with delight, as I see
>> My enemies crushed,
>> Satan baffled, defeated, destroyed,
>> Sin buried in the ocean of reconciling blood,
>> Hell's gates closed, heaven's portal open.
>
> Go forth, O conquering God, and show me the cross,
>> Mighty to subdue, comfort and save.

—⁂ CHAPTER 4 ⁂—

If I'm a Christian, Why am I Depressed?

Blessed be the God and Father of our Lord Jesus Christ,
who according to His great mercy has caused us to be born
again to a living *hope* through the resurrection of Jesus
Christ from the dead. (1 Peter 1:3)

The question that heads this chapter and this book was on my mind in the midst of the depression. I was asking myself, "If I am a Christian, why am I depressed?" This led to many other questions. What caused my depression? Can I get out of it? Now that time has passed and I have been able to process what I went through, I offer these thoughts that I believe will enable you to see meaning in your suffering and enable you to give glory to God in the midst of it. Just as we did with Elijah, let's look first at the causes of depression.

What Are the Causes of Depression?

The causes of depression can be as numerous and varied as the people that they affect. But they can fall into three main categories. The pressures of life, physical infirmities, and sin can all lead to depression.

Like Elijah, you may encounter depression in the line of duty as you serve your family and the church, as wave after wave of opposition comes at you until you collapse in exhaustion, crying out for God to take your life.

Depression can come from overwhelming grief from marriage failure, a rebellious child, severe financial problems, the death of a loved one, or a number of other stress-related issues. A violent assault, an accident, terrorism, military combat or a natural disaster can precipitate depression. Depression can also originate from disappointments—hope that has been dashed over and over again. "Hope deferred makes the heart sick, But desire fulfilled is a tree of life" (Prov. 13:12).

We are vulnerable not only because of certain outside factors but because we live under the general curse on creation that came through Adam and the fall. Our bodies are vulnerable to disease, our hormones malfunction, our adrenal systems can fail, and chemicals that we take to treat one illness can have bad side effects. Of course our enemy Satan is involved; he is the accuser of the brethren and will quickly turn these physical issues into spiritual issues as he tempts you to despair. We can find hope in the fact that we have a compassionate God. "He knows our frame. He is mindful that we are but dust" (Ps. 103:14). He cares about our bodies and their weaknesses. We will deal with treatment for the physical factors in detail in chapter 6.

Depression can also come as a consequence of sins such as worry, anxiety, fear, sinful dealing with relationships, or not taking care of our bodies properly. It can come from outright rebellion and sins such as adultery, homosexuality, perpetual lying, stealing, using pornography, or other flagrant sins. In chapter 5 we will discuss how to deal with the guilt that causes depression.

So we see that external pressures, physical ailments, or a burden of guilt can all tempt us toward depression. However, outside factors alone are usually not sufficient to cause depression. These circumstances have to happen in conjunction with an internal belief system that interprets them in such a way as to plunge you down into the slough of despond. Our interpretations of our circumstances will determine how we respond.

When we take an honest look into our hearts, we find that we are proud and self-centered. This may seem surprising for a person who feels low, but in my depression I found that the focus was always on me. I craved to be in control; I wanted to know the reasons for what was going on instead of just trusting God for them. I was surprised, once again, by the sinfulness of my own heart. But I was happy to know that I could repent and get back on the path to healing.

In the rest of this chapter I want to give you the tools that you need to avoid the sinful responses that will lead you into depression or keep you there. This should give you hope that even though a Christian can become depressed, he doesn't have to stay there because he can change his response to his circumstances and find freedom.

How Can I Get out of Depression?
Avoid Fear by Rejoicing in Persecution

If we think back to the Elijah story, we will remember that his first sinful response to persecution was fear. This is such a prevalent cause of depression that I am going to treat this temptation with a whole chapter. But for now let's look at one way to avoid fear through the proper perspective on persecution.

If some kind of persecution for righteousness sake has precipitated this depression, you actually have a lot to rejoice in. Meditate on Jesus' words in Matthew 5:10-12 and purpose to rejoice because you are in good company with Jesus and with the prophets before you. Jesus predicted this when He said, "You will be hated by all because of My name, but it is the one who has endured to the end who will be saved" (Matt. 10:22). You can rejoice because you have a reward coming in heaven. If you fix your eyes on eternity, you will not be able to fear your persecutors, *instead you will fear for them.* "Do not fear those who kill the body but are unable to kill the soul; but rather fear Him who is able to destroy both soul and body in hell" (Matt. 10:28).

"*Blessed* are those who have been persecuted for the sake of righteousness, for theirs is the kingdom of heaven. *Blessed* are you when people insult you and persecute you.... *Rejoice* and be *glad*, for your reward in heaven is great ..." (emphasis mine) (Matt. 5:10-12). Preach this to yourself, dear sufferer, when you want to give up, when your conscience is confused by all the slander or self-recrimination, when you think that you must have done something wrong

71

for your life to fall apart like this. Remind yourself that this suffering is a badge of being a true disciple and it is a privilege to suffer with Christ! Depression cannot survive where rejoicing prevails.

Avoid Self-Reliance by Trusting Our Sovereign God

Elijah tried to fix his problem with Jezebel by doing the sensible thing and running away. In the past, he had waited for the word of the Lord. God had told Him exactly where to hide and how he would get his food. But this time, he didn't wait, he just ran. Sometimes, that is how it is in depression. Our minds have been racing trying to figure out how we got into this situation and how we are going to get out of it. The wheels spin. We demand answers. They don't come and we get stuck deeper and deeper.

The solution is not to rush off for a quick fix but to wait on God and trust His sovereignty. I had to learn that God's ways are not always our ways (Rom. 11:33). At the time, I didn't know why I was depressed. I had no hope that I would ever recover. But I had to learn to trust a sovereign God in the midst of it. I had to learn to view my adverse circumstances through the eyes of faith, trusting in God's immeasurable love and wisdom. God was in control of the physical issues that brought me face to face with depression. The question then was, how do I respond to it—in faith or in doubt? I had to choose to believe that God had a good purpose for it even though that purpose may remain a mystery. Recognizing and thanking God for His sovereignty and goodness is the first step in avoiding self-reliance.

In the book of Job, God gives us a glimpse into His secret counsels. In chapter one, we see Satan enter into the throne room. God starts the contest by pointing out the qualities of His servant Job. Satan counters with an accusation that if God takes away His hand of blessing, Job will curse Him to His face. God takes the challenge and gives Satan permission to put Job to the test. God sets his limits.

Job passes the test. He declares, "Shall we accept good from God, and not trouble" (Job 2:10)? He chose to trust God even though he didn't know what God was doing. As God intended, Job proved that God is worthy to be worshipped and praised, not for what He gives but for Who He is. I too had to learn to say with Job, "I have accepted good from my Father for all these years and shall I not accept trouble now? He is worthy to be worshipped and praised in the midst of this!"

Our suffering may remain a mystery to us. Job asked God a lot of questions. God could have pulled back the veil and shown Him what was happening in the spiritual realm. But He didn't give Job the answers he was looking for. Instead, He answered him out of the whirlwind, "Now gird up your loins like a man, and I will ask you, and you instruct Me! Where were you when I laid the foundations of the earth" (Job 38:4)? God went on to show Him His own greatness. He let Job know that it wasn't right for him to condemn God to justify himself. If there were so many things that Job did not understand, why should he think that he should understand his own suffering (Job 38-41)? Job had to let God be God with no explanations needed. Job needed a bigger vision of God.

Job repented—not for sin that brought on his suffering, for this was not the case, but for his arrogance in thinking that God was obliged to give him an answer. He repented of not knowing his God in the full sense of His sovereignty. He said, "I have heard of You by the hearing of the ear; But now my eye sees You" (Job 42:5).

I too wanted to know God in that way—humbly accepting what He had for me with no explanation needed. I had walked with him for forty years of ministry, and I needed to trust Him even in this! I had witnessed many inexplicable things throughout those years and God had kept my faith firm. Could I not trust Him to get me out of this dark valley in His time? Job is quite a testimony to trusting in God, his Redeemer, through the worst possible circumstances, although he only saw through a glass darkly.

Mary and I had to trust God as Job did. He put his hand over his mouth when he realized that God was God and he was not. He said, "But He knows the way I take; When He has tried me, I shall come forth as gold" (Job 23:10). By faith we also had to acknowledge that God was up to something good. He was pressing us closer to Himself. He became all our hope.

Ligon Duncan writes in *Does Grace Grow Best in Winter?*

Some people do not want to think that God is involved in their suffering. It is so painful, they cannot conceive of a good and loving God having anything to do with it. In order to protect the goodness of God, they, ironically, push him as far away as they can from their suffering. But think about it—if God is removed from suffering, then our painful experiences, which generate some of the most significant moments we have in this life, are outside the reach of our God. That is not very encouraging at all. I want God right in the middle of my suffering. But it's not just a matter of what I want; it's about what the Bible says, God is sovereign even over suffering."[1]

I could have the confidence that God was in control and that what we were going through was part of His loving plans for me. His major plan for me is to deliver me from sin, not to give me an easy life—to make me hate my sin and to keep me growing in His grace. Is God accomplishing His goal in my life through this adversity? That's the big question! By faith in his Word we know the answer is, "Yes!"

As you learn to stop relying on your own understanding of the situation and begin to trust God, your question might even change from "Can I get out of this?" to "What does God want me to learn from this?" You might even realize that this depression is good for you. "Trust in the Lord with all your heart and do not lean on your own understanding, in all your ways acknowledge Him, and He will make your paths straight" (Prov. 3:5-6).

Avoid Self-Reliance through Prayer

Elijah entered into his depression because of a tiny space of prayerlessness between great prayer victories. But he came out of his depression when he poured out his soul to the Lord and heard the answers that the Lord had for him. You too can cry out to our Father. He already knows what you are going through. You don't have to suffer in silence. Listen to David's cry, "My voice rises to God, and I will *cry aloud*; my voice rises to God, and He will hear me. In the day of my trouble I sought the Lord" (Ps. 77:1-2a, emphasis added).

David did not try to run away from his trouble through self-reliance. He did not drown it in drink, reason it away, or laugh it off. He cried out to his God.

In D.A. Carson's book *How Long, O Lord: Reflections on Suffering and Evil* he assures us, "God does not blame us if in our suffering we frankly vent our despair and confess our loss of hope, our sense of futility, our lamentations about life itself. One cannot read chapter 3 (of Job) without recalling that God will later excoriate the miserable comforters, but insist that Job himself said right things (42:7)."[2] God is not shocked by our pain or questions. He wants us to bring them to Him.

When we don't even know how to express the agony of our souls, we open the Psalms to find that David has gone before us. God allowed this man after His own heart to go through every kind of trial and to record the full range of his emotions in song to bring light into our darkness even three millennia later! I sought to read at least one Psalm per day and to journal a prayer of thanksgiving. That is still my goal for my daily quiet time.

Sometimes David confessed that he could not see God. He laid bare his doubts, his fears, his anxieties, his anguish, and his sin; and God pulled him up out of the miry pit and set his feet upon a rock, making his footsteps firm. God put a new song in his heart, a song of praise to His God (Psalm 40). His words can be prayed back to God and be springboards for our own prayers. (See chapter 8 which helps you use the psalms of lament as templates for expressing your grief to God.)

Although our souls are bereft of feeling we need to seek God through prayer. That is why we have included *The Valley of Vision* prayers at the beginning of each chapter to aid in that pursuit. These godly men from the past warm our hearts that are cold with depression to adoration of our great God. They remind us of our great guilt before God but immediately take us to the Gospel where we find the only remedy for our sin. As we pray, we can take courage that we are communing with our Father who loves us and is mighty to work in our lives. We can pray with hope because "His great mercy has caused us to be born again to a living hope through the resurrection of Jesus Christ from the dead" (1 Pet. 1:3).

I was challenged to memorize portions of scripture and pray them back to God. One such passage was 1 Peter 5:5b-11. This was what I needed to focus on—the God of power promises to *"perfect, confirm, strengthen* and *establish"* us as we *"humble ourselves* under His mighty hand."* I prayed to that end—that I would humble myself before Him. God doesn't call us to do anything that His Son was not willing to do. Jesus, the very Son of God humbled Himself, taking the form of a bondservant and became obedient unto death to redeem us (Phil. 2:3-8)!

We cannot clothe ourselves in humility and bear our anxieties on our own. One of the ways we humble ourselves is to pray and seek His strength in everything, casting our anxieties on Him (1 Pet. 5:5-7). Why? Because God cares for us! We don't have to suffer in silence. We can cry out to our Father. David did, "Out of the depths I cry to you, O Lord" (Ps. 130:1). He hears and will answer.

Avoid Isolation by Seeking Fellowship

Although you feel like withdrawing, you need to fight for your life. You do this by utilizing the provision God has made for this very purpose—His church (Heb. 10:24). As the apostle Paul said, if one member suffers we all suffer (1 Cor. 12:26). In fellowship with believers you will find strength to persevere as others share the comfort they have received from the Lord (2 Cor. 1:4).

Before I was able to go to church, the church came to us. Many came and brought meals. One such meal especially touched my heart. In came the couple bringing the meal. The husband was pushing his wife in a wheelchair carrying the dinner that the husband had made. My wife asked them to stay and share the meal with us. These people knew suffering. They loved us in our pain. Men came to sit with me to give my wife a break and to lend support. I received calls from my pastor and pastors out of our area expressing concern and support. I received many cards and notes of encouragement from our church and my students. Although the kind words didn't instantly lift my depression, they assured me that I was not alone in it and gave me hope through promises from God's Word. I have kept them all and return to them and am encouraged again.

After my surgery before I was physically recovered enough to go to church, we listened to messages online from our own pastor, our son in law who pastors in South Africa, and other well-respected pastors on the topic of affliction.

When I had recovered enough physically but was still in depression, I went to church out of duty. It was like taking medicine that tastes terrible but brings healing. Obedience brings blessing.

When communion was served I told God that I didn't feel saved and I did not want to take communion in an unworthy manner. What would I do? Communion was being served. My thoughts went something like this:

> Lord you see who will be serving communion to me. He is one of our elders, and he is also the Chief Financial Officer of the college where I teach. He signs my payroll checks. What will he think if I don't take communion? Lord, that doesn't matter. It's not what he thinks that matters; it is what you think that matters. What should I do? *Bob, what would you tell someone who was not saved?* I would tell them to believe in Christ and to trust in him alone for salvation. I cannot see how I can be one of the elect and be this depressed, but that is what I believe will bring salvation to someone who genuinely puts their faith in Christ. *What does communion represent?* It represents the body and blood of Christ given for our salvation. *Then take communion and proclaim that you believe that the body and blood of Christ were the sacrifice needed to bring salvation to man even though you are not sure you are saved.*

I took communion. You will need to wrestle with your own doubts and make decisions to act against your feelings in obedience to God's Word as you understand it. Do what you know to be right by the Word of God whether you can feel the rightness of it or not.

Avoid Self-Reliance and Isolation through Seeking Counsel

Even in church you can still maintain your isolation if you don't let anyone into your life. You must find a mature Christian friend, an elder or biblical counselor, who can help you as you struggle with your depression. He or she can help you interpret the causes and find God's way out. If personal sin is the cause of this depression, your counselor can help you see your blind spots and make a plan to over-come that sin. He will be able to ask you good questions to examine your heart as my counselor did. Ask him or her to help you find Scripture passages that apply to specific areas in which you struggle. Pray together for the Holy Spirit's power to enable you to walk in victory as you memorize and meditate on His Word. Ask your friend to show you how to replace the sin in your life with patterns of obe-dience that will please God out of a heart that has been enraptured by His love. Remember that this is a moment-by-moment battle and a process. And again, you will have to act against your feelings and ask God for the will power to obey.

You may need to seek forgiveness, and go back and be reconciled to one you have offended or do other hard things in order to take care of your sin. God will strengthen you for the steps of obedience. You are helpless to solve your sin problem on your own. But God can radically change your heart by His Spirit if you surrender to Him, and He can lead you to a place of obedience and His blessing.

If persecution or other external pressures or physical ailments led to your depression, your counselor can help you to know best how to handle the trials you are facing in a God-honoring way. He can hold you accountable to avoid some of the responses I have described (and others that the Scriptures make us aware of) and train you to respond in a way that glorifies God.

Avoid Despair by Fighting Thoughts of Suicide

Depression often leads to thoughts of taking your own life. Even godly men in scripture longed for death. Who could blame Job when he said that he longed for death and searched for it more than for hidden treasures (Job 3:20-26)? Moses also pleaded with God to kill him because his burden was too great (Num. 11:14, 15). Jonah got angry at God and said, "O Lord, please take my life from me, for it is better for me to die than to live" (Jonah 4:3).

But these valiant men, even in their misery knew that God was the author of life and it was He alone who could give it and take it. To long for death at God's hands is understandable, but planning suicide is a sin that we must run from. We must remind ourselves that taking one's own life is murder. There is hope for any situation that you are facing through your powerful, sovereign God who will help you sort out what led you to this place and who will see you through. Suicide is never the answer.

Have a loved one help prevent you from sinning in this way. My son came to our house and removed everything that could be a danger. I admitted to the elder from our church who was counseling me that I was dealing with suicidal thoughts. When I considered stepping off of the curb into traffic I counseled myself as I had counseled others. This would be sin against God as the author of life and death (1 Sam. 2:6), the One who has numbered our days (Psalm 139). This would be sin against my wife and family whom I would be forsaking. It would destroy my testimony by telling the world that God cannot give us strength to persevere. This would also be a sin against the driver of the car who might be injured and could end up blaming himself for my willful sin.

John Bunyan was familiar with this temptation over 300 years ago. In his Christian classic, *The Pilgrim's Progress*, he writes about Christian and Hopeful being captured by Giant Despair who beats them mercilessly and then throws them into a dark, nasty, and stinking dungeon far from friends and in a hopeless state. He told them "that since they were never likely to come out of that dungeon, their only way of escape would be to make an end of themselves, either with knife, rope, or poison. 'For why,' said he, 'should you choose life, seeing it is attended with so much bitterness?'"[3] Christian who has triumphed over Apollyon and braved the Valley of the Shadow of Death and unflinchingly faced martyrdom at Vanity Fair is now ready to give in to the darkness and despair.

> "Brother," said Christian, "what shall we do? The life that we now live is so miserable. For my part I do not know which is best: to live like this, or to die and escape this misery. 'My soul chooseth strangling rather than life,' and the grave seems

more desirable than this dungeon.' Shall we be ruled by the giant?"

Hopeful suggested, "Indeed, our present condition is dreadful, and death would be a relief. But still let us consider that the Lord of the country to which we are going has said, 'You shall do no murder.' And if not to another man, how much more then are we forbidden to take the giant's counsel to kill ourselves? Besides, he who kills another can only commit murder upon a body; but for someone to kill himself is to kill body and soul at the same time. Besides, my brother, you talk about the ease of the grave. But have you forgotten the Hell to which murderers go? For 'no murderer has eternal life.' And let us consider again that the outcome of this is not in the hands of Giant Despair.... I am determined to gather all my courage and try my utmost to escape. I was a fool not to attempt an escape during the first fit. So, my brother, let us be patient and endure for a while longer. The time may come when we have an opportunity to escape, but let's not murder ourselves."[4]

Eventually Christian remembers that he has a key in his pocket called Promise which will open any lock in Doubting Castle, and they make their escape. I know through experience that hope is found in God's promises. As John Bunyan pictured it, God's promises are the key to unlock the door to Doubting Castle and set us free from Giant Despair.

There is more to your struggles than you can see. Scripture says that you are wrestling against the rulers, authorities, cosmic powers, spiritual forces of evil in the heavenly places (Eph. 6:12). Satan is our adversary and wants to destroy us when we're down. Jesus said that he is a murderer and the father of lies (John 8:44). Satan is telling you that you are done and that God has abandoned you and that everyone would be better off without you. Perhaps you believe that your sins are too bad for God to still love you. *Don't believe Satan's lies.*

Realize your helplessness, come to the Cross and turn to Jesus for rescue. In the Scriptures He assures you of His love—that He is with you and will never desert you nor forsake you (Heb. 13:5b). He is your Savior who is come to rescue you from yourself and your desires that are destroying you. He enters your world and understands what you're going through. Jesus grieves with you over the brokenness of your life. He is your sympathetic High Priest who understands temptation and suffering (Heb. 4:15). He drank the full cup when He went to the cross. He gives you His Spirit so you can grow through this trial and overcome the sin that may be destroying your life. You can come to realize He has allowed this for your good and His glory.

Commune with God through His Word

Take time each day to get into his Word with pen and paper at hand to note down a wonderful thing that God impresses on your mind (Ps 119:18). This forces you to be definite about what his Word is saying. *What truth in this text prompts me to take action in obedience and/or praise?* Take comfort from the promises of hope that abound. God's Word is ultimate truth—an antidote to distorted negative thoughts leading to hopelessness. Journal the lessons you are learning. This will help to bring meaning and purpose into your suffering.

Dig into the biblical accounts of godly men who experienced the depths of despair. We see how God met these men at their lowest point both physically and spiritually. He brought them out of their doubts through faith in His promises so that they were able to continue serving Him. Jeremiah's eyes were a fountain of tears and his heart was faint (Jer. 8:18–9:1). But in the midst of his sad lament, he gives one of the greatest expressions of hope found in the Bible. Let this key promise bring you out of the dungeon of despair:

> The Lord's lovingkindnesses indeed never cease, For His compassions never fail, They are new every morning; Great is Your faithfulness...For the Lord will not reject forever, For if He causes grief, Then He will have compassion according to His abundant lovingkindness. For He does not afflict willingly or grieve the sons of men (Lam. 3:22, 23, 31-33).

We can't stop being depressed just by telling ourselves to be happy. The only way to change how we feel inside is to change what occupies our minds—to "renew our minds" with the Word (Rom. 12:2). Our minds are renewed through the truth about our merciful and loving God as we do battle with our hearts to believe the promises of God. God's Word will wash you and draw you back to Himself and in His presence is fullness of joy (Ps. 16:11).

Look Outside Yourself

We must ask God for the strength to look beyond our own needs and pray for others who are suffering or who are in need of God's help. Remember that God's grace is made perfect in our weakness and just as Paul could boast in his weakness, we too can reach out to others in our weakness with the strength that He supplies.

Pray for and reach out to someone else on a daily basis no matter how you feel. My counselor held me accountable to do this through a phone call or email note of encouragement. The small mustard seed of the love of Christ was in me, and I needed to let it grow even in my depression. If the love of Christ is in us we will love one another (1 John 4:7). You may be surprised by the joy that you receive from giving to others. Again, I had to do this in obedience as I did not feel like I had anything to offer to others.

Joni Eareckson Tada gives the example of having a "Pain Pal" in her excellent book *A Place of Healing*. She prays for a very poor fellow believer in Africa who is paralyzed. She keeps his picture next to her desk. Her prayers lead to action through her ministry—Wheels for the World.[5] When one member of the Body suffers, we all suffer. His suffering has become hers. This is a way Joni fights against her own depression when her wheelchair begins to get her down. Why not get a Pain Pal to whom you can minister?

Avoid Despair through Perseverance

In my depression I was like the author of Ecclesiastes who after searching for meaning cries out,

"So I turned about and gave my heart up to despair over all the toil of my labors under the sun, because sometimes a person who has toiled with wisdom and knowledge and skill must leave everything to be enjoyed by someone who did not toil for it. This also is vanity and a great evil." (Eccles. 2:20-21 ESV)

I saw everything as vanity. It was as if my mind could only think in terms of despair and hopelessness. But even the author of Ecclesiastes did not stop there. Solomon kept searching until he could summarize his quest for meaning in this way, "The conclusion when all has been heard, is: fear God and keep His commandments, because this applies to every person" (Eccles. 12:13). Every act will be brought to judgment; nothing is futile in the end. You must not give up!

Perseverance is very important when dealing with depression. We must persevere in suffering and run the race set before us, just as we await the coming of the Lord (Rom. 5:3; Heb. 12:1; James 1:3; 5:11; 5:7). We are called to persevere in faith even when we can't see the why or the way before; avoiding bitterness and resentment. The proper response to our depression is to keep on trusting in our good God and not try to get revenge or turn back to evil. You don't persevere in your own strength but through the strength that He supplies. His promise is that, "He who began a good work in you will perfect it until the day of Christ Jesus" (Phil. 1:6). He keeps us! Our salvation is all of Him and He perseveres with us. It brings God glory when we walk by faith and not by sight, persevering to the end. God rewards perseverance (Rev. 2, 3).

What did not make sense while in the trial is beginning to make sense now. This will come true for you as well. I can hear you saying in your mind right now, *Sure, Sure! That is fine for you to say, and maybe that is true for you but it cannot be true for me. I can't believe that! You don't know how bad it is for me!* I can tell you that I thought those exact same thoughts when someone told me the truth. Now I know that they were right and I needed to persevere. So read on and believe the truth of God's Word rather than the lies of your own understanding.

Our afflictions help us draw closer to Christ and enable us to become more like Him and less centered on ourselves so in the end we experience more joy. It doesn't mean that God is happy about depression and all that goes with it. In an evil world, God allows evil to take place for His ends and purposes.

This trial has given my wife and me a deeper understanding of the nature of depression and a greater empathy for those going through it. We can see now how God is using what we went through as a platform for ministering to others, just as God used what Paul went through. Students come to me who are themselves struggling with depression, and I am able to give them encouragement and support. God has given both Mary and me numerous places in which to share our story and hopefully encourage others. Some of the stories we share were contributed by people who were touched by our lives. If God can use our trial to encourage someone else in the Gospel in their journey—praise God! What a joy!

Conclusion

So back to our question, "If I am a Christian, why am I depressed?"

I am depressed not because God has forsaken me but because a sovereign God has a plan to use this for good in my life. God can bring good out of depression as he conquers my fears, crushes my self-trust, barges into my isolation, and diffuses my despair. He can bring good out of depression as He teaches me to rejoice in affliction, to trust Him implicitly, to pray fervently, to rely on His church, to fight evil and to persevere. "In this you greatly rejoice, even though now for a little while, if necessary, you have been distressed by various trials, so that the proof of your faith, being more precious than gold which is perishable, even though tested by fire, may be found to result in praise and glory and honor at the revelation of Jesus Christ..." (1 Pet. 1:6-7).

Response

In the end each one must examine his own heart by asking, *Lord, you have allowed this trial, what do you want me to learn?* These are some ways to do that:
- Examine the contributing factors to your depression.

- o Make a list of the external pressures you are facing.
- o Make a list of the physical difficulties you are dealing with.
- o The next chapter will help you examine and deal with sin, but if deliberate sin was an issue, record that as well.
- o Make a list of your wrong responses to those contributing factors.
- Take steps to avoid those wrong responses
  - o If this chapter has made you aware of sinful responses to life's pressures, repent specifically and write how you will put off the sins of fear, self-reliance, isolation, or despair.
  - o Read Job 38–41. Ask God to give you a bigger vision of Himself. Record prayers of praise in your journal. Ask this God to help you trust Him with the circumstances that you are tempted to be depressed about. Ask Him to teach you to rely on Him through this difficult time.
  - o Make a plan to put on the new man. Choose which area you are going to work on and pick a verse to memorize regarding your need to rejoice, trust, pray, seek fellowship, seek counsel, fight suicidal thoughts, or persevere.
- Plan to go to church. Purpose to speak with at least one or two people, asking them about themselves and be willing to tell them how you are and ask them to pray for you.
- Reach out and do a loving thing each day for someone with whom you are close.

A Story of Post-Partum Depression and Triumph

Summer was over. We had just returned to our little west coast apartment after enjoying a visit with loved ones in Florida. Somehow we managed to sandwich a brief vacation in between nonstop summer school and fall classes. We had three years of seminary life under our belt and only one more to go. Tommy and I learned to cope with the little down time, little money, and little living space. Our kids never knew differently. We learned the art of savoring simple pleasures like McDonald's apple pies, free library videos, and peaceful evening drives. Our ever-expanding family of five grew to enjoy and embrace this life as semesters of my husband's seminary classes came and went. We witnessed the faithfulness of God in marvelous ways as He cared for our every need.

With graduation finally in sight, we dreamed of what was to come and hoped to soak up all that remained of our time there. Over the years we had concocted a much unchecked list of the touristy things we wanted to do before leaving California. Hopefully our long awaited trip up north to the big Redwoods would materialize. Or maybe it would be the San Diego Zoo or Tahoe slopes. During our plan-making we even laughed about squeezing in one more baby while we still had good insurance. "Why not?" we pondered.

Just as classes got underway, I developed a serious infection due to a recurring breastfeeding issue. This led to a short hospital stay and a round of strong antibiotics incompatible with nursing. Between the exhausting illness and potent meds, we believed it best for me to wean our eight-month-old son. Without a second thought I abruptly ended all feedings. My body had been producing milk around the clock so discomfort was inevitable—but I knew it would pass. I simply wanted to get on with life and put the whole hassle behind us.

Within days the infection began to heal. As my energy returned I jumped back into the swing of things, happy to roll up my stay-at-home mom sleeves again. A few nights later I found myself struggling to fall asleep. This was a strange occurrence since I typically dozed off before the lights were even out. I awoke the next day puzzled by the experience but not the least bit concerned. I got into bed that night feeling beat, but surprisingly I did not fall asleep. Again, I lay awake for hours, eventually drifting off just before morning. Waking up in a fog, I wondered what had provoked such a sudden disruption in my sleep.

By the end of the week I reached a melting point as my sleep spiraled into a complete nosedive. Crawling out of bed after a grueling night, I broke down in Tommy's arms. As we talked and prayed, he encouraged me to call a close family friend. Many seminary wives considered her a mother figure, including myself. She answered the phone to the sounds of sobbing as my composure collapsed. I finally managed to recount my terrible week of sleeplessness. She responded in a concerned voice, "Sarah, this is *not* you, something is *very* wrong." She urged me to call my doctor, which I did without hesitation.

Convinced my recent infection triggered the sleep disturbance, my doctor assured me the insomnia would eventually fizzle out. In the meantime, he prescribed a mild sleeping pill to take as needed. At last I obtained a little rest, but it proved short-lived. With or without the pills, my sleep remained unstable. Hourly, this unexpected trial tested my body, mind, and soul. The days painfully crept by while I dreaded each lonely and tortuous night.

Although far from my best, I attempted to maintain some regularity about our home life for the sake of my family, but it grew harder each day. Our busy life with three young children could not compete with the relentless insomnia. Tommy frequently took off work and missed classes to relieve the strain on our family. As the pressure mounted, we fervently prayed for relief— and expected it. We hadn't anticipated things getting worse.

One afternoon while I mindlessly dusted our living room, a wave of intense darkness suddenly engulfed me. The very light of my soul seemed extinguished, and I felt trapped in a black hole. I found myself helpless to escape the unshakeable terror, no matter what I did or prayed. I called my husband in desperation. He prayed for me and left work early to take us out to dinner, hoping a change of scenery would direct my mind away from the struggle. The blackness slowly faded that evening, and I sighed in deep relief. I would have gladly traded a thousand nights of sleep to avoid experiencing that again. It wasn't long before we realized the harrowing encounter was merely a foretaste of what lay ahead.

The dark episodes continued to overtake me, unannounced and unflinching to my defenses. My stability started to unravel fast as life became a carnival of nightmares. I began to suffer from extreme anxiety, obsessive fears, and compulsive thoughts—all the while with no relief from the chronic insomnia.

My mental state became a constant frenzy of chaos. Unwelcome thoughts harassed me day and night. Troubling images plagued my mind like a song stuck on repeat. I avoided the television and computer, afraid of being haunted by what I saw or read. I became hypersensitive to background noise. I could not bear the sound of a ticking clock, so my mother's wedding gift had to come off the wall. Running our dishwasher terrified me as its incessant humming drilled through my brain—likewise the refrigerator motor kicking on and off. Even the trickling of the courtyard fountain threatened my sanity.

My physical state rapidly deteriorated. Eating became a major chore as my appetite disappeared and my clothes began to hang on me. The exhaustion and lingering side effects from sleeping pills made it hard to function normally, so I could no longer drive. We arranged for people to be with our children and me as much as possible because of my fragile mental and physical condition. We converted our bedroom into something like a bunker—sound-proof, light-proof and even child-proof. Nightly, I retired there and lay alone with earplugs, black-out curtains, and a rolled-up towel pressed against the bottom of a locked door. Tommy slept in the living room with our baby in an attempt to shield any interruption and protect my sleeping environment at all costs.

In six weeks' time only a semblance remained of my former life. Tommy officially withdrew from classes and the spring graduation we anticipated faded away like a distant memory. We had never been so blind-sided and watched helplessly as our life and plans seemed to fall apart. I held on tightly to whatever was spared in the rubble—my children, my husband, and most importantly, my faith.

I clung to God's Word with every waking breath, plastering the walls with verses, even scribbling or taping them on my hands. I desperately fought to fix my thoughts on truth—the only stable voice in my mind. Everything seemed to shout my demise so I staked all my hope on God's promises such as, "Never will I leave you, never will I forsake you." Assailed with, "*You will not survive this ...,*" I repeated, "My heart and my flesh may fail but God is the strength of my heart and my portion forever." Grasping for my sanity, I even kept a card with these words written across, "You are not crazy!" At times I stared at it to keep myself from believing otherwise.

Even with all we had faced together, a foreboding fear remained: *Perhaps we had yet to touch the bottom of this pit. Would Tommy be forced to abandon seminary, possibly even ministry? Would I end up unfit to care for my family or infinitely worse, be taken away from them?* On several occasions I keenly felt only one slight nudge existed between me and a hospital bed.

Then the day arrived, when in the words of Job, "the thing I greatly feared had come upon me." We planned to attend church that morning but instead I lay crumpled on the floor in my husband's lap with our children gathered around. Sobs of anguish shook my body as Tommy prayed over me with tears. The excruciating sleeplessness had issued its deathblow. My soul and body could endure no more. We paged my doctor, and he advised me to check into the ER in the hope of securing a new prescription for some much-needed sleep.

Lying on the triage bed, I encountered an onslaught of questions regarding my mental health. Panic set in as I realized the doctor wanted to admit me for a psychological evaluation. Instinctively, I wanted to bolt for the door, but I couldn't forfeit my only option for immediate prescriptive help. The doctor insisted I spend the night because the chair of their psychiatric ward would not arrive until morning. This left me terror-struck. Faced with an impossible choice, Tommy encouraged me to stay while he kept the kids at home. Every preceding moment of this trial had been bathed in prayer so we held fast our confidence that God would not lead us astray at such a desperate hour—no matter how counter-Christian and petrifying this all seemed.

I begged the staff to put me anywhere but the psychiatric unit, knowing I was in no position to handle a potentially traumatic environment. Much to my relief, they complied. I faced the moment of truth as they wheeled me into a room and handed me a gown and booties. I was given a grooming basket but warned not to use anything without supervision. My worst fears of becoming a mental patient were unfolding before me.

I sat in eerie silence until noticing the big, ticking clock staring at me from across the room. In that moment, I was convinced this place would result in my final undoing. I scrambled for the small Bible in my purse and began to devour page after page of Scripture. I shudder to imagine that night without this God-sent escape. Powerful truth washed over my dread and soothed my anxiety-ridden heart. I knew that if God could uphold me through *this*, He could sustain me through anything. I pulled up my blanket in peace, closed my eyes and securely rested in His faithfulness.

I met with the hospital's leading psychiatrist the next day. After hearing me rehearse the past two months she confidently stated that I was in a textbook post-partum depression with classic symptoms such as insomnia, anxiety, loss of appetite and rapid mood decline. This was not a staggering revelation. We already felt sure that my abrupt weaning had caused the hormonal landslide I was experiencing. Her confirmation was reassuring, but her prescribed solution was not. I later experienced a very adverse reaction to the dose of medication she recommended.

In God's perfect providence, this faith-testing turn of events paved the way to an amazing Christian doctor who firmly believed in the sufficiency of Christ and a conservative use of proven medicine when necessary. Up to this point we had tried every natural sleeping remedy known to man while bolstering my diet with the best depression-combating foods and supplements. I strongly resisted the idea of using any prescription other than a sleeping pill—which I reluctantly took and received little benefit from. After two long, miserable months, I could bear no more. We trusted this doctor and were willing to try whatever he recommended. And above all, we trusted God, continually seeking Him for help and guidance.

Our primary goal was to reestablish my sleep. Incredibly, the worst of my anxiety and dark spells had already begun to vanish as God's Word gained control of my hijacked mind. But in spite of this victory, the insomnia hadn't budged. My new doctor believed a low-dose antidepressant could help me overcome the sleeplessness. After a rough week of adjusting to the medicine, we witnessed steady improvement in my sleep for the first time. Within three weeks, it gradually began to resemble normal.

My sleep continued to stabilize, my appetite returned, and my mind remained sound—thanks be to God and the power of His Word! I overflowed with immeasurable gratitude as each day brought further healing and restoration. Within eight weeks of starting the antidepressant—with my doctor's consent—I successfully weaned off the medicine without the slightest relapse.

We stood in awe of God's kindness and mercy. It was the first time I felt like myself in five months, even though I knew life could never truly be the same again. This rugged journey exposed unimaginable frailties in me. I no longer felt safe in the former myths I once rested in—that I was incapable of such instability and personal weakness. I discovered a new default: resting in the indestructible refuge of God's perfect strength.

Three years past this trial, I am still daily impacted by it. Nothing in my Christian life has been more instrumental in drawing me closer to God. I have a greater confidence in His hold on my life and how He uses all things, *even awfully hard things*, for my ultimate good. Those truths have sustained me through subsequent times of testing and have continued to grow my faith in significant ways.

Tommy and I now possess a much greater compassion for others in turmoil, especially those in the clutches of depression. I've prayed for *battlefield wisdom* to impart to anyone facing this dark struggle. I am keenly aware that we'd all be one breath away from an asylum if not for God's mercy. Each happy and sane moment our Redeemer provides is cause for praise. No person, Christian or not, is safe from depression or a mental crisis.

When the wrecking ball of depression hits, confusion and panic often ensue—especially when it happens unexpectedly. I was desperate for answers. My husband taught me to *deal with what we knew and trust God for what we didn't know*, instead of frantically searching the Internet for help. Determining how we got here—and every confusing detail in between—mattered little. Resolving how to trust God and move forward made all the difference.

Trusting in God's promises was the only thing keeping me afloat in the floodwaters of despair. Like David, if I had not known His Word I would have perished in my affliction. The Word of God is depression's greatest enemy. Scripture won the battle for my sanity and hope.

A very wise and compassionate pastor counseled me to resist morbid introspection and over-spiritualizing every aspect of my depression. Attempting to untangle each emotion or assigning some profound meaning to each struggle was an endless maze of confusion and distress. I found myself simply saying, "Lord, I am yours—me and all these struggles—we are all yours!"

I learned how to grab hold of today's mercies for today's difficulties. Grace for the moment became my anthem. In the middle of a depression, one day at a time becomes one hour—even one minute at a time. Fear was always whispering, "The worst is yet to come." Each day had enough trouble of its own, but God supplied every ounce of grace I needed.

Depression is a dream-crippler. It dashed our hopes for more children. I couldn't risk tampering with my hormones again. It killed our plans for a seminary degree. Tommy couldn't finish school, knowing that the pressure could derail my recovery. But "the counsel of the Lord stands forever." One year later, we welcomed our fourth child as Tommy wrapped up his final semester in seminary!

I learned not to blame well-meaning friends or respond sinfully when they offered ground-shattering insight such as, "Try to think of something happy when you can't fall asleep." I needed life-anchoring assurance that God would see me through this trial, not casually tossed-out platitudes. God helped me to simply smile, nod, and thank them for their care and especially their prayers.

There is a lot of sunshine even in the storm. Our family in Christ rallied around us in such touching ways—baking cupcakes for my daughter's birthday, assisting us with meals, cleaning our apartment, and providing company when I needed it most. Even a simple gift of flowers for my windowsill added a bright spot in all the dreariness. The Lord also provided a dear sister in Christ whose medical background and personal battle with depression helped me invaluably. She walked me through every step and the darkest of moments. God also gave me the sweet and unexpected gift of the Somervilles. They held my hand, looked me in the eye, and promised God's grace would be sufficient and that He would see me through this. And from beginning to end, God sustained us through the faithful prayers of our family and friends.

Depression does not wait for the right time to invade a person's life. It does not spare presidents, pastors, or busy mothers from its pain. Depression does not care if it ruins our lives. But we are not at the mercy of depression. It operates under the dominion of our sovereign God, who determines its pre-appointed boundaries. I've never felt more weak, desperate, and vulnerable than when passing through this darkness; yet each day God grew my confidence that if He is for me, nothing can successfully plot against me—nothing. He loves me more than I can fathom. The trial was fierce, but in the end God prevailed. And as Paul writes in 2 Corinthians 2:14, "Thanks be to God, who always leads us in triumph in Christ."

Sarah Clayton, Wife and Mother

Self-Depreciation

O Lord,
    Help me to approach thee
        with becoming conception of thy nature, relations and
designs.
    Thou inhabitest eternity, and
        my life is nothing before thee;
    Thou dwellest in the highest heaven and this cannot contain thee;
        I live in a house of clay.
    Thy power is almighty;
        I am crushed before the moth.
    Thy understanding is infinite;
        I know nothing as I ought to know.
    Thou canst not behold evil;
        I am vile.
    In my ignorance, weakness, fears, depressions,
        may thy Spirit help my infirmities
        with supplies of wisdom, strength and comfort.
    Let me faithfully study my character,
        be willing to bring it to light,
        observe myself in my trials,
        judge the reality and degree of my grace,
        consider how I have been ensnared or overcome.
    Grant that I may never trust my heart,
        depend upon any past experiences,
        magnify any present resolutions,
        but be strong in the grace of Jesus;
        that I may know how to obtain relief from a guilty conscience
        without feeling reconciled to my imperfections.
    Sustain me under my trials and improve them to me;
        give me grace to rest in thee,
        and assure me of deliverance.
    May I always combine thy majesty with thy mercy,
        and connect thy goodness with thy greatness.
    Then shall my heart always rejoice in praises to thee.

─────── ⚘ CHAPTER 5 ⚘ ───────

How Do I Handle My Guilt?

What happiness for those whose guilt has been forgiven!
What joys when sins are covered over! What relief for
those who have confessed their sins and God
has cleared their record.
(Psalm 32:1, LB)

Guilt Has a Purpose

A friend recently told me her story of a narrow escape. She had stayed up late studying for exams. It was freezing cold, so she had the electric heater close to her bed. Lying down for a second to warm up, she was soon fast asleep. As her body was just starting to feast on this delicious bit of sleep and warmth, she was rudely disturbed by noise in the hallway. But this time she could not block out the raucous college students. They started pounding on her door louder and louder until she roused to find that her hair was on fire! The smoke detector had gone off and saved her life!

Guilt is the smoke detector in our lives. God has written His Law on our hearts. He has given us the gift of a conscience. Our consciences tell us that there is a God and we are accountable to Him (Rom. 1:20; 1 Pet. 3:16). If we do not deaden our consciences through ignoring them, they will make us miserable when we sin. The heart will cry out, "Guilty! Condemned! Lost!" This is a good thing because guilt is warning us of judgment. That's originally what helps bring us to Christ for salvation.

Real, true guilt is more than a feeling. It is *culpability before God for breaking His standard of righteousness*. It dates back to when the first man, Adam, sinned. God gave him only one command, "Of every tree of the garden you may freely eat, but of the tree of the knowledge of good and evil you shall not eat" (Gen. 2:16, 17). Even though Adam lived in paradise and had everything he could ever need or desire, he still disobeyed God and ate the fruit. When he disobeyed God, he was guilty. God had warned him that consequences would follow. He declared, "On the day you eat of it, you shall surely die." When Adam sinned he showed what every one of us would do if given the chance. And every day when we are given the chance we also choose to disobey. "And thus death spread to all men, because all sinned." (Rom.5:12).

We are all in a state of guilt before a holy God. Our hearts are sinful, and we cannot please God on our own. We all fall short of His glory (Rom. 3:23). We break His law. Jesus summed up the law like this, "You shall love the Lord your God with all your heart and with all your soul and with all your mind. And ... you shall love your neighbor as yourself" (Matt. 22:37-39). Just two rules and we have all broken them not just outwardly but in our hearts as well. He demands not only our obedience but our love for Him. He looks into our hearts and sees our very motives. If they are tainted, our obedience is worthless.

We are guilty of breaking God's righteous law. That means we have sinned against the infinitely holy Lawgiver Himself (Ps. 51:4). Therefore we owe an infinite debt that we can never pay! This guilt should drive us to put our faith in Jesus who took the payment for our law-breaking on the cross and kept the Law perfectly in our place. When that transaction is made—my sin for His righteousness—God declares me "Not Guilty" or justified (Rom. 8:1). Now my desire is to walk in the righteousness that He purchased for me with His death and resurrection. I am no longer a slave of sin. I can do what is right (Rom. 6). But when I go back to my old master and willingly serve the flesh, I experience guilt again. It is warning me that I am sinning against the Lord who bought me! If I continue in sin and trample Christ's sacrifice, I show that I was not truly saved. If I am saved, God will discipline me in order to bring me back into fellowship with Himself.

From my many years of counseling, I know that God sometimes uses tough means to get our attention. Depression gets our attention. It can sometimes come from forgetting our main purpose here on earth and going after worldly gain, pleasures, and things which do not satisfy. Depression can be a warning to take stock of what is important—not our own selfish desires or self-aggrandizement, but His glory. We can trust the good purposes of God in bringing us to a place of depression (although it is a very painful thing) if it helps to reveal what we value, what we think will make us happy outside of Him. We come to a crossroads. Are we going to rebel against God's purposes in our lives or accept what God is doing and seek His strength to put Him in His rightful place in our lives?

There is hope in calling sin "sin" because that's why Jesus died and rose again—to break the power of sin in our lives and to give us His righteousness and joy. David is our biblical example of depression caused by sin. You can read his story in 2 Samuel 11–12. He confessed, "When I kept silent about my sin, my body wasted away through my groaning all day long. For day and night Your hand was heavy upon me; my vitality was drained away as with the fever heat of summer" (Ps. 32:3, 4). David was depressed because God was using guilt to draw him back to Himself.

John Piper admonishes those in darkness to start at the easiest place.

> Start with despair. Despair of finding any answer in yourself. I pray that you will cease from all efforts to look inside yourself for the rescue you need. I pray that you will do what only desperate people can do, namely, cast yourself on Christ. May you say to him, "You are my only hope. I have no righteousness in myself. I am overwhelmed with sin and guilt. I am under the wrath of God. My own conscience condemns me, and makes me miserable. I am perishing. Darkness is all about me. Have mercy upon me. I trust you."[1]

Confess and Forsake Your Sin

David thought he had done a pretty good job of covering up his secret sin with a beautiful woman. Bathsheba was pregnant, but she was now his wife. Her husband had died honorably in battle. No one was the wiser. But he knew what he had done and he was miserable. The best thing that happened to this guilty king was when God sent Nathan the prophet to point his icy finger at David's nose and declare, "You are the man!" Then the brave prophet brought it all out into the light. He exposed David's treachery to the God who had appointed him as king and preserved his life and blessed him with all he could ask for. He exposed his adultery and his betrayal of Uriah the Hittite. He rendered God's judgment.

David's high tower of pretenses crumbled around him and he admitted, "I have sinned against the Lord." In Psalm 32 he goes on to say, "I acknowledged my sin to You, and my iniquity I did not hide; I said, 'I will confess my transgressions to the Lord'; and You forgave the guilt of my sin" (Ps. 32:5). That is where we need to start!

You also need a Nathan who is not afraid to call sin "sin." This is where it is good to have a biblical counselor or another compassionate believer to help you sort it out. Now remember that I had practiced biblical counseling for thirty-seven years when I was overcome by depression. I had counseled possibly a few hundred depressed people, but now I needed to receive counsel. I needed to humble myself, admit my depression, and ask for help! No matter how well you have known the scriptures, or how long you have walked with the Lord, just like David you still need counsel. As that counselor opens up God's Word to you, he can help you with the examination process. He can ask good questions to see if there is sin behind the guilt that needs to be confessed. He can hold you accountable for change.

Turn from Willful Sin

Perhaps you are following your flesh like David did. You know that your lifestyle is not honoring to God. You might be involved in a life-dominating sin like those that Paul listed in Galatians such as "immorality, impurity, sensuality, idolatry, sorcery, enmities, strife, jealousy, outbursts of anger, disputes, dissensions, factions, envying, drunkenness, carousing, ..." (Gal. 5:19-21). You must bring these things out into the light. You must agree with God that these are the "deeds of the flesh" and "those that practice such things shall not inherit the kingdom of God." Take radical measures to deal with these sins. Jesus said, "So if your hand or foot causes you to sin, cut it off and throw it away. Better to enter heaven crippled than to be in hell with both of your hands and feet" (Matt. 18:8, LB). In other words, do anything necessary to cut that sin out of your life and to put on righteousness in its place.

You cannot free yourself from these powerful sins. The only recourse is to despise your filth and cry out to God to wash you. The Bible asks you:

Do you not know that the unrighteous shall not inherit the kingdom of God? Do not be deceived; neither fornicators nor idolaters, nor adulterers, nor effeminate, nor homosexuals, nor thieves, nor the covetous, nor drunkards, nor revilers, nor swindlers, shall inherit the kingdom of God. And such were some of you; but you were washed, but you were sanctified, but you were justified in the name of the Lord Jesus Christ, and in the Spirit of our God. (1 Cor. 6:9-11)

Then you will be able to say with David, "What happiness for those whose guilt has been forgiven! What joys when sins are covered over! What relief for those who have confessed their sins and God has cleared their record" (Ps. 32:1, LB).

What if No Willful Sin is Involved?

Sometimes depression does not come from unconfessed, willful disobedience. It is possible that you are suffering like Job. God singled him out as a righteous man to demonstrate to Satan that there is such a thing as innocent suffering. Not all suffering is directly related to a specific sin. (For further study in this area see *How Long,*

O Lord? Reflections on Suffering and Evil, Chapter 9 "Job: Mystery and Faith" by D.A. Carson.)

If you, at the end of the day, cannot identify any specific sin that led up to your depression that needs to be confessed, you need to know that you are not alone. God justified Job to his miserable counselors. They thought he was guilty because he was suffering. But he was genuinely serving God from a pure heart (Job 42:7-8). God was not punishing him but using the trial to reveal Himself in a greater way to Job and to all of us.

Exposing Idols of the Heart

What about you and me? Most of us are not quite as righteous as Job. The depression can still reveal idols of the heart. Even though it was not willful sin that got me into the depression, God was working in my heart to show me that I needed to put off sins such as pride, idolizing comfort, and craving control. I had also sinned against my body by taxing it beyond its limits. Ask God to show you what you are treasuring more than Christ. Ask him to reveal your hidden faults. Plead with the Psalmist, "Search me, O God, and know my heart; try me and know my anxious thoughts; and see if there be any hurtful way in me, and lead me in the everlasting way" (Ps. 139:23, 24).

The best way to avoid self-deception (Heb. 3:13) is to make sure you are a member at a church where God's Word is preached faithfully. You want the searchlight of Scripture shining into your life. You don't want Sunday morning sermons that are superficial and comfortable. Israel had this problem just before being exiled into Babylon.

Everyone is greedy for gain, and from the prophet even to the priest everyone deals falsely, and they have healed the brokenness of My people superficially, saying, "Peace, peace," but there is no peace. "Were they ashamed because of the abomination they have done? They were not even ashamed at all; they did not even know how to blush. Therefore they shall fall among those who fall: at the time that I punish them, they shall be cast down," says the Lord. Thus says the Lord,

"Stand by the ways and see and ask for the ancient paths, where the good way is, and walk in it; and you shall find rest for your souls." (Jer. 6:13-16)

You don't need a pastor who is innovative. You just need someone who will show you the ancient paths, a man who watches his life and doctrine closely (1 Tim. 4:16). If God's Word is preached verse by verse, your heart idols will be exposed and thrown down before they gain greater mastery over you.

I want to encourage you to confess what you are guilty of and receive the forgiveness that is available in the cross of Christ (1 John 1:9). Then take steps to make things right. If you have sinned against another person you will need to seek forgiveness from that person and if possible make restitution. Jesus recognized that salvation had come to rich Zaccheus the chief tax gatherer when he heard him declare, "Lord, half of my possessions I will give to the poor, and if I have defrauded anyone of anything, I will give back four times as much" (Luke 19:8-10). The law only required the extortionist to make restitution by giving back one fifth above what he had stolen (Lev. 6:4-5; Num. 5:7). But joy over Jesus' invitation made the new man rush to do much more than was required.

How will you show your repentance? If you cannot speak to each person that you have wronged face to face, write a letter. Tell the offended party that you sinned against them. Call it what God calls it. Do not make any excuses. Tell them what you plan to do to make restitution and ask if there is anything else you need to do to restore trust. Do not take communion until you have done as much as you can on your side to be reconciled (Matt. 5:23-24). You can do all things through Christ who strengthens you (Phil. 4:13). We have this great hope, "He who conceals his transgression will not prosper, but he who confesses and forsakes them will find compassion" (Prov. 28:13b). What hope that brings!

Inappropriate Guilt

It may be that some of us in depression are living under a measure of guilt and shame that is not appropriate in light of our redeemed state. If you have confessed your sins and turned to Christ in repentance and faith, the verdict is in: Not guilty! Your sins were covered by the blood of Christ. "He made Him who knew no sin to be sin on our behalf, that we might become the righteousness of God in Him" (2 Cor. 5:21). Not only are you not guilty but you have Christ's righteousness imputed to your account. You are seen by God as someone who has always pleased Him by keeping all His commandments from the heart. Jesus' perfect obedience has been accredited to you. Even if you don't feel it, know that the transaction has taken place. You are justified!

Rest in Your Position in Christ

Dear friend, rest in the forgiveness you have in Christ. If your emotions are telling you, as mine did, "Things are hopeless, Bob. God is sorry He made you. You are a failure. You could not be saved and think as you are thinking," don't believe it for a second. You can't trust your subjective darkness. You have an objective hope based on God's Word that tells you that He couldn't love you more. "But God demonstrates His own love toward us, in that while we were yet sinners, Christ died for us. Much more then, having now been justified by His blood, we shall be saved from the wrath of God through Him" (Rom. 5:8-9). Your salvation does not rest on your performance but on Christ's accomplishment.

Find Mercy By Reeducating Your Conscience

If you are still feeling guilt after you have confessed all known sin and welcomed conviction from those who might point out your hidden sins, then you must reeducate your conscience with God's Word. To continually feel guilty is not what God intended. The conscience is not basing its judgment upon the truth and is therefore false. To have a standard different from God is wrong. The convictions of our heart must be subjected to God's Word and the Gospel. The bottom line is to believe God at all times and not our feelings.

I found that, when I was in severe depression, my conscience was telling me, "You should be working; you shouldn't be down and discouraged; that is sin." The fact was that I couldn't have worked because of my physical and mental state. It was not a sin to take time to rest and recover. My thought processes needed to be corrected by my wife and others.

Conclusion

So, how do I handle guilt? I run to Jesus. I confess any willful sins. I examine my heart to see if there are any idols that I need to destroy. I repent and forsake my sins and find mercy through His cross. "Thanks be to God through Jesus Christ our Lord! ...There is therefore now no condemnation for those who are in Christ Jesus. For the law of the Spirit of life in Christ Jesus has set you free from the law of sin and death" (Rom. 7:25a, 8:1, 2). The accuser of the brethren who wants me to dwell on my guilt cannot keep me in despair over my sin when I dwell on my perfect position in Christ because of His shed blood and His intercessory work for me right now.

Response

Guilt is a good thing if it drives us to Jesus. It's an alarm that we should not try to silence. Here are some important responses:

- Have you dealt radically with any deeds of the flesh that are hindering you from entering the kingdom of God? Read through the lists in Galatians 5:19-21 and 1 Corinthians 6:9-11. If you are still struggling with one of these sins, thank God that you feel guilty! Use David's prayer of repentance in Psalm 51 to help you cry out to God for pardon. Find a wise Christian who can help you to cut everything out of your life that tempts you to fall back into that sin. As you start to walk in the Spirit, you will not fulfill the deeds of the flesh and the Spirit will assure you that you are God's child.
- Ask a biblical counselor or a wise and godly friend to help you to examine your heart. Ask them if they have seen the fruit of the Spirit in your life in the past? Have they observed in you what they believed to be a genuine walk with Christ? Ask your spouse. Listen to their counsel.

- In your journal list the doubts that you are currently facing and evaluate them with your counselor one at a time.
- Ask God to reveal to you anything that you are treasuring more than Christ. The Holy Spirit's work is to let us know what grieves the heart of God in our lives. Perhaps we've idolized beauty or health or security. Or, maybe we worship being in control of our circumstances. There are many things that can easily gain higher priority than Christ—whether intentionally or not. Here are some questions you can ask yourself to help see if this is the case:
  o What do you think you must have in order for your life to have meaning again?
  o Are you making a place in your heart for what you know to be sin in the Lord's eyes?
  o Have you sought worldly success at the expense of everything else?
  o Do you seek the approval of people more than approval from God?
  o Have you neglected the spiritual leadership of your family?
  o Have your disappointments, busy lifestyle or other issues led to sin in the area of not caring for your body, the temple of the Holy Spirit?
  o Are you filled with anger and bitterness, and are you unwilling to forgive someone?
  o Are there other sins that came out of these idolatries of the heart such as dishonesty, slander, use of pornography, adultery, unbiblical divorce, or even murder as in the case of David?

Did you answer yes to any of those questions as I did? If so, you need to come to the Lord, the One who loves you, with a broken heart over your sins, confessing them to Him. When you confess your sin there is forgiveness—no matter what! Scripture says, "Such were some of you; but you were washed ... sanctified ... justified" (1 Cor. 6:9-11). Talk this over with your friend and pray together (James 5:16).

A Story of Sinful Response to Trials and God's Deliverance

*F*rom the vantage point of a senior citizen, I can look back over my life and see *events* that, from a secular viewpoint, may have caused my depression. However, after several years of study, the guidance of a biblical counselor and a renewed relationship with the Lord, I now realize that my *sinful response to* those events led to thirty years wasted in the bleakness of depression.

My father was an alcoholic, and my parents divorced when I was three years old. Depression is evident on my father's side of the family in his alcoholism and my half-brother's suicide. My mother was married and divorced two more times by the time I reached adulthood. When I was five, we moved from the home of my grandparents to another state so my father wouldn't be able to find us. So you see that my childhood was anything but happy and normal.

I married and became a mother as an immature teenager. My response to an out of control life, was to attempt to be in control. When I encountered a situation where someone I cared about was being abused, it angered me that I was unable to stop it because I wasn't in control. Later guilt over my perceived inadequacy in this situation plagued me. When my family and I encountered major trauma, illness, and various other trials, I made decisions based on what I thought was best but often not biblically directed, which led to consequences that complicated my life still more.

My early symptoms of depression were mild, including frustration and crying spells. My physician recommended increased exercise, psychological counseling, and relaxation therapy. These band-aides didn't address the root of the problem. About five years later when I returned to college for my nursing degree, my husband was in a major automobile accident. Then my symptoms became more severe, interfering with my studies and my daily life. My instructor in the psychiatric rotation of my nursing studies recommended a Marriage and Family Counselor (MFCC), who referred me to my family physician who prescribed a tricyclic antidepressant. I was on this medication for about five years, through periods of major change in my life. I started seeing a psychiatrist when my symptoms worsened. He put me on a newer class of antidepressant, a serotonin reuptake inhibitor (Zoloft). Later, my doctor added another tricyclic antidepressant for insomnia. My symptoms persisted but to a milder degree.

My husband also went through a period of depression after he lost his job and never looked for another one. We did some traveling and relocated to another state, and then I came down with an illness which causes insomnia due to chronic pain. Nevertheless, I continued to work until my retirement almost ten years ago. We continue to travel, spending summers in our home in West Virginia and winters in southern California with our children.

I saw a Marriage and Family Counselor, who was a Christian, for several years. His method of counseling was looking at my personal life and stressors, but his treatment was secular. He recommended antidepressants, which were again prescribed for me by my family physician. I was on antidepressants from 1989 until 2012. On two occasions, each under the care of a different psychiatrist, I attempted to "wean off" as the drugs were damaging my liver. Neither attempt was successful. I went through difficult times when I was tempted by suicidal thoughts. I had to ask my husband to remove all of the handguns from our home. Because of my faith, suicide was not an option to consider, but I was taking no chances.

In His timing God brought help to me through our son Scott who entered the master's degree program in biblical counseling at The Master's College. During his graduate studies there, Scott took courses from Dr. Robert Somerville and sought his counsel on how to help me. Dr. Somerville helped me connect with a biblical counselor who met with me weekly to walk me through the steps of biblical counseling and monitor the progress of my withdrawal from antidepressants (with the help of my doctor).

I had read my Bible regularly since being saved at age fourteen but never on a consistent daily basis or with such a focused plan. I have learned to search God's Word on issues in my daily life and to seek the wise counsel of biblically sound authors. I have been off antidepressants for over two years now. Praise God I can now look back and see how He has guided me step by step through this process over the years, especially the last ten years.

One of the benefits of being off of antidepressants is that I feel emotions, both lows and highs, that I am supposed to feel. I now see them as "normal" rather than something that needs to be medicated. I continue with daily focused Bible reading, participate in Bible studies as well as a worship service each week, and I am usually reading at least one book by a biblically sound author all the time.

My current focus is on improving and expanding my time in prayer. I also keep in touch with my counselor and know I can contact her as I did recently to discuss issues related to some major changes in my life. All of these things keep me grounded in the Word, which I feel is the most important stabilizing influence in my God-centered life. That's the key: God is now the center of my life, not I or my husband or my children or my circumstances. Everything else revolves around Him and His teachings.

I now have come to realize that it was my response to the events in my life rather than the events themselves that led to my depression. My sins of anger and false guilt were the real causes. Without realizing it, I allowed these sins to overshadow my life, separating me from the peace God promises in His Word and the Gospel of Jesus Christ. I praise Him for forgiveness through His blood and freedom from the guilt and penalty of all my sin!

I would recommend these three things as most important to someone else dealing with depression:

1. Seek God and make Him the center of your life.
2. Seek wise biblical counsel. If necessary, seek wise medical counsel. I believe antidepressants can be helpful in some cases on a temporary basis.
3. Be diligent in pursuing the things you learn through counseling for the rest of your life. Trials will continue to come into your life. God has the answers, but you won't find them if you don't keep seeking.

Jane Meadows

The Deeps

Lord Jesus,
    Give me a deeper repentance,
        a horror of sin,
        a dread of its approach;
    Help me to flee it,
        And jealously to resolve that my heart shall be thine alone.
    Give me a deeper trust,
        that I may lose myself to find myself in thee,
        the ground of my rest,
        the spring of my being.
    Give me a deeper knowledge of thyself
        as savior, master, lord, and king.
    Give me deeper power in private prayer,
        more sweetness in thy Word,
        more steadfast grip on its truth.
    Give me deeper holiness in speech, thought, action,
        and let me not seek moral virtue apart from thee.
    Plough deep in me, great Lord, heavenly husbandman,
        that my being may be a tilled field,
        the roots of grace spreading far and wide,
        until thou alone art seen in me,
        thy beauty golden like summer harvest,
        thy fruitfulness as autumn plenty.
    I have no master but thee,
        no law but thy will,
        no delight but thyself,
        no wealth but that thou gives,
        no good but that thou blesses,
        no peace but that thou bestow.
    I am nothing but that thou make me,
    I have nothing but that I receive from thee,
    I can be nothing but that grace adorns me.
    Quarry me deep, dear Lord,
        And then fill me to overflowing with living water.

─────⋙ CHAPTER 6 ⋘─────

What's Going on with My Body and Mind?

But if we *hope* for what we do not see, with *persever-ance* we wait eagerly for it (the redemption of our body). (Romans 8:25)

S o what is going on? I see everything through the grid of this depression! Nothing looks good! The light at the end of the tunnel is a train coming straight at me. I am like the author of Ecclesiastes who when after searching for meaning cries out,

> So I turned about and gave my heart up to despair over all the toil of my labors under the sun, because sometimes a person who has toiled with wisdom and knowledge and skill must leave everything to be enjoyed by someone who did not toil for it. This also is vanity and a great evil. (Eccles. 2:20-21 ESV)

I saw everything as vanity. It is as if my mind could only think in terms of despair and hopelessness. My head literally felt fuzzy. It was as if my thinking was in slow motion. I could not make up my mind about the simplest decisions.

So what was going on in my body? I had absolutely no appe-tite—not even a desire for ice cream and that had been a treat all of my life! People would observe my weight loss and say, "Bob you look great!" I would think, *I might look great but I don't feel great and if this is a diet plan you surely don't want to be on it!* All of this started with the herniated disc in my back and the pain that came with that, but then how did this relate to loss of appetite and a fuzzy sensation in my head?

Our bodies and minds/souls are so intertwined that one affects the other. In order to understand each of their contributions to the problem, we will talk about them separately. In this chapter we will focus on the physical factors which can be addressed.

A Look at Our Physical Person

Just as God, the Counselor, met Elijah's physical needs first when Elijah was suffering from suicidal depression (1 Kings 19:4-8), we must examine our own physical conditions and strive to improve them in order to find relief. Dr. Martyn Lloyd-Jones, a former medical doctor and one of the greatest pastors of the twentieth century, wrote in his book *Spiritual Depression,* "Does someone hold the view that as long as you are a Christian it does not matter what the condition of your body is? Well, you will soon be disillusioned if you believe that." He goes on to say,

Physical conditions play their part in all this… There are certain ailments which tend to promote depression…. Take that great preacher who preached in London for nearly forty years in the last century—Charles Haddon Spurgeon—one of the truly great preachers of all time. That great man was subject to spiritual depression, and the main explanation in his case was undoubtedly the fact that he suffered from a gouty condition which finally killed him. He had to face this problem of spiritual depression often in a most acute form. A tendency to acute depression is an unfailing accompaniment of the gout which he inherited from his forebears. And there are many, I find, who come to talk to me about these matters, in whose case it seems quite clear to me that the cause of the trouble is mainly physical. Into this group, speaking generally, you can put tiredness, overstrain, illness, any form of illness. You cannot isolate the spiritual from the physical for we are body, mind and spirit. *The greatest and the best Christians when they are physically weak are more prone to an attack of spiritual depression than at any other time and there are great illustrations of this in the scriptures (*emphasis mine*).*[1]

Paul compared our bodies to a clay jar (2 Cor. 4:7). A clay jar is fragile and easily broken or chipped. We get tired and ill and are subject to sicknesses and diseases that limit our ability to fulfill our responsibilities at times. The weakness of our flesh can even lead directly to spiritual depression. Therefore, we as believers are under obligation to be good stewards of our God-given bodies, not by worshipping the body but realizing that because we only have one body in which to obey the Lord, care and protection of health are essential. A great preacher who died young was purported to have said with regret, "God gave me a message and a horse. I wore out the horse, so I can no longer carry the message."

God brought angels to minster to Elijah under the juniper tree and to Jesus in the wilderness and then under the olive tree when his soul was grieved to the point of death. Those angels did not minister by playing harps or singing songs. They brought much-needed food and drink—physical refreshment. God is in favor of natural nourishment and ministry to your body. He may want to use that to also restore you to drink the cup that He has for you, to go on and do His will in His power.

The following are some principles to use as guidelines to help you get a handle on this important area. Your spouse, a friend, or a counselor can help you implement these things and hold you accountable to do them. When in depression, it is especially hard to implement change.

Take Care of the Body Medically

It is important to determine what is going on physically. It is good to start with a thorough physical exam, including a thyroid test. If you are in a transitional time of life hormonally, take that into consideration. There are no blood tests to determine whether one has depression. It manifests itself in emotions, thoughts, and observable behaviors. It can impair immune function, hinder digestion, and disrupt sleep. It can be diagnosed through asking questions but there is no test to determine it. There are however physical conditions that can bring it on.

Improper diet or eating disorders can be a great contributing factor in depression. Excesses of refined carbohydrates, alcohol, and tobacco, as well as nutrient deficiencies have been linked to depression. Irregular sleep patterns, insufficient sleep, or sleep apnea can lead to slowed thinking which may appear as depression. Diseases such as hypoglycemia or thyroid issues should be examined. Hormones directly affect the brain chemistry that controls emotions and moods. Hence women have an increased risk for depression after giving birth and during the transition into menopause.

Alcohol and drug abuse are the most common causes of depression (although hopefully not among Christians). Depression can also result as a side effect of medications for pain and a number of other prescription medications. These contributing factors must be investigated and addressed by medical doctors.

What about Psychotropic Medicines?

What if your physician recommends psychotropic medicines? Are they always necessary to bring restoration? We must consider that these drugs deal with the outer symptoms of depression, not necessarily the underlying cause. Dr. Edward Welch in his book *Blame It on the Brain* counsels us to use them carefully and sparingly:

> If the person is not taking medication but is considering it, I typically suggest that he or she postpone that decision for a period of time. During that time, I consider possible causes, and together we ask God to teach us about both ourselves and him so that we can grow in faith in the midst of hardship. If the depression persists, I might let the person know that medication is an option to deal with some of the physical symptoms.[2]

While the medical, psychiatric community focuses on the physical factors primarily, we must focus on the whole person while not ignoring the physical. We know that the answer to our deepest needs is not found in a pill. Medication should never be our first and only plan of attack. Our spiritual needs must also be addressed. Welch further clarifies, "The bottom line is this: don't put your hope in medication. Be thankful if it helps, but if it becomes just another place to put your hope instead of Jesus, you are just perpetuating the cycle of hopelessness."[3]

After a considerable period of time, with the advice of biblical counselors and physicians, I realized that an antidepressant would help my body regain its emotional and physical balance quicker. It very gradually took effect, and when combined with everything I was doing spiritually, the depression began to lift. My thoughts and feelings finally returned to normal. I was able to get back to teaching and off of the medication in six months (after a year of suffering). The medication was not my first or only course of action, but it was a gift of God's grace in my case.

If you are on medication, you should know that the Bible doesn't condemn you. There are negative side effects to using it over a long period of time so the goal is to get off of it as soon as possible. However, weaning your body from the medication should be done only under a doctor's supervision. The body needs time to adjust, and he knows the proper timing for the best results. In my experience, there have been some cases where we weaned the counselee to a certain point but found that a minimum of continued medication was needed. If this is your case you should trust God and continue to serve Him for His glory. As you grow in health and strength, you can try again to drop the medications at a later stage.

Take Care of the Body Naturally

Have a Diet of Nutritious Food

Part of my recovery plan was to eat nutritious meals and take supplements that would help restore my health. I tried all the natural means first. Whether we feel like eating or not, we need to eat balanced meals with plenty of protein, eating both raw and cooked vegetables and fruit, and cutting out sugars and refined foods. Since the body has extra stresses on it, vitamins can help make up for any gaps. This is good counsel:

> A poor diet doesn't cause unipolar major depression, but inadequate nutrition can result in deficiencies of amino acids, fatty acids, vitamins, and minerals that impair your health, upset bodily processes, disturb the function and growth of brain cells, and worsen your depressive symptoms. Being overweight or underweight can cause physiological discomfort in the short term and can truncate your life in the long term.[4]

We want to glorify God in all this, even in our eating and drinking, vital components in our restoration process (1 Cor. 10:31). Our motivation must not merely be avoidance of the consequences that can come from abuse of the body, but the real prize—Christ Himself. Therefore, with Jesus in view and by the grace of God, we must keep the desires of our flesh under control by the power of the Holy Spirit. We must run so as to win. The apostle Paul said, "I buffet my body and make it my slave ..." (1 Cor. 9:27).

Get Rest and Recreation

I needed to take time off from teaching to recover. My body needed time to recover.

We must give our body periods of needful rest. Sleep is often elusive in depression. Medication may be needed to induce sleep for a time. I had to learn to simply set my mind on the fact that even though I was not sleeping soundly, I was resting and therefore I needed to stay in bed and just rest even though my mind was not completely at rest. At a reasonable hour each night we set aside time before bed to prepare our minds and hearts so as to be able to go to sleep. Despite our best efforts, I didn't always sleep. During the day it is easier to drown out negative thoughts with activities, but at night you are at their mercy. It is good to take a look at your sleeping environment. Wear a sleep mask if your bedroom is not dark enough. Is the temperature conducive to sleeping? Is your bed comfortable or too hard or too soft? I needed a hard bed for my back. Are there disturbances? These must be removed. When in depression, sleep is vital in order to get well!

Maybe you need to adjust your sleep patterns. Sleep loss can impact your health and mood. In my opinion, most Americans do not get the proper amount of sleep as they allow television programming or social networking or extra work to delay their sleep schedule rather than listening to their own body clock.

Recreation is important as well. We need to find time to relax and enjoy God's creation. We can read and enjoy good stories and take part in different sports and enjoyable activities. God has also given us fellowship with fellow believers to cheer our days. Although we feel like withdrawing, we need to get together with those who care and can lift us up.

My physical therapist recommended that we watch two or three comedies a week just to put my mind on something humorous. We were ready to try anything. Mary rented some comedies, and we tried to watch them. As I watched I would think, *I used to think this is funny. If I was normal I would laugh at this! What is wrong with me? Funny isn't funny anymore!* I got more depressed because I didn't think the comedies were funny. Mary couldn't laugh because she saw it wasn't funny to me. We gave up on the comedies, and in fact we watched almost nothing on television for nine months. We especially avoided the news broadcasts as all the news was depressing. However, I did play Hearts and Solitaire and we played board games like UpWords and Chinese checkers. You need to find some form of recreation.

Exercise

In the midst of the depression it took every ounce of will power to take a walk or to get in the pool for exercise, but we needed exercise. I had physical therapy which was required to help my back. My wife and I took walks together when I was able after the back surgery, which helped both my body and mind. The endorphins produced from exercise give us an emotional lift. Our bodies need exercise. Get a plan for exercise and stick to it. Now that the depression has lifted I have found that I feel better and have more energy when I work out several times a week. Exercise improves our energy, endurance, and physical well-being. This comes from a medical report:

The psychological and emotional benefits from exercise are numerous, and many experts now believe that exercise is a viable and important component in the treatment of emotion disorders. A 1999 review of multiple studies found, across the board, that exercise advances the treatment of clinical depression and anxiety."[5]

Live a Structured Life

I was encouraged to keep moving on things that I could do. Those who are not in such severe depression should continue in their normal duties. Pulling back from meaningful work can add to the depression. If you are like me, you may not feel like getting out of bed in the morning, but I knew that I must not operate on the basis of my feelings. I must remind myself of the gospel and God's power. I'm His and I can get up by His grace and strength and I can do what He calls me to do. I can add up this trial to be a joy by faith. I might even need to confess my sin of self-pity in bemoaning my plight. God hasn't forsaken me, and I can serve Him by doing my work with the strength that He supplies.

Living a structured life is very important. I had a schedule of things that I did every day. I was not called to do great things but to be faithful in the things that I could do (Matt. 25:21). Besides the reading, journaling, and doing some minor work-related things, I had to do the physical therapy which was required to help my back.

My counselor had me write some notes of encouragement to others each day by email—to look beyond my own needs. I did not feel like doing this! I did not think I had anything to offer because my own thoughts were so negative, and I was not even sure of my own salvation. But I could obey the command, "encourage one another day after day as long as it is called today." I could write and set someone's mind on God's truth.

So just obey. If you wait until you feel like doing something encouraging when you are depressed, then you will never do anything! I could reach out to others who could be suffering as well and in need of God's help. As we reach out to others, God ministers to us and gives us the joy of knowing the smile of His approval. When we think that we are unable to do what is necessary, we can ask God for His strength (Phil. 4:13). We need to think of the things we can do instead of the things we can't do.

Reading to my wife was something I could do as it had been my pattern for our whole marriage. During the long days I read book after book on the Gospel, soaking us in the truth about what Jesus Christ has already done on our behalf. As I read these amazing Gospel truths to my wife I would think, *Why isn't my heart moved by this truth? This is the amazing story of God the Father's love in giving the Son and God the Son's amazing love in giving Himself! This is good for my wife to hear, but I don't think I am elect so it can't apply to me!*

However I kept reading. I was blessed to have a wife who directed her energies to helping me get through this in every way — being there to feel my sorrows, to listen to me, and to encourage me with who I am in Christ! Needless to say, this time drew us closer as a couple. As I look back now I know that those words did nourish my soul even though I could not believe the truth or accept it or feel it at the time. Keep saturating your soul in the truth of the Gospel.

Prioritize and Organize

We get the principle of putting first things first from Jesus. He said to seek first His kingdom and His righteousness and all the other things would be added to us (Matt. 6:33). What comes first? Our relationship with Christ comes first. If we have no time for Him, then we are too busy. Even while in the severe depression when I could not work, I had to carve out a time to be in God's Word because my feelings were telling me it was useless for me to seek God.

Since over-commitment and overwork led in part to my situation, it was necessary to evaluate and set new priorities. Because depression can be brought on by physical and emotional exhaustion we need to avoid being trapped by the tyranny of the urgent. Create a plan for making the best use of your time. By the power of the Holy Spirit you can exercise self-control to do those things that are important, true, and good, rather than those things that feel urgent but are ungodly or less important.

Let me encourage you to take a very careful look at all the commitments you've made. Do you need to say *no* to some things? Yes, you do! You must say, "Yes" only to the things that are a part of your God-given calling, and say "No" to the extras. That may be difficult to do at first. But it's much better for us to fulfill our priorities well than to try to do everything poorly or relapse back into depression.

Accept Help from Others

When you find yourself in depression you need to evaluate your life in regard to the physical demands put upon you. A biblical counselor from our church helped me make a plan for the ongoing care of my body to avoid a relapse into depression. In evaluating my situation, I came to realize that I had sinned against my body by taxing it beyond its limits. The consequences were that everything was taken from me—my job and ministry and even the ability to think and feel in a normal way. I needed to set guidelines for the future.

I also needed to realize that God was more interested in my heart before Him than all my service for Him. If I could never serve Him again outwardly, I could give Him the sacrifice of praise by praising Him by faith whether or not my feelings ever returned. I had a very challenging conversation with Joni Eareckson Tada. I expressed to her that my feelings were starting to come back, but they were far from normal. I was wondering if I would ever think normally again or laugh at a joke as heartily as I used to laugh—or be able to sense real feelings of empathy for another. I still did not know if I would be able to return to teaching. I was planning to start the new semester in two months but would I be able to do it? Joni stated to me that after her accident she had to adjust to a "new normal." She would never walk again or have feelings below her neck. She had to answer the question, "Will I serve God with this 'new normal' and give my life to Him for his glory with the 'new normal?'" Then she asked me point blank, "Bob, if your feelings never return to normal and a lack of feelings are your 'new normal,' will you still live for His glory?" I did not want to even think about my feelings not returning to normal. However, I wanted to answer her question in the affirmative and serve my Lord with or without "normal" feelings.

I resolved to remember my vulnerability and weakness and by God's grace to not trust in my own strength. My main focus had to be Jesus Christ no matter what! I have thought back to that conversation many times and to the one asking me that penetrating question who reminds me by her life that it's possible. Read anything you can that she has written, and it will strengthen your soul for the adversities of life.

It's good to set limits. Enough is enough. We can only do so much. With my new normal, I have to keep a little mat in my office so I can take a nap each afternoon. You, like me, may have been there for others in their need, and now the situation is reversed and you need their help. We tend to be independent by nature and since we receive more joy from giving to others than from receiving, we tend to refuse the help we need. However, we must allow others to minister to us. Then they can experience that joy, too. Paul allowed the Christians to minister to his needs. He went on to tell them that they would be enriched by their liberality in giving (2 Cor. 8:3-4; 9:11; Phil. 4:10-19). If we don't allow others to minister to our needs, we are robbing them of a blessing.

Rest One Day in Seven

The best way to manage stress is to observe one day of rest every week—that is, obey the fourth Commandment. What a basic solution to a big problem! Resting one day in seven is not only a nice idea; it is God's idea—a creation ordinance (Exod. 20:9-11). God always knows what's best. I can't overstate this truth. We must rest. It is for the good of our own bodies and souls and increased productivity that we must follow the pattern that God established. It is especially important because of the constant weight of responsibilities upon our shoulders as men and women. Understanding our bodily limitations is part of taking care of our bodies that are the temple of the Holy Spirit (1 Cor. 6:19-20).

There is no doubt that we need to make a priority of getting the proper amount of rest. Seek to implement a plan to get the rest that you need. God said that one day in seven is for worship and rest, but we seldom genuinely rest. Repent and take one day in seven to really rest. In addition stake out some time each day for rest while you are in this depression—a time to calm your soul, relax, and be renewed. Take a good, hard look at your schedule and limit it to your priorities.

For a thorough examination of this body/soul connection, see *Will the Medicine Stop the Pain?* and other resources in the Annotated Bibliography which cover this subject in detail.

Conclusion

Since our bodies are not our own because they have been bought with the price of Christ's precious blood, we need to take care of them (1 Cor. 6:19, 20)! Taking care of that temple is a wise course of action. Then you can rest in the knowledge that you are doing all you can physically for healing to take place.

Yes, we identify with what the Apostle Paul said in his treatise on the Gospel, that he and all believers groan within ourselves waiting for a new body (Rom. 8:23). He had suffered the ill effects of bodily weakness including fear and depression as the result of ministry (2 Cor. 7:5), but he didn't lose hope. He went on to say "But if we *hope* for what we do not see, with perseverance we wait eagerly for it" (v. 25, emphasis mine). He had the hope of the redemption of his body. Someday our bodies will be resurrected and be beyond the pain and suffering we go through here. That gives us perseverance to go on. Why? David concludes, "My flesh and my heart may fail, But God is the strength of my heart and my portion forever." And Paul writes, "For I consider that the sufferings of this present time are not worthy to be compared with the glory that is to be revealed to us" (Rom. 8:18). There's glory coming when we see Jesus!

Response

In seeking to be a good steward of your health I suggest the following things which I found very helpful:
- Get a thorough physical exam.
- Ask your doctor if nutritional supplements could be helpful?
- Check with your doctor to see what kind of exercise is right for you and how much. If you have no restrictions, set a time—at least twenty minutes per day of walking, jogging, swimming, or whatever appeals to you and make a plan and stick to it.

- Examine your eating habits. Are they nutritional? Plan nutritious meals and eat right.
- Examine your sleep patterns. Plan for sufficient rest. Set a reasonable time for bed and stick to a plan that helps you rest.
- Memorize Exodus 20:8 and answer the question: How do I keep one day separate for rest and worship? In your journal list how you will practice rest and worship on your Sabbath day.
- Do a "Discovering Wonderful Things" study of 1 Corinthians 6:19-20. Specifically ask the question: *How can I better care for my body as the temple of the Holy Spirit with regards to nutrition, exercise, sleep, and rest?* Make a plan. (See Appendix 2 for a sample of the "Discovering Wonderful Things" study guide.

A Story of Chronic Pain and Restoration

I am a Christian wife and mother to six, soon to be seven wonderful children. I always felt like I lived a charmed life, getting to live out my dream which was to be a wife, mother, and homemaker. The Lord had blessed me so much. Up until this point I had not experienced any really big trials, but I was in no way prepared for what was to come.

My story began a few years ago with what had seemed to be a toothache. I spent the next year trying to get to the bottom of what was causing the pain; which included countless fillings, root canals, and even getting my tooth eventually pulled hoping that would fix it once and for all. When the pain continued after the tooth was pulled, my doctor determined that this was starting to look like a neurological problem and not a dental problem. So, I was referred to a neurologist.

He determined that I had a chronic nerve pain called Trigeminal Neuralgia. We then spent the next six months trying different procedures and medicines to help the pain and eventually ended up doing two surgeries one month apart. During this whole time I was on pain medication. I had to take even more at the end, when the pain was very severe due to the surgeries and some complications from the surgeries. At that point I had been on pain medications for a little over a year, but I had no idea how dependent my body and mind were getting on them. After my second surgery, I determined that I would try to get off of the meds. I did not need them as much, and I really did not like being dependent on them just to get through my day. Weaning off of them proved very difficult. It sunk me into a terrible depression. I figured since the weaning wasn't working, I might as well get off of them cold turkey and get it over with.

The withdrawal from the medicine launched me into an unbearable state of depression, anxiety, and despair that I could never have imagined. My body, mind, and soul literally started breaking down.

I completely lost my appetite, and it took all the strength I had just to take a bite of food. It felt as if I had the worst flu I had ever had in my life. There was no relief. My body ached and burned constantly. My intestinal system was completely out of whack.

As bad as I felt physically, I felt more tormented mentally and emotionally. All I could feel was emotional pain. There was no joy. The anxiety I felt overtook me. Many times I told the Lord to please take me home. I did not want to live like that. I told my husband the same thing, which was very hard for him to hear. I felt like an empty shell and could not even remember what it felt like to feel joy.

Spiritually I was broken also. In the beginning I could not read the bible or pray at all. I felt a complete disconnect from God. I believed His truths but couldn't experience any sort of relationship with Him. I would hear sermons that I knew should encourage and help me, and yet I felt nothing. My husband, friends, parents, and kids literally had to take care of me. I was like a child: stripped down to nothing, humbled, embarrassed, and desperate. I was in this state for several months, and it was the absolute worst time of my life. I had always been the mom and wife who lived to take care of her family, and I thrived on running my home in an organized and efficient way. I home schooled our children. I love them so much and was always very involved in every aspect of their lives. But now, all I could do was lie in bed, not being able to have a conversation let alone think straight.

In my mind, my kids were literally slipping through my fingers, and there was nothing I could do to change it. I kept thinking, *My brain is broken and this is what I am going to be like for the rest of my life.* My family and doctors would tell me that it would just take time for the medicine to work its way out of my system and for my brain to start to produce its own serotonin again. Serotonin is the chemical in the brain that allows you to feel joy. Evidently when you take pain medicines for an extended period of time your body stops producing serotonin, and it's replaced by the medicine. I was encouraged to take an antidepressant for a short period of time to bring about the proper serotonin balance needed. I finally agreed to this course of action.

During the dark hours and days all I could do was try to cling to scripture. One passage that I repeated to myself constantly was Psalm 23.

The LORD is my shepherd,
I shall not want.
He makes me lie down in green pastures;
He leads me beside quiet waters.
He restores my soul;
He guides me in the paths of righteousness
For His name's sake.
Even though I walk through the valley of the shadow of death,
I fear no evil, for You are with me;
Your rod and Your staff, they comfort me.
You prepare a table before me in the presence of my enemies;
You have anointed my head with oil;
My cup overflows.
Surely goodness and lovingkindness will follow me all the
days of my life
And I will dwell in the house of the LORD forever.

I could not feel Him leading me beside still waters or restoring my soul, but I had to believe that He would. When the physical anxiety was almost unbearable, I would recite it to myself over and over. After a couple weeks I could start to read the Psalms. I saw in Psalms the suffering that other men of God endured. I could completely relate to David when he said he felt like his body was wasting away.

I would find very small bits of comfort from these passages, and I clung to them for dear life. I had to just believe what people were telling me, "You will get better once the medicine works its way out of your system." I had to force myself to believe it because I did not see how it was possible, and I was having to come to terms with the fact that it wasn't going to happen overnight like I wanted it to.

After about a month, I started going to church again. That was not easy either; I knew I should be growing through the worship and learning so much from the preaching, but instead I felt dead inside, unable to grow or even absorb and put into practice what I was learning. But the wonderful part is that in time and very slowly over several months, I started getting bits of myself back. After five of the worst months of my life, I started to feel joy again and I started to feel myself again.

I truly never thought I would be able to say these words and mean it but I am grateful for the trial that God allowed in my life. There are so many ways that my thinking has been changed through the experience. I have a new compassion toward people going through mental or emotional problems. Before, I was probably a little too judgmental, thinking it was something they brought on themselves or some sort of spiritual problem. The experience has also humbled me and hopefully made me a more real person. It was very difficult for me to let people know that I did not have it all together. I was forced to put my pride aside and let friends and family see what I was going through and how desperate I was.

I wanted to talk to someone who had been through this dark valley who would understand, but I knew no one. Thankfully, someone in church told me that Bob and Mary Somerville (who are members of our church) had been there. I called them up and we met together several times. It was wonderful to know that they understood and could give me hope and counsel from first-hand experience.

Other trials now pale in comparison to what I went through. I have a new perspective. I know that God has strengthened my character. I still struggle, but I know that if He could get me through that trial, He could get me through anything. Looking back through my journal I am reminded of the verses that I clung to (usually by my fingernails) at the time:

- "Rest in the Lord and wait patiently for him" (Ps. 37:7).
- "Wait on the Lord, be of courage. And he shall strengthen your heart. Wait I say on the Lord" (Ps. 27:14).
- "My grace is sufficient for you. For my power is made perfect in weakness" (2 Cor. 12:9).
- "Consider it pure joy, my brothers, whenever you face trials of many kinds, because you know that the testing of your faith develops perseverance. Perseverance must finish its work so that you may be mature and complete, not lacking anything" (James 1:2-4).

Stefanie Hartung

Worship

Glorious God,
 It is the flame of my life to worship thee,
  The crown and glory of my soul to adore thee,
  Heavenly pleasure to approach thee.
 Give me power by thy Spirit to help me worship now,
  That I may forget the world,
  Be brought into fullness of life,
  Be refreshed, comforted, blessed.
 Give me knowledge of thy goodness
  That I might not be over-awed by thy greatness;
 Give me Jesus, Son of Man, Son of God,
  That I might not be terrified,
  But be drawn near with filial love,
  With holy boldness;
 He is my mediator, brother, interpreter,
  branch, daysman, Lamb;
  Him I glorify,
  In him I am set on high.
 Crowns to give I have none,
  But what thou hast given I return,
  Content to feel that everything is mine when it is thine,
  And the more fully mine when I have yielded it to thee.
 Let me live wholly to my Savior,
  Free from distractions,
  From carking care,
  From hindrances to the pursuit of the narrow way.
 I am pardoned through the blood of Jesus—
  Give me a new sense of it,
  Continue to pardon me by it,
  May I come every day to the fountain,
  And every day be washed anew,
  That I may worship thee always in spirit and truth.

─────── ◦§ CHAPTER 7 §◦ ───────

How do I Deal with My Fear, Worry, and Anxiety?

For I *hope* in You, O Lord; You will answer, O Lord my
God. (Psalm 38:15)

*D*epression can often come from a spiral of worry and anxiety
that lands a person in a horrible morass of negativity. In a flash
your thoughts can go down roads you'll never actually need to travel
and cross bridges you'll never need to cross. You end up like Elijah
in a deep pit of despair and depression in which there is no peace to
be found! In my depression this was my state of mind. There was
always an anxiety factor present. It manifested itself in a wild imagination. I worried about everything in life. I was never going to teach
or preach or earn a living again. I would probably end up living in
my brother in law's basement. Who would take care of my wife?

I lived with the constant fear or dread that something bad was
going to happen. I wondered if my faith was real. Then I became *convinced* that I had been deceived, and my faith had never been real. I
had stood in front of my congregation and told them that Jesus calms
storms and they should not fear, yet now I was full of fear. I hated
the hypocrisy of my own heart.

I even experienced an anxiety attack as the physical therapist
gave me the simplest of directions for the mildest of exercises that
I was to do after my back surgery. What was wrong with me? I had
played high school football, basketball, and baseball and college
baseball. The exercises being described to me were the mildest I

had ever heard of and yet in the negative grid of the depression they were overwhelming and impossible. I hyperventilated and thought that I would pass out. I had heard many counselees describe this but now I was in it! How could this be happening?

I had to find the cure for my fear, worry, and anxiety. It was not enough for me, however, to tell myself to quit worrying, because that would never capture this thief of joy. Worry is an "inside job," and it takes more than good intentions to get the victory. The antidote to worry is God's peace. Paul says, "And the peace of God ... shall keep [garrison, guard like a soldier] your hearts and minds through Christ Jesus" (Phil. 4:7).

We want that kind of peace—one that is a soldier to fight off worry, anxiety and depression! So in this chapter we are going to study God's prescription for peace found in Paul's letter to the Philippians. If anybody had an excuse for worrying, it was the Apostle Paul. He was under house arrest in Rome, chained to Roman guards. Some were preaching Christ from envy and rivalry seeking even to afflict him in his imprisonment. His beloved Christian friends who had worked alongside him in the ministry, Euodia and Syntyche at Philippi, were disagreeing with one another, and he was not there to help them. Along with that, Paul had to face division among the believers at Rome (Phil. 1:14-17). Added to these burdens, he was facing the very real possibility of his own death! Yes, Paul had many good excuses to worry—*but he did not!* Instead, he took time to explain to us the secret to victory over worry.

Rejoice in the Lord

Paul put it out there in Philippians 4:4 "Rejoice in the Lord always; again I will say, rejoice!" This is an unqualified command. We are to rejoice. "Rejoice" is in the present imperative and could be translated, "Keep on rejoicing in the Lord always." This is repeated, "Again, I will say rejoice, or "Again I will say, keep on rejoicing." What are we to rejoice in? "In the Lord!" In Jesus Christ and His cross—the blazing center of the glory of God where He poured out His wrath on His own Son so you could become His child. Rejoice that you are a blood-bought child of God! Rejoice in all the riches you have in Christ. You are joint-heirs with Jesus! Rejoice in the gospel!

The sphere, in which your joy as a believer exists, is totally unrelated to your circumstances of life or your feelings about them but related to your unassailable, unchanging relationship to your *sovereign* Lord. Paul was writing to them about peace from a prison cell! Do you think they listened? If Paul can have peace in prison, can't I have it in freedom? He found peace in the fact that Jesus is Lord, that God is sovereign!

Why does God's sovereignty give us so much hope? What does it mean? Our Lord is absolutely free to do whatever He wants. Jerry Bridges defines it for us in his book *Trusting God*:

> No plan of God's can be thwarted; when he acts, no one can reverse it; no one can hold back His hand or bring Him to account for His actions. God does as He pleases, only as He pleases, and works out every event to bring about the accomplishment of His will. Such a bare unqualified statement of the sovereignty of God would terrify us if that were all we knew about God. But God is not only sovereign He is perfect in love and infinite in wisdom.[1]

Bridges goes on to state how God's sovereignty and providence come together to work all things for good: "God's providence is His constant care for and His absolute rule over all His creation for His own glory and the good of His people."[2]

Knowing that He is sovereign gives us cause to rejoice! When we're facing the difficulties of life, when we're filled with fears and anxiety and when we're feeling as though our lives are coming apart at the seams, it is the truth that God is *sovereign* and that God is *good* that will bring us hope, peace, and confidence. How good is our God? He forgives our sin by placing His wrath upon His own Son at Calvary and exchanges our death for eternal life to those who receive salvation (Gal. 4:5). The Lord's goodness is promised in Romans 8:28. Any of us who suffer any kind of affliction or wrong committed against us can cling to this promise of hope. So rejoice in the Lord's sovereignty and goodness!

It's the truth that He is perfectly holy, just, loving, wise, and good, coupled with His perfect power that will be our mainstay during times of trial. He knows what is best for us, and He has the power to bring it to pass. This gives hope to us when we're in the midst of it. .

The first step to victory over worry is to choose to rejoice. How do we rejoice? We rejoice in the Lord through our tears. We rejoice by faith. God is on the throne and He is in control. He is working all things together for our good and His glory. We talk to the Lord and tell Him how much we love and trust Him just as David did when he wrote, "For I hope in You, O Lord; You will answer, O Lord my God" (Ps. 38:15). We count the trial up to be a joy, by faith (James 1:2). We keep our minds stayed on Him (Isa. 26:3). I will say it again, "Rejoice in the Lord!"

Resolve to be Gentle, Patient, and Reasonable

Paul continues, "Let your forbearing spirit be known to all men" (Phil. 4:5).

Paul is commanding us here to be gentle, patient, gracious, and reasonable toward others. "Forbearing" may refer to being merciful toward the faults and failures of others. It can even refer to patience in submitting to injustice or mistreatment without seeking revenge. Gentleness and patience are a fruit of the Spirit. Paul wants Christians to be well known before all men for this attitude.

Maybe you feel like lashing out. Don't. When you are depressed, you may be more tempted to focus on the faults of others and be irritable. Ask God to help you to be supernaturally patient. Are you bitter because of injustice that you have been served? Look at the next phrase. You can be forbearing because the Lord is near. Jesus is coming back to right every wrong. Wait for God's vengeance to be carried out. Pray for your enemies; if they don't trust in Christ their sins will be judged (Rom. 2:16). Remember how much you have been forgiven. Because of the gospel, because of God's forbearing or gentleness and patience with you, you can be like that with others.

In my depression I especially needed to be reminded of this. I was counseling someone close to me who was being abominably treated by other Christians. This was causing me emotional and physical pain. I felt it even in my back. I was carrying this injustice. I wanted to lash out and set the wrongs right. Instead, I needed to cast it on the Lord and leave it there, trusting in His flawless and matchless character to handle the situation. I needed to remind myself that God loves my dear ones even more than I love them. He was putting them through the oven of affliction. He had the power to deliver them and make them to stand. I had to ask God for His grace to be patient and forgiving and rest in what He was up to in their lives and my own. The outcome? It is several years later and God has done just that—made His servants to stand. We see now how God has worked it together for His own glory.

If you try to fix all the evils in the world yourself, you will end up a nervous wreck. You must let God be God and wait for Him to act. "Never take your own revenge beloved, but leave room for the wrath of God, for it is written, 'Vengeance is mine, I will repay,' says the Lord. But if your enemy is hungry, feed him, and if he is thirsty, give him a drink; for in so doing you will heap burning coals upon his head. Do not be overcome by evil, but overcome evil with good" (Rom. 12:19-21).

If I trust the judge, then I can be patient and forbearing even with my enemies. How much more then can I be patient and forbearing with those who love me and accidentally rub me the wrong way? We see that the second secret to victory over fear, worry, and anxiety is supernatural patience that stands out to everyone as you overcome evil with good and bear up under difficult circumstances.

Remember the Lord Is Near

Paul reassures us that the "Lord is near" (Phil. 4:5b). His bodily return could happen at any moment. I really do not have to be patient for long. The evil that oppresses me now is seen by the God who judges righteously. Soon He will come back to destroy all evil. He will "judge the secrets of men" (Rom. 2:16). He will reward every man according to his deeds (1 Cor. 3:9-14). As His blood-bought child I can be confident that "this momentary light affliction is producing for us an eternal weight of glory far beyond all comparison" (1 Cor. 4:17).

Jesus' Second Coming is near, but also His daily presence is near! You can experience the nearness of Jesus through the person of the Holy Spirit. His very presence is as near as your own breath. Jesus referred to the Holy Spirit as the Comforter. He is in you to comfort you! You must allow Him to do that. His grace is sufficient! He is near to you to help and comfort you no matter what you're going through. He can give you joy and patience as you wait for His return.

Jesus understands. He was acquainted with our sorrows and is a sympathetic high priest we can go to in time of need (Heb. 4:15). How can One so holy sympathize with one so sinful? How can He possibly know what I'm going through? He was tempted in all things as we are. He knew fear. He dreaded the cup of His Father's wrath that He had agreed to drink from before the foundation of the world. But He endured the cross for the joy set before Him (Heb. 12:2). He literally understands everything we go through but, as important as that is, He is there to help in time of need (Heb. 4:16). "He has said, 'I will never leave you nor forsake you.' So we can confidently say, 'The Lord is my helper; I will not fear; what can man do to me'" (Heb. 13:5-6 ESV)? The Lord is near! I can rejoice! I can be patient!

Refuse to be Anxious (Fearful) about Anything

Paul gives us this command, "Be anxious for nothing" (Phil. 4:6a). Just what does it mean to be anxious or to worry? "Anxious" in this verse means *to be pulled in different directions*. Our hopes pull us in one direction; our fears pull us the opposite direction; and we are pulled apart! The Old English root from which we get our word "worry" means "to strangle." If you have ever really worried you know how it does strangle a person! In fact, worry has definite physical consequences: headaches, neck pains, ulcers, even back pains and yes, even depression. When we're stressed, we tend to drink too much caffeine, eat too much sugar, and not get sufficient rest or exercise. Worry affects our thinking, our body, and our behavior. To fret and worry is to exhibit a lack of trust in God's love, wisdom, sovereignty, and power.

"Be anxious *for nothing*." Let's think about all the "nothings" that we worry about and commit to set them aside. I will not worry how I am ever going to get through this depression. I will not fret over if I will ever teach or preach again. I will not be anxious about what will happen to my wife or about my reputation. By the power of the Holy Spirit, I can be anxious *for nothing*! That doesn't mean that it is wrong to have concern for all these things. Anxiety, worry, and fear are different from concern. Paul had concern for all the churches (2 Cor. 11:28).

We can avoid allowing our concerns to become worries by following Paul's next bit of advice. There is certainly no switch to turn off worry and anxiety but Paul tells us how to change worry into peace through prayer!

Rely on Prayer

Paul instructs us: "But in everything by prayer and supplication with thanksgiving let your requests be made known to God. And the peace of God, which surpasses all comprehension, shall guard your hearts and your minds in Christ Jesus" (Phil. 4:6b, 7).

Whenever I catch myself worrying, it should be like the red light on the dashboard of my car coming on and it says, "Check your connection" So, check your connection with Jesus! Worry is a sign that I have lost my connection with Jesus—I've taken my eyes off of who He is and gotten my focus on all my circumstances that seem to be swirling out of control. I forget who can calm the sea or even walk on its most tumultuous waves. Like Peter who got out of the boat to walk to Jesus, I have faith ... until I take my eyes off of Jesus and look down at the waves. Then I start to sink in unbelief. I must call out like Peter, "Lord, save me" (Matt. 14:31)!

We must remember who Jesus is and what He can do! "Immediately Jesus stretched out His hand and took hold of him, and said to him, 'You of little faith, why did you doubt?' When they got into the boat the wind stopped. And those who were in the boat worshiped Him, saying, 'You are certainly God's Son!'" (Matt. 14:31-33) Prayer reconnects us with God's son! He can save you. He can calm your sea. Don't doubt his purposes or His power.

133

Now Paul doesn't just say, "Pray about it!" He uses three different words to describe the sort of prayer he's talking about—*prayer, supplication,* and *thanksgiving.*

The word *prayer* is the general word for communicating with God through adoration, devotion, and worship. Whenever we find ourselves worrying, our first action ought to be to get alone with Jesus and ask Him—"What have I forgotten about who You are?" When I do this, then I go to the written Word to meet the living Word—I search its pages to find the Jesus I've lost—evidences of His power, of His kindness, His love, His caring, His ability to do the impossible. I get my eyes reopened to who He is, and then I worship Him. We must see the greatness and majesty of Jesus! We must realize that He is big enough to solve our problems!

Too often we rush into His presence and hastily tell Him our needs, without giving any thought to *beholding* Him and regaining our sense of all that He is able to do in the face of our weakness! It's good to read over the accounts of Jesus' crucifixion and resurrection to refresh ourselves with this glorious news. We have not been utterly forsaken by God, but Jesus was. We will never experience the wrath of God, but Jesus has. The more we dwell on the price that was paid for our redemption, the more we will love and trust Him. I can pray, *Yes, Lord this cup you've given me to drink is terrible, but Your sufferings were greater. Thank You for suffering and dying for my sins on the cross. Thank You for rising from the dead.*

The second word for prayer is *supplication.* Once one regains his focus through adoration, devotion, and worship, he is free to make supplication—to pour out his heart like a child to his father, earnestly sharing his needs and problems. We have seen that He can really do something—He is able! Therefore, I can pour out my need to Him and in faith leave it with Him! Jesus told His disciples just prior to His death, "Until now you have asked for nothing in My name: ask and you will receive, so that your joy may be made full" (John 16:24).

Just pray specifically about everything. *Lord you know I don't feel that I can take a walk right now but I need to exercise so help me to walk for Your glory.* Or *Lord, You know I don't want to go to services this morning but enable me by your strength to go and worship You*

134

even though I may not feel any different in doing it! Or *God just help me grade this exam in a way that will be pleasing to You and helpful to the student even though I do not feel I have anything to offer.*

We need to commit *all* things to Him in prayer. In fact isn't this what Paul meant for all of us when he said, "pray without ceasing" (1 Thess. 4:17)? (For some excellent help in this area, see the book *A Praying Life* by Paul Miller which was an encouragement to me in the midst of the depression.) We have assurance that we will receive abundant answers to our prayers!

When you come to your merciful Father He will not give you a stone when you ask for bread. Don't give up on asking God to help you to enjoy the pleasures of life that He has provided—his masterpiece found in a sunset, the flavors of different foods, and the smiles of your friends that reflect His goodness. Ask Him to restore to you the joy of your salvation. Earnestly petition Him for healing, accepting that it will come in His time and His way. He hasn't promised all ills to be healed in this life, but you know for sure that ultimate healing was purchased for us by Jesus' work for us on the cross. In heaven we will have perfect bodies, with perfect emotions.

God knows the suffering associated with depression and He cares. He will relieve you of it in His time and way. Of course we want Him to answer immediately but remember that we are to resolve to be patient even with our depression. But prayer is a means by which we ask our Father to give us the desires of our hearts as they are submitted to His will.

The third mode of prayer that Paul prescribes is, *"with thanksgiving."* We can offer gratitude in advance knowing that God hears and will answer our prayers according to His will. Surprisingly, we must also thank God for this trial, this depression! That is hard to do.

Joni Eareckson Tada sets the example for us. She became a quadriplegic at age seventeen, and now in her sixties she is facing cancer. The day after discovering that it was cancer she was trying to compose an e mail to her staff at "Joni and Friends" to let them know of her condition and ask for their prayers. She prayed for guidance,

"Lord, give me words. Your words. Where should I start?"
Almost immediately the answer came. *Start with gratitude.*

Of course. That was where so many good things began. ...
You have often heard me say that our afflictions come from
the hand of our all-wise and sovereign God. And although
cancer is something new, I am content to receive from God
whatever He deems fit for me, even if it is from His left
hand. Better from His left hand than no hand at all right?!
Yes, it's alarming. But rest assured that Ken and I are utterly
convinced that God is going to use this to stretch our faith,
brighten our hope, and strengthen our witness to others.[3]

Can I pray that same kind of prayer? Can I thank Him by faith for
what He is going to do even through my depression? *Lord, I thank
You for this depression as we are to thank You in every circumstance
and even add it up to be a joy when we fall into various trials and
tests of our faith. Thank You for the strength you will give to endure.
Enable me to glorify You through this time of depression.*

Without faith it is impossible to please God (Heb. 11:6). I know
for certain that when you thank God for your trial, you are expressing
the kind of faith that pleases our Heavenly Father. You are opening
yourself up for all He would have you to learn and receive from Him
through the trial. And *then*, Paul says, "the peace of God, which surpasses all understanding, will guard (like a Roman guard over Paul)
our hearts and our minds" (v. 7). Why? Because they are grounded
where? "In Christ Jesus"—in our knowledge of Him! What peace
that brings!

This reminds me of the great hymn,

What a Friend we have in Jesus, all our sins and griefs to bear!
What a privilege to carry *everything* to God in prayer.
O what peace we often forfeit, O what needless pain we bear,
All because we do not carry *everything* to God in prayer!

God promises peace—an inner calm or tranquility, freedom from
mental agitation or anxiety, perfect peace to those whose minds are
stayed on Him.

Dear sufferer, your feelings may not tell you that you have
this peace, but *it is yours in Christ.* I could not feel this peace for

months but you must rely on prayer no matter how you feel. Many are seeking their peace in the world. It's not there. When you can't sleep, instead of counting sheep—talk to the Shepherd. Roll all your concerns over onto Him. Remember that He actually commands you to cast all of your anxieties on Him because He cares for you (1 Pet. 5:7). The peace will come, but in the meantime just keep praying. As you cast your fears on Jesus, you can be assured that He will take care of it in His time and way.

Rest your Mind on What is Excellent or Praiseworthy

And to sum up Paul says, "Finally, brethren, whatever is true, whatever is honorable, whatever is right, whatever is pure, whatever is lovely, whatever is of good repute, if there is any excellence and if anything worthy of praise, dwell on these things" (Phil. 4:8). This is Paul's further directive for peace.

I used to spend a lot of time trying to figure out what each of these eight filters meant. And then I hit upon it!—*Jesus* is all of these things! *He* is what we are to put our minds on! Jesus is true, Jesus is worthy of respect/honorable, Jesus is just, Jesus is pure, Jesus is lovely/kind or gracious, Jesus is of good report! Let's search the Scriptures to find the Jesus we've lost. Let's find evidences of His character—let Him fill our thoughts and think on Him first!

Then think on His Word and His promises. Make a list of the truths of Scripture to replace wrong thinking. For example, in the depression you feel completely overwhelmed and not capable of any task. So instead, set your mind on, *"I can do all things through Christ who strengthens me"* (Phil. 4:13).

In the depression you believe that everything that can go wrong will go wrong and nothing will turn out for good so set your mind on the truth of God which states, *"And we know that God causes all things to work together for good to those who love God, to those who are called according to His purpose"* (Rom. 8:28).

In the depression you believe that you are condemned and lost forever so set your mind on the truth of God's word that states, *"Therefore there is now no condemnation for those who are in Christ Jesus"* (Rom. 8:1).

In your depression you believe that you are separated from the love of God; that God has deserted you. Therefore you must set your mind on the truth of God's word that says, *"for He Himself has said, 'I will never desert you, nor will I ever forsake you'"* (Heb. 13:5). We must not lean on our own understanding (Prov. 3:5) but on the very truth of God's Word. Set your mind on what is true.

We must run all our thoughts through the Philippians 4:8 grid. When I worry, I must ask myself, "Is it true? Most of our worries can be eliminated with this question because they concern future possibilities not present realities. Is it honorable, right, pure, lovely, reputable, excellent, and praiseworthy? I know I am safe when I am thinking about Jesus. But when I am not thinking specifically about Jesus and the Scriptures I can still be thinking about things that pass the test and will build me up. I can cut out all movies, news, conversations, books, and daydreams about things that don't measure up to Paul's standard. I can replace them with uplifting stories of noble deeds, movies exalting right actions, conversations full of pure speech, daydreams about lovely nature scenes, and magazines that give me admirable skills and hobbies. Taking control of your thoughts and what you let influence your thoughts is a large part of the battle.

Do you think that I would have had a measure of peace if I had not set my mind on Jesus and the promises of God that we read or that my wife posted all around our apartment during my depression? No! I had to actively do these things that Paul prescribes for peace: rejoice in the Lord, remember His presence was with me, rely on prayer by taking my needs to God on a moment-by-moment basis and resting my mind on Jesus: who He is and what He can do.

That doesn't mean that I had the *feelings* of peace very much of the time. Depression affects the ability to process the truth and know it experientially in one's emotional make up. Between the struggles of our flesh and the way Satan would cause us to doubt God's goodness, we have to constantly bring our focus back to the knowing of Christ and what He can do. Our sanctification is a process of dependent responsibility—depending on God and being responsible to obey His Word and leave the feelings to follow.

Reach out and Practice What is Good

Paul ends this portion of his letter to the Philippians by saying: "The things you have learned and received and heard and seen in me, *practice* these things; and the God of peace shall be with you" (Phil. 4:9). To paraphrase it: "All the things I have taught you about Christ and you've seen me live by—you live by them too! And if you do, the God of peace shall be with you."

Paul is not afraid to say imitate me. He was living a life that could be copied. They had seen Paul's life. They had heard his message. He said, "For me to live is Christ, to die is gain." He testified, "I count all things as rubbish, if I may gain Christ." They saw him forsake all the prestige of his pharisaical background. They saw him pour out his life as a drink offering upon the sacrifice and service of their faith. They saw him earning his own living with calloused hands, preaching the gospel to all, chased out of city after city, beaten, stoned, shipwrecked, imprisoned, yet rejoicing because the gospel could not be shackled, rejoicing because he could share in the sufferings of Christ and in the resurrection glory of Christ. Now they were to follow his example. What an intimidating example! But the result would not be stress. The result would be that the God of peace would be with them. They could rest in the knowledge that God was working with them in this.

Do you find yourself forgetting the riches that are in Christ and like me going down the path of worry and fear as I did? Does your mind center on all the problems instead of the goal—God's glory? I needed to meditate on what Paul taught and put into practice the things that Paul did: knowing Jesus better and the power of His resurrection (Phil 3:10).

Paul wrote, "Now I want you to know, brethren that my circumstances have turned out for the greater progress of the gospel" (Phil. 1:12). His focus was on the gospel, not his own suffering. His life was summed up in knowing Jesus and making Him known by life or by death (Phil. 1:21). Friend, when you catch the vision of Christ that Paul had, your circumstances will take on new meaning. You will see them as divine opportunities for the furtherance of the Gospel. Then, like Paul, you will know His peace that passes understanding.

We were living in a small apartment in a large senior complex through our wilderness of testing. That was just the place to be a witness among others who were experiencing the same afflictions! It gave us a platform for the gospel, and we were able to touch many lives out of our weakness. Look around you and see how God may want to use you in your weakness as well.

Conclusion

Let your enduring hope be in the One who calmed the Galilean Sea who can calm and still your soul. Rejoice in Him, refusing to be anxious, resisting the temptation to be impatient with others. Rest in his nearness. Adore Him, thank Him, and call out to Him in prayer. Think on Him and His good gifts. Find ways to turn your suffering into a platform for the gospel. Then God's peace which transcends all understanding will guard your hearts and your minds in Christ Jesus. Worry and anxiety will be cast out and peace will come to take their place!

Response

How can you incorporate Paul's approach to worry into your own life? Here is a plan that you could use. In the midst of your depression if this seems like too much, then just try one aspect of the plan per week and add to the plan week by week.

- Read one chapter a day in the book of Philippians. (Plan to do this for the next two months.)
- Journal the portion read for the day by noting the most striking thought from the chapter.
- Read Philippians 4:4-9 every day.
- Review the following outline each day:
  o Rejoice in the Lord. Philippians 4:4
  o Resolve to be gentle/patient. 4:5
  o Remember the Lord is near. 4:5
  o Refuse to be anxious (fearful) about anything. 4:6
  o Rely on prayer. 4:6,7

- o Rest your mind on whatever is excellent or praise-worthy. 4:8
- o Reach out and practice what is good. 4:9
- Meditate on and do a "Discovering Wonderful Things" study sheet on Philippians 4:6. (See Appendix 2 for a sample study sheet.)
- Practice reviewing these principles each time you are tempted to spiral into anxiety, fear, worry, or depressed thinking.

A Story of God Using Depression for Good

Approximately two years ago I began experiencing depression, which began to escalate. Nothing specific happened in my life at the time but now as I look back, this is what I see. There had always been an underlying sadness in my life which started with abuse as a child. I covered it pretty well. I looked to people to make me happy, including my husband and children. I was a people pleaser, turning from one idol to another.

In God's providential timing He began stripping me of friends and anything I thought that I needed for enjoyment, or I now see that I idolized. Subsequently I had no appetite, lost weight, and my hair thinned. I wanted to isolate myself but was afraid to be alone. I began to think of my grandmother and mother who had committed suicide. Fears crept in, whispering that perhaps it was hereditary. Yet in the recesses of my heart I clung to the fact that I had Jesus and they didn't.

The day I was going to try a prescription medication for depression, my daughter emailed me that Dr. Somerville had spoken at their church and she took the liberty to write to him of me. Well, he wrote me and sent what I thought was a year's course study on depression— homework and all. I listened to a seminar he gave on his own personal battle with depression, and I wept because finally someone understood how I felt and what I was going through, while giving me biblical hope. For the first time I had *hope*. I had not understood what hope meant, but now I do.

I began my study and was slowly feeling better, then upon reading in one book "when the depression returns...." I frantically wrote Dr. Somerville, and I could feel his gentle smile through the email when he said, "Yes, sometimes the battle with depression does go on! But God gives us strength and grace for each day." Then he told me that I should look for and expect opportunities to share what God was teaching me to encourage others. As I began emerging from the darkness, other women in need began coming out of the woodwork. I have always had a heart to help younger women, but now I have a longing to help those in need just like I was. I can easily see the sadness in them. The Lord now has led me to turn some of my other responsibilities over to others so I would have more time to disciple five or six women. I am not a scholar but I can teach and encourage them from the Word of God and from my experience.

God has also been replacing my idolatrous desires with desires to love and please Christ. I am so thankful for what He has done. My attitude toward my husband is becoming more loving and compassionate just as Jesus is toward me.

When dark, depressing thoughts come back into my heart, I remind myself that I am in a spiritual warfare and bring up my favorite passages from His Word; especially the Psalms as they center on the beauty of my God and Savior. I obey the command to "be anxious for nothing" and then I experience the "peace which passes all understanding" flooding over me (Phil. 4:6-8).

The three most important things I would recommend to someone facing depression are:

1. Find favorite Psalms and have them on 3x5 cards with you in the kitchen, car, and bedside until you have them in your heart. Remember the heart, which is deceitful above all things, is an idol factory; but Christ came and paid the penalty for our sin by His death on the cross, is greater than our sin, and sits at the right hand of the Father interceding for us. We are no longer alone but have Christ as our friend, husband, and savior. He is better than all those idols. We also have the Spirit to comfort and empower us to overcome our sin—putting other things before Him.

2. Pray for God to give you one or more intimate, loving friends who will have compassion on you in your condition and who will pray for you. Invite them to call you occasionally and come along side you with hope from God's Word. Let them help you carry your load and hold you accountable to do what is right biblically.

3. Seek to minister to someone else in some small way. Continue to do this for it will bless you greatly.

Mary Annoni

Grace in Trials

Father of Mercies,
    Hear me for Jesus' sake.
    I am sinful even in my closest walk with thee;
        It is of thy mercy I died not long ago;
    Thy grace has given me faith in the cross
        By which thou hast reconciled thyself to me
        And me to thee,
        Drawing me by thy great love,
        Reckoning me as innocent in Christ though guilty in myself.
Giver of all graces,
        I look to thee for strength to maintain them in me,
        For it is hard to practice what I believe.
Strengthen me against temptations.
My heart is an unexhausted fountain of sin,
        A river of corruption since childhood days,
        Flowing on in every pattern of behavior;
Thou hast disarmed me of the means in which I trusted,
        And I have no strength but in thee.
Thou alone canst hold back my evil ways,
        But without thy grace to sustain me I fall.
Satan's darts quickly inflame me,
        And the shield that should quench them
        Easily drops from my hand:
Empower me against his wiles and assaults.
Keep me sensible of my weakness,
        And of my dependence upon thy strength.
Let every trial teach me more of thy peace,
        More of thy love.
Thy Holy Spirit is given to increase thy graces,
        And I cannot preserve or improve them
        Unless he works continually in me.
May he confirm my trust in thy promised help,
        And let me walk humbly in dependence upon thee,
        For Jesus' sake.

---── CHAPTER 8 ──---

How Do I Express My Grief to God?

Though He slay me, I will *hope* in Him. (Job 13:15a)

When my eight-year-old granddaughter was doing her quiet time this week, she had to read Job chapter 1. She came to me and expressed, "Did you know after all the servants came and told Job that his donkeys and sheep and camels were all destroyed and all ten of his children were dead, Job tore his robes and *worshipped* God?!" Through her big eyes and expressive face I was made to try to imagine that scene again. Job gets the bad news. Bam! Bam! Bam! Everything and everyone that he loves is gone. He tears his robe, shaves his head, and falls on the ground—not in self-pity, not in rage, but in worship. Then this poetry comes out of his mouth. Was he singing? "Naked I came from my mother's womb and naked I shall return there. The Lord gave and the Lord has taken away. Blessed be the name of the Lord" (Job 1:21).

He turned his pain into praise. He turned his weeping into worship. This is the kind of faith that makes the world stand still as the angels and demons (and even the eight year olds) stop and watch. A little later Job cried out, "Though He slay me, I will *hope* in Him" (Job 13:15a).

If you want that kind of faith, then you need to learn to sing the kind of songs that Job sang. And you don't even have to write them yourself like he did.

The American slaves didn't invent the *blues*; they began with Job and the Israelites in ancient Palestine. In fact all lovers of the true God have been able to sing in their sorrow and know that God knows. God sees. God cares. God is still there on the throne. In the book of Psalms we can see that it is possible to praise God when you are counting God's abundant blessings or when you are making your couch swim with tears; when you are surrounded by friends and encouragers or when you have been deserted by your closest friends and are surrounded by enemies; when you feel like you could jump over a wall and defeat an entire army or when your bones are wasting away, when you feel God's smile or when you feel forsaken and it feels like God is far off.

The psalms are the hymn book for ancient Israel and for all believers. They are meant to be sung. "For the choir director" is found at the beginning of fifty-two of them. They are music to be used in praising and worshiping our great almighty God and Redeemer. Ronald B. Allen, in his excellent book *And I Will Praise Him* says,

> Consider any of the familiar lines of the Psalter meditatively, and you will discover how appropriate they are in mirroring the variegated moods of the life of faith. We who so often find our tongues stammering, our emotions choked, and our minds muddy, find our very necessary expressions of reality in these lines from the Psalms.[1]

While in depression, I found in a new way that the psalms of lament expressed my feelings (or lack of them) as they became my lifeline to worshiping God. Those who wrote these songs in the minor key communicated their honest feelings and hard questions to God. By reading these psalms, you enter into their experience that is like your own. They express how you're feeling and it is appropriate. God used this poetry to communicate truth. By living in it and making it your own you can have an authentic experience with the God who can be trusted at all times.

Even Jesus prayed one of David's psalms of lament–Psalm 22—when on the cross. When God abandoned Him and poured out His wrath upon Him for our sins, He prayed, "My God, My God, why have You forsaken Me?" He was quoting Psalm 22, verse 1. That psalm goes on to describe Jesus' exact situation two thousand years before it happened. It says he was surrounded by dogs, evil scoffers, His hands and feet were pierced, and people were staring and casting lots for His garments. Yet the psalm goes on to declare that God will deliver Him and all the ends of the earth will remember and turn to the Lord. That psalm was written for Jesus, to comfort Him in His most excruciating moment! Jesus knew the rest of the psalm so even His cry of despair was inextricably bound up with the exclamations of trust in God that are found in the same psalm!

D.A. Carson in his marvelous book *Scandalous* on the ironies of the Gospel expresses it this way,

> (Jesus') cry of desolation is of course a quotation from the Davidic Psalm 22:1. But that psalm is rich in expressions of confidence and trust in God. If David can utter such an anguished cry while demonstrating his own steadfast trust in God, why should it be that unthinkable that David's greater Son should utter the same cry while exercising the same trust?[2]

What irony, the man who cries out in despair trusts God! We too can use the Psalms to turn our cries of despair into declarations of faith, especially knowing that we will never be abandoned by God like Jesus was. The songs of lament are given to us as a ladder that can lead us out of the deepest pit of depression up to the heights of praise. So ... when you are depressed, sing!

Psalms with which to Lament

I am going to walk you through two Psalms of Lament so that you can see how to use all of them. You can climb the same ladder out of depression as you (1) give vent to your own lament, (2) express your trust, (3) cry for deliverance, and (4) vow to praise God again. Take out your Bible and your journal now and respond to the Word as we study it together. Don't rush through these psalms. Let them inform your heart that is sad and weighed down. If you can't do it with the joy that you would like, just do it as you can. Express the praise by faith even though you cannot feel the praise.

Psalm 142
Prayer for Help in Trouble
Maskil of David, when he was in the cave. A Prayer.

1 I cry aloud with my voice to the LORD; I make supplication with my voice to the LORD.
2 I pour out my complaint before Him; I declare my trouble before Him.
3 When my spirit was overwhelmed within me, You knew my path. In the way where I walk They have hidden a trap for me.
4 Look to the right and see; For there is no one who regards me; There is no escape for me; No one cares for my soul.
5 I cried out to You, O LORD; I said, "You are my refuge, My portion in the land of the living.
6 "Give heed to my cry, For I am brought very low; Deliver me from my persecutors, For they are too strong for me.
7 "Bring my soul out of prison, So that I may give thanks to Your name; The righteous will surround me, For You will deal bountifully with me."

Read this psalm over twice aloud asking God to allow it to express your heart to Him.

David writes a Maskil or contemplative poem or prayer from the cave in which he had run to hide from King Saul (1 Samuel 22). He is teetering on the brink of despair. He models for us how to pray with total dependence on the mercy of the Lord.

(1) Vent Your Lament

Read verses 1, 2 again. What is David doing? David is crying aloud, making supplication, pouring out his complaint, and declaring his trouble. He is intense about it. We're to be intense in our relationship and love for God. It's to involve all of one's heart, mind, strength, and soul.

Prayer, in its most basic form is just communicating with God—telling Him what is on your heart. If your heart is sad, your prayer will take on the form of a lament. Declare your trouble! Talk to God about it. We can be so quick to complain to our friends and family. Shouldn't we rather bring our woes to God? He cares and He is the One who can do something about it. Through prayer we grab hold of the first wrung on the ladder out of depression by showing our utter dependence on God's mercy through pouring out our hearts to Him. Sufferer, let this trial of depression drive you to intense prayer.

David's prayer is specific. He pours out his complaints, his troubles (what was going on in his life: the turmoil of losing his best friend Jonathan and running for his life from his friend's father who fears that David will steal his throne). He expresses his helplessness—spirit overwhelmed, trapped, no one to help, no escape, in despair as no one cared for him. Does that resonate with you? No escape, no help! Whatever you do, it seems there is no way out of the emptiness—all exits are blocked. That's why there are suicidal thoughts. But David didn't allow himself to go down that path; instead he cries out to the Lord. You too must stop hiding your struggles, disguising your pain, and covering your burdens. Tell it to the Lord. Vent your lament!

It is time to respond. First read Psalm 142:1-4 again. Pray those words with David. Now write in your journal your own cries of desperation to God—tell Him exactly how you feel or don't feel right now. Tell Him all about your fears and your desperate situation. But don't stop here. You must go on to the rest of the Psalm to find the way out.

(2) Express Your Trust

We see the first hint of David's faith in the middle of his lament when he says "You knew my path." He recognizes that God knows the journey he is on. God is not surprised about the traps that are hidden along the road. He is not surprised by the pain or difficulty. He has put David on that path for a purpose and He will show him the way out. You can also say, *God you know my path. You planned it. I wouldn't have chosen it, but you did and you must have a good design even though I can't see it.* After the brief expression of faith, David is complaining again about his defenselessness and the hidden traps along his way. He says, *look God, there is "no one"—not on the right or left to help.* "No one cares for my soul." But then he looks up.

Read verse 5a "I cried out to You, O Lord..." David addresses his prayer to the LORD, Yahweh, the God of the burning bush, the God who said to Moses, "I am who I am." He is the God who created the universe and is the same yesterday, today, and tomorrow. He is the God who heard the cries of His people in slavery in Egypt and sent them a deliverer before they even asked. He is the God who saw us in our bondage to sin and sent a savior even though we would spit on Him. Do you have a relationship with the God of the burning bush? Can you stand on holy ground and cry out to him for deliverance?

Jesus is the only mediator. Remember he was forsaken so you could be brought near. If you have trusted Him to take away your sins, then you can come boldly into the throne room to ask for grace to help in time of need (Heb. 4:16). He even asks you to come (see John 14:13, 14; 15:16; 16:23-28). Don't run to any other refuge when you are in trouble and despair. Cry out to the Lord!

David has to remind himself that God is his refuge. Even if no man will help him, God will take him up. God will not allow anything to happen to him that is not for his good. He can hide in God. He can trust God. Peter showed this same kind of dependency on Christ when he said, "Lord, to whom we shall go? You have words of eternal life" (John 6:68). Take refuge in the One who can give you eternal life!

David moves on from trust in God's providence and His ability to provide refuge to expressing His trust in God as a person. He says, "God is my portion in the land of the living." In other words, he is saying, "God is the starving sailor's ration. If God is all I have, that is enough for me!" Tell God He is enough for you. He has stripped you of all other joys, but He is enough! Express your trust!

Read Psalm 142:5 again. Put David's expression of trust into your own words.

David trusted in God's grace and the promised Messiah to save him but we live with more revelation. Tell God on what basis you come to Him—only through the shed blood of your Savior Jesus Christ and on the basis of His mercy and grace. Confess to Him if you have forgotten aspects of His character or the Gospel. Behold

Jesus! Saturate your soul in His love for you! When you have spent time meditating on His goodness and love for you, tell Him how you trust Him for all you are and what you're going through.

Write out your own prayer of trust to the Lord.

(3) Cry for Deliverance

The third wrung on the ladder is to cry for deliverance. Let your trials drive you to God. Like David, cry aloud with your voice, make supplications, and pour out your complaint. If you think God is not listening, beg Him to listen. Say with David, "Give heed to my cry, for I am brought very low."

Ask for specific deliverance, "Deliver me from my persecutors, for they are too strong for me. Bring my soul out of prison" (v. 6). Affirm that God alone is your help. Yes, you are low. You are weak. You are chained. But God is on His throne. He is almighty. His arm is not so short that it cannot save (Num. 11:23). Your doubts might fight back, *God may have wanted to deliver David from prison, but he won't deliver me.* Search the scriptures to see if that is true. You will find promises like these:

- He is working all things together for my good (Rom. 8:28)
- He foreknew me, predestined me to become conformed to the image of His Son, He called and justified me and will glorify me (Rom. 8:29. 30)
- He will freely give me all things that He knows that I need (Rom. 8:32).

God wants to deliver you from fear, from sin, and ultimately from all suffering—after he has used that suffering to accomplish His perfect work.

In the melancholy of your situation with everything stripped away, you can turn to the God who loves you and has given His Son as your sure defense and refuge. God can deliver you from your persecutors whether they be human or imaginary. Your persecutors may be an unsaved husband or a rebellious three year old, they may be a mountain of laundry or a difficult boss, they may be fears of facing life alone or the oppression of constant pain. Ask God to deliver you! He can give you victory and joy in the situation you are in. He is honored when we depend on Him through prayer.

Read Psalm 142:6,7a and boldly write out your own petitions. *Lord, I ask ... in the powerful name of the* resurrected *Jesus. Amen.*

(4) Vow to Praise Again

Finally, at the top of the ladder, the song turns from a dirge to a dance, from a lament to a joyful shout. David realizes that his deliverance is not for his sake alone. He says, "Deliver me... *so that* I may give thanks to Your name" (vv. 6, 7). The goal is God's glory and God's praise. David looks forward to the day when he will publicly praise God among His people. Praise is the natural outcome when God has heard and delivered. What else could the Israelites do when the waters parted and their enemies were drowned, other than take out their tambourines and dance and sing? Some day you will also dance and sing. This brings glory to God's name. You may not feel like God is dealing bountifully with you right now, but like David, you know He will someday. And if you think about your salvation, you can say with Paul "He has given us every blessing in the heavenly places in Christ" (Eph. 1:3). Keep in mind that we deserve only God's wrath, but He has given us eternal life through the perfect life, death, resurrection, ascension and intercession of Jesus Christ. Whatever we get above that is icing on the cake. We can praise Him no matter what! Praise Him for the bounty you have now in your salvation. Praise Him for the rewards that are coming.

David began with a cry of anguish and ends with a song. Remember, dear sufferer, the ability to praise God in the dark does not come naturally. It comes from God's mercy and grace to help in time of need. We walk by faith. You can praise Him through the pain of your suffering. You can praise Him even through the dark lens of depression that is saying, *Yes, this lament is surely true of me, but I will never again be able to give a song of genuine praise.* Stand against those thoughts and, based on the truth of God's Word, write a prayer like this based on Psalm 142:5-7

Lord, you know that I cannot feel this truth in my heart right now. But, Lord, you deserve this praise whether I can feel it or not so I cry out to you, You are my refuge, my portion, and my only hope in this land of the living. Please, Lord, pay close attention to my cry. You know how very low I feel. You know that I have no feelings. Deliver me from these thoughts that persecute me and pull me down. Bring me out of this prison of emotions that overwhelm me. Help me to genuinely believe that the righteous will surround me again and that you will deal bountifully with me. Then I will give thanks to your name for your glory!

Take out your journal again and pray and give thanks to your God for what He will do; for His love and mercy toward you! (How could God use this trial for good in your life and for His glory? How will you praise Him with others?) Write out your vow of praise.

Let's look at another Psalm of Lament.

Psalm 13
Prayer for Help in Trouble.
For the choir director. A Psalm of David

1   How long, O LORD? Will You forget me forever? How long will You hide Your face from me?
2   How long shall I take counsel in my soul, having sorrow in my heart all the day? How long will my enemy be exalted over me?
3   Consider and answer me, O LORD my God; Enlighten my eyes, or I will sleep the sleep of death,
4   And my enemy will say, "I have overcome him," And my adversaries will rejoice when I am shaken.
5   But I have trusted in Your lovingkindness; My heart shall rejoice in Your salvation.
6   I will sing to the LORD, Because He has dealt bountifully with me.

Read this psalm over twice aloud asking God to allow it to express your heart to Him.

(1) Vent your Lament!

This Psalm of David reflects the very feelings of the person going through depression who may not dare to voice them. His pain is so severe that he feels like the omniscient God has a memory block! He thinks God has forgotten him. He asks four times, "How long?" This is an expression of darkest terror when he feels cut off from God. Does this express your pain?

David pictures God not only having His attention elsewhere but deliberately avoiding him (v. 1, 2). If you feel forgotten by God, you can know that a believer can feel that way at times. You might even think that God has abandoned you. David is called a man after God's own heart and yet he feels abandoned. He asks God four times, "How long?" He is in good company, for even the martyrs around the throne in heaven are also asking, "How long?" (Rev. 6:10). Do you ever ask God, "How long?" When a trial is resolved quickly, we don't have any trouble trusting God but when a situation drags on with no end in sight, we are tempted to think that God has abandoned us.

David expresses that he has no hope day after day—only sorrow to look forward to. He can't think of any way to end the pain even if he counsels himself all day long (v. 2). He dreads seeing his enemies gloating over his misery. He is sure they are going to get the victory.

We learn from David here that the first step in getting out of the pit is to realize that you are in one. You must admit that you cannot climb out by yourself. If God doesn't remember you and come looking for you and throw you a ladder, you will sink into the mud at the bottom of the well while your enemies are dancing around above you. Call out to God!

Turn your cries of despair into prayer. Of course there are wrong things to say to God that are blasphemous while we are in our misery. Thankfully, Job did not take the counsel of his wife to curse God and die (Job 2:9). D.A. Carson states:

But within certain boundaries ...it is far better to be frank about our grief, candid in our despair, honest with our questions, than to suppress them and wear a public front of puffy piety. God knows our thoughts in any case....Without (Job's) questions, there would have been no responses.[3]

Instead Job was praised because "in all this Job did not sin, nor did he blame God" (Job 1:22). But he did ask questions. He did wrestle with God. You too must be frank about your grief, honest with your questions and candid in your despair if you want to find true help.

Read vv. 1-2 and write out your questions for God.

(2) Express Your Trust

Despair turns to trust as you take your hopeless situation to the only One who can rescue you. David prays, "Consider and answer me, O Lord (Yahweh) my God!"

Here we see David exercising his weak faith to uproot his despair. If the source of his grief is God's abandonment, then the cure is God's attention. If God has truly abandoned him, it is hopeless to ask God to consider and answer. But David at least has enough faith to *ask* that God not forsake him utterly. Maybe the stories of the past strengthened him to ask for the same God to remember him. Did God forget Noah when he was tossed about in the ark on the stormy seas? Did God forget his people in bondage in Egypt? Those 430 years may have seemed long, but when they were up, He brought them out on the very day! (Ex. 12:41; Gen. 15:13, 16). Did God forget Abraham and leave him childless? No he gave him a son in his *old age* who would father peoples more numerous than the stars.

We have even more scriptures than David did to prove God's faithfulness to us. When Israel was sent into captivity, was it forever? No, God promised that it would be seventy years, no longer. "But Zion said, 'The Lord has forsaken me, and the Lord has forgotten me. Can a woman forget her nursing child, and have no compassion on the son of her womb? Even these may forget, but I will not forget you. Behold, I have inscribed you on the palms of My hands ...'" (Is. 49:14–16a). God did not forget. He moved a pagan king's heart to send them back to their land at just the right time. And best of all, we have Jesus' own words before He ascended into heaven "… and lo, I am with you always, even to the end of the age" (Matt. 28:20). So when you feel like God has forsaken you, remember that He may turn His face away in anger for a moment, but His lovingkindness is forever (Ps. 30:5). Call out for him to consider and answer you. Even this calling shows your trust.

What kind of God did David call out to? He confesses that the great I AM is *his* God. Yahweh is the only one to whom he can go. This God who has always existed and who will never change has the answers! It's the same for us! He alone has the power to save and give life and hope. Is He your God? Then claim Him and express your trust in Him. Cry out, "Consider and answer me, O LORD my God!"

(3) Cry for Deliverance!

Now we come to the middle of the Psalm, and we find that it is the hinge or turning point. As David prays, the whole tone of the psalm changes. David began his petition almost timidly, asserting that God *is* his God and he hopes that God will hear and answer. Now he gains boldness and goes on to present his specific requests, "Enlighten my eyes, or I will sleep the sleep of death, And my enemy will say, 'I have overcome him,' And my adversaries will rejoice when I am shaken" (vv. 3-4). He even becomes so daring as to give God three reasons for responding. He is assuming now that God doesn't want him to die or to have his enemies overcome him or rejoice at his demise. Throughout this prayer we actually see David's faith triumphing.

What now does this new David ask for? He petitions God to enlighten his eyes. He doesn't ask for a change of circumstances or comfort. He only asks for life and hope. The darkening of the eyes infers that he's about to die — reminiscent of a man breathing his last on the battlefield and his eyesight is failing, a premonition of the end. He needs new life infused into him. He cannot die now or his enemies will win and God's promises to make him king and establish an everlasting kingdom will fail. David wants to live because he knows that is the best way for him to serve God and further his kingdom at this time. Our prayers for life must also be similarly kingdom focused like Paul modeled for us,

> For to me, to live is Christ, and to die is gain. But if I am to live on in the flesh, this will mean fruitful labor for me; and I do not know which to choose. But I am hard-pressed from both directions, having the desire to depart and be with Christ, for that is very much better; yet to remain on in the flesh is more necessary for your sake. And convinced of this, I know that I shall remain and continue with you all for your progress and joy in the faith...." (Phil. 1:21-25)

You too can pray for restoration of health in order to serve Christ and His kingdom.

In another sense enlightening of the eyes can refer to a spiritual restoration of hope through seeing God and his purposes. Remember when the king of Aram sent a great army with horses and chariots to surround the city where the pesky prophet Elisha was giving away his secret plans, Elisha's servant started to panic. So Elisha prayed and said, "'O Lord, I pray, open his eyes that he may see.' And the Lord opened the servant's eyes, and he saw; and behold, the mountain was full of horses and chariots of fire all around Elisha." (2 Kings 6:17) The servant's fear was banished with that sight. You also can cry out to God to "enlighten my eyes" and He will show you that you aren't outnumbered like you thought. He is on your side. You just need to see more of Him as you look into His Word and claim His promises. Pray with David Psalm 119:18 "Open my eyes, that I may behold wonderful things from Your law." Get a glimpse of God's power, love and goodness! Read His Word and proclaim it even when in the depression you cannot feel it.

Lay out your petitions before your God. First use David's prayer:

> "Consider and answer me; O Lord my God; enlighten my eyes, or I will sleep the sleep of death and my enemy will say, 'I have overcome him,' and my adversaries will rejoice when I am shaken."(vv. 3-4)

Now write out your petitions, be bold. Ask God to enlighten your eyes, to restore you physically and spiritually, to show you Himself. Lay before Him the reasons you have for wanting this deliverance for His glory. (How could God use this trial for good in your life and for His glory?)

Examine your motives and claim His promises.

Make a plan for studying His Word daily and searching the Scriptures so your eyes can be opened to your God.

(4) Vow to Praise Again

"I will sing to the Lord, because He has dealt bountifully with me" (v. 6). Here, David began with a sob and ends with a song. He began with an accusation and ends with a refutation. He began by stewing over God's apparent forgetfulness and ends by rehearsing God's loyal love! He began with questions. He ends with declarations. His situation has not changed but somehow his desert has become an oasis.

Even the structure of the psalm shows us the transformation that has taken place in the psalmist. The first stanza started out with five lines of tumultuous and emotional lament. The next two stanzas move "through an increasingly calm prayer (expressed in four lines), to a final expression of trust in God and harmony (expressed in three lines). Franz Delitzsch, one of the great nineteenth-century commentators on the Psalms, wrote, "This song, as it were, casts up constantly lessening waves, until it becomes still as the sea when smooth as a mirror, and the only motion discernible at last is that of the joyous ripple of calm repose."[4]

David's enemies were still surrounding him, but his eyes were opened to see that "those who are with us are more than those who are with them." (2 Kings 6:16). "Greater is He who is in you than he who is in the world" (1 John 4:4). You too can experience this transformation of heart even if your depression is not suddenly lifted and your circumstances remain indefinitely.

Your final response is a vow to praise, a promise to sing even from the bottom of the pit. You can now wait patiently for deliverance because you know it will come. And as you wait you have a heart that rejoices in suffering, like Paul and Silas who sang in prison (Acts 16) and like the apostles who considered it a privilege to be counted worthy to suffer for the sake of the Name (Acts 5:41).

Pray and give thanks to your God for what He has done for you and for His love and mercy toward you. First use David's prayer: "I will sing to the Lord, because He has dealt bountifully with me" (v. 6). Make a list of all the ways that God has dealt bountifully with you. Lord, I praise You for …

You can even include in your list God's gift of the Psalms of Lament that give you a ladder out of the pit into His very throne room where we find mercy to help in time of need.

Response

In turning your pain into praise and your weeping into worship I invite you to respond in this way:

- In your journal write out the template used in the Psalms of Lament: (1)Vent your lament, (2) Express your trust, (3) Cry for deliverance, and (4) Vow to praise again. Now write your own psalm of lament to God by filling in each part.
- The next time you cannot sleep at night, get up and make yourself a hot drink and turn to the Psalms. You can go directly to the Psalms of Lament (Psalm 3, 5, 6, 7, 13, 32, 44, 60, 69, 74, 77, 79, 80, 83, 85, 88, 90, 123, 130, 137, and 142, and others; see Appendix 3 for two more examples) or you can just read consecutively until one strikes a chord with you and your soul finds rest as you pray it back to God.
- Not just the Psalms of Lament are beneficial when going through depression but all the Psalms. Why not read through the Psalms consistently beginning with Psalm 1. Read them aloud to someone else or just to yourself. Read them every day. Pray them back to God. Listen to them sung and learn to sing them yourself. Turn your pain into praise, and even the angels and demons will stop and take note!

A Story of Betrayal and a Renewed Trust in God's Providence

As a believer from a young age, it has been and still is my desire to serve Christ with my life. When I was planning to marry, I looked for a partner who was committed to serving the Lord and raising a godly family. The Lord brought me that beautiful partner in life and we have been married thirty-two years. The Lord has blessed us with three lovely, godly daughters who are all married to godly young men, and each one is serving the Lord in ministry at church and in their homes. We are truly blessed.

My life growing up was about family and the family business. I was four years old when I lost my dad, so my mother started a restaurant and my brothers and I worked alongside of her in the restaurant from my childhood through my college years. I was saved in my community church early in my childhood and felt a strong desire for ministry from my youth. I entered seminary briefly until called home by my family to help with the family restaurant. Most of my life has been in that business. However, prior to my marriage, we decided as a family to sell the business and property in order for each of us to pursue different opportunities in life. Personally, I knew it was very difficult to work in the business, serve the Lord and raise a godly family, so at the time I felt most likely I would not be in the restaurant business after I married.

After a year into our marriage, it became apparent that I needed to have my own business again and do what I felt I was good at. So, since my family restaurant was still for sale, my wife and I agreed to purchase it from my family and run it as our own business. So, with a verbal agreement from my three brothers and mother, my wife and I set out on opening, managing, and building our own restaurant business. We started with nothing more than a desire to spend our time together working to build our future and raise a family all under the direction of scripture.

We had twenty-four successful years in our business. It was a blessing to have our children grow up working in the business alongside of us as well. We welcomed friends, family, church, and community into our business with great joy. During the later years we were able to home-school our daughters and help plant a church in our community, all while caring for our aging parents. Again we felt very blessed to be surrounded by God's people, supportive extended family, and community. We joyfully watched our daughters growing and serving family and church as well. We were and are so grateful for all God allowed us to be a part of in His plan. Our days and hours were long and oftentimes filled with many trials throughout the years, but our reward has been much more than a paycheck.

Although there had been times in my life of significant trials and testing from the Lord, nothing was as sharp, sudden, and all-encompassing as the devastating crisis which came as an attack in February, 2007. Everything I was doing, had known, and worked for changed completely. Within in few short hours, the business my wife and I had worked twenty-four years together to build, support our family, and prepare for retirement was stolen from me. The ones who stole it from me where the very ones I grew up alongside and knew as well as I knew myself: my brothers. They claimed the verbal agreement made twenty-four years ago never happened and used old documents to say they were the rightful owners and operators of the restaurant property and my business. I loved them as much as anyone could love a brother, and they claimed to love me, too. However their greed and desire for power and control caused them to be used by Satan to cause harm to me and therefore my family.

I was completely blind-sided. In one afternoon and with one meeting, my business, my job, my income, my career, my retire-ment, and the access to my business's bank account were all gone. I never expected this action from them, nor did I ever dream such a thing was possible from someone in my family. The lies, hate, anger, jealousy, and just plain evil that came out of them was utterly shocking. I had always felt very close to them throughout our lives. We were all raised by a widowed mother who taught us to look out for each other, with the premise that family always comes first. I had never witnessed any of this behavior from them and had always thought nothing could ever come between us. We would always stick up for each other. Nothing could have been further from the truth. To my further sadness I learned this attack on me had been planned for some years. They were actually waiting on our mother to pass away to carry out their devious plan. When she continued to live into her nineties, they decided to not wait any longer but instead go ahead and act on their plan.

Not only did I lose my business and income but, in God's sovereignty, at the same time, the stock market had a historically record low. Everything I had worked for, every place I thought and planned to put my finances to grow into retirement, were all gone. I think at the time I was too scared of all that was happening to question God. However, I did search the Scriptures looking for help to make sense of my devastation. I was very worried to the point of insomnia. I could not eat. Questions regarding the future flooded my mind and controlled my thoughts: What was I to do? How would I support my family? How would I rebuild my finances? Nothing made sense. The very family that I had always trusted betrayed me and stole my business from me. My future looked very bleak and frightening. I had a wife, two daughters in college, my mother, and my mother-in-law, all dependent on me to provide for them. How was I going to do it? What was I going to do so as not to let them down?

Everything I tried failed; I was unable to get a job anywhere. I was told that I was "over-qualified" with "too much experience." After spending forty-plus years in my own business, having my college degree, and being sixty years of age, I was unable to find a job. I kept asking myself, what was I going to do? All the while I was trying to make sense of what had happened to me and why. My own elderly mom died of a broken heart from what my brothers did shortly after. How was I to go on?

I finally gave into the pains screaming from my body. I let the weakness take over. It became harder to get out of bed. I became sad inside and out. I could not make sense of how the brothers I grew up with, loved, and trusted could devise to cause me harm. I could not comprehend that they would carry out such a purposefully hurtful, life-changing attack on me that would devastate my family as well. I began to have thoughts of my family being better off without me and prayed the Lord would take me. It was becoming too hard to watch them look to me for leadership that I felt inadequate to give. The desire to just sleep and not get up grew stronger, and I felt no one understood what I was going through. No one understood the thoughts I was having or knew how to help me.

I was very depressed and thought the only way of getting help was to go to the hospital. I told my wife one day I thought she should take me there. I desperately wanted to talk with someone who could help; someone who understood. I was feeling very trapped with no help. I have never known a man to deal with depression, so I had no one to ask all of my "How do I deal with this?" questions. It's not something that people I knew talked about. Besides that, I didn't feel comfortable admitting that I was depressed. It was as if I was failing again in some other way.

I knew in my head that God was in control and even in charge of the events in my life. I just did not know how to handle them or understand them. I did not have the ability to see any good coming from me or my life anymore. I prayed fervently, my family prayed with me and for me, as did my friends, my pastor, and my elders at church. They had not experienced what I was experiencing and did not understand how to help either, outside of reading scripture to me and praying for me. I still was overcome by the feelings of uselessness, failure, complete loneliness, and the terrible inability to support my family.

I am so very thankful that my wife and daughters did not give up hope on me or let me stay in a place of depression. They never gave up on me, nor would they let me give up. They would tell me, "There is always hope!" Though they were suffering with all the same losses as I, they stayed by me and with me anyway. My wife had sought out our pastor for personal counseling and asked for other men in our church to come pray with me. All was appreciated and I was grateful for them. Though they had not gone through the same losses, they knew God's Word. They knew it was sufficient, and they encouraged me by sharing it with me. But I still was battling with my feelings and lingering questions.

During this time, one of my daughters was going through some counseling classes in California. She reached out for help from one of her professors, Dr. Somerville about my situation one day. She explained all we had been going through and my current state of depression. She heard him mention in class that he had done phone counseling before, and she inquired to see if he would consider counseling with me. He said he was willing if I wanted the counseling. When my daughter told me of his offer, I knew I wanted his counsel. So my wife and I together began speaking with him on a weekly basis for over a year. He was and is a very caring individual, very wise, a great listener, and offered very helpful advice as we worked through many of the trials I was experiencing.

Something that struck me right away when speaking with him was that he understood me! This is what encouraged me to continue. He was a pastor and is now a teacher, and yet he had been very depressed in his life as well. He had gone through his own very difficult trials with many of the same feelings I had. And he came through it. Praise God! Now he is helping others, like me, and my wife too, grow through the pain and be able to truly "count it all joy when you encounter various trials" (James 1:2). His desire was to help us see how we could grow through the trials God had allowed to come into our lives, "knowing that the testing of our faith produces endurance" (James 1:2). Through weekly phone counseling, he guided us through scriptures that I have read so many times before. But through his biblical instruction, those verses became very real and relevant to me. Through his assignments, guidance, and instructions, we were able to read several wonderfully biblical and applicable books as a couple and began to see how God was working through all the devastation. Though my brothers had abandoned me, God never left my side. They "meant evil against me, but God meant it for good" (Gen 50:20).

Our caring counselor listened, prayed, extended compassion, held us accountable to the assignments, talked plainly, lovingly and biblically with us. As we counseled with him, I could see God's Word become real in my life in a new way. I began to regain strength, the pain subsided, and hope was being restored for a future designed by God for my life. A future that was all for God's glory and submitted to His plan for my life. My wife and I were growing in a fresh new way spiritually. Sermons became more alive, hymns of praise came to mind, and out of our mouths with true sincerity we cried "The LORD gave and the LORD has taken away; blessed be the name of the LORD" (Job 1:21).

I developed an insatiable appetite for the Word. I had been reading about Job's life for quite some time. Though I had not lost all that Job lost, I could see how God had grown His servant Job's faith through his trials and I could see how God was developing in me a stronger faith. Then I began reading more closely about Joseph's life. Again, a story I have known all my life and have read many times; however now it was like his story came alive in my life. I could now relate very much to Joseph. I wanted to understand as much as I could about him and how he handled all that he went through because of his brothers.

It is clear that nothing happens in our life without God ordaining it or allowing it all for His purpose and glory (Rom. 8:28). He has a plan for our lives and is working that plan out until the day that it is completed (Phil. 1:6). Yet, He never promised we would not suffer, struggle, go through trials, or have pain; in fact we are taught to expect trials and suffering in this life (John 16:33; 1 Pet. 4:12). However, He did promise He would be with us always (Matt. 28:20) showing His constant love and care.

My trust has always been in God, but now it is a deeper, wider, all-encompassing trust. My life is completely surrendered to God's will. I realize I can only control what God wants me to control, and rely on Him for everything. God is my refuge and strength (Ps. 18:2).

Using an old metaphor, God "removed all the trees in the forest" so I could see Him and only Him. By removing those people and things that I had placed as more important at times than my Lord, I now see Christ more. Every day I gain a deeper understanding of Jesus, believing in His Word, completely relying on His Word, being committed to prayer even as I continue to walk through the trials of rebuilding my life. I understand through painful experiences now, how to completely depend on Christ. My desire is to have others see Jesus in me in all I do and say, no matter what my circumstances.

My understanding of His love and sacrifice for me is so much deeper than ever before in my life. I praise God for His unconditional, limitless love for me. I am thankful for His amazing grace. I love to talk about what Jesus has done (and is doing) for me and through me, all for His glorious purpose. My Savior brought me out of depression and allows me to serve Him and tell of what He has done for me. "For I am confident of this very thing, He who began a good work in you will perfect it until the day of Christ" (Phil. 1:6). Thankfully, God has provided me a way to support my family through a new business. The reality of my life is that the circumstances with my brothers have not changed, but my response has changed. I now trust in God's Word, persevere through His leading and the power of prayer. I continue to be encouraged through reading Scripture and recommended books written by wonderful godly authors. To God be all glory and honor. Amen.

The most important things that I would recommend are:

1. Read the Bible. There are always going to be things that try us, challenge us, hurt us, anger us; and we may never understand why we have to walk through a certain trial. There is always hope and strength and help in God's Word. I sincerely believe that regular daily reading from the Bible is mandatory to fight and survive the spiritual battles we face in life. It is vital that we remember God is our stronghold and our wisdom. We must face our daily trials with the Word of God. Scripture reminds us that our security rests firmly and always in Christ's faithfulness; then comes believing, trusting and submitting to His will.

2. Desire God. Learn all you can about God: His character, His love, His forgiveness, and then seek Him and you will be saved (Ps. 34:4). Desire to know Him and trust Him.

3. Pray. Be committed to daily prayer in all things. Bring all your requests and petitions to God without anxiety (Phil. 4:6-7). Prayer is worship. Worship God. Pray without ceasing (1 Thess. 5:17), and pray for one another (James 5:16).

4. Seek counsel. Remember we are a part of a body of believers and are not meant to be on our own. Seek out godly counsel and find a biblical counselor who can help you apply the Scriptures through your struggles.

An Elder and a Businessman

Joy

O Christ,
    All thy ways of mercy tend to and end in my delight.
    Thou didst weep, sorrow, suffer that I might rejoice.
    For my joy thou hast sent the comforter,
        Multiplied thy promises,
        Shown me my future happiness,
        Given me a living fountain.
    Thou art preparing joy for me and me for joy;
    I pray for joy, wait for joy, long for joy;
        Give me more than I can hold, desire, or think of.
    Measure out to me my times and degrees of joy,
        At my work, business, duties.
    If I weep at night, give me joy in the morning.
    Let me rest in the thought of thy love,
        Pardon for sin, my title to heaven,
        My future unspotted state.
    I am unworthy recipient of thy grace.
    I often disesteem thy blood and slight thy love,
        But can in repentance draw water
        From the wells of thy joyous forgiveness.
    Let my heart leap towards the eternal Sabbath,
        Where the work of redemption, sanctification,
        Preservation, glorification
        Is finished and perfected forever,
        Where thou wilt rejoice over me with joy.
    There is no joy like the joy of heaven,
        For in that state are no sad divisions, unchristian quarrels,
        Contentions, evil designs, weariness, hunger, cold,
        Sadness, sin, suffering, persecutions, toils of duty.
    O healthful place where none are sick!
    O happy land where all are kings!
    O holy assembly where all are priests!
    How free a state where none are servants except to thee!
    Bring me speedily to the land of joy.

————— ⚜ CHAPTER 9 ⚜ —————

Is Joy Out of the Question?

> Consider it all joy, my brethren, when you encounter var-
> ious trials, knowing that the testing of your faith produces
> endurance. (James 1:2-3)

All good feelings are completely lacking when you're in depression. Can you have joy when you feel so miserable? How can sadness and joy go together? How can you "count it all joy" when you are not experiencing any positive emotion? This is one of the things that so convicted me in my depression. Joy seemed completely missing. I tallied this up as another reason to believe that I was not a Christian. Had not Jesus said, "These things I have spoken to you that My joy may be in you, and that your joy may be made full" (John 15:11)? And yet, my heart felt empty and my life was characterized by anything but joy. There was no "zoom and boom" in my life—only "gloom and doom" and I was completely engulfed in that gloom. No matter how much I read from the Bible which admonished me to "Rejoice always" I felt no joy. What could I do? I wanted it desperately.

In this chapter I will seek to define joy according to God's Word and then explore how joy can grow even through depression.

What then is joy? Peter tells the believers who were suffering in the early church about joy, "Though you have not seen him, you *love* him; and even though you do not see him now, you *believe* in him and you greatly *rejoice* with *joy* inexpressible and full of glory, obtaining as the outcome of your faith the salvation of your souls" (1 Pet. 1:8-9, emphasis mine). Taken from this passage, John Piper gives a definition of joy: "Joy in Christ is the deep good feelings in *loving* Him and *believing* Him. It's the echo in our emotions—our hearts—of experiencing Christ as *precious* and experiencing Christ as *reliable*. It's the deep good feelings of being attracted to Him for who He is and the deep good feelings of being confident in Him for what He will do."[1] This can hold us through any circumstance in life because it's not based on our *circumstances* being "just so" or our emotions affirming it, but on our *rock-solid relationship with Jesus Christ*.

So from this passage we see that joy is the experience of good feelings that flow from a relationship with Jesus Christ. Joy is based on the truth of who Christ is, and it is experienced as we love Him and trust Him. We must keep in mind that in severe depression there seems to be a physical breakdown of the body's ability to experience the feeling of joy. This does not mean that you should give up on joy. On the contrary, you should work all the harder to cultivate the relationship that is its source. The feelings will come as a natural by-product. If my tongue is burned so that I cannot taste good food, that doesn't mean I can't eat and my body can't absorb the food. I must keep eating and as I continue to nourish my body, the tongue will heal and the flavor will be restored. Even so, you can keep clinging to Christ and cry out to God, "Restore to me the joy of Your salvation! (Ps. 51:12).

Dr. Greg Harris who has drunk from the cup of suffering, gives us this challenge if the feeling of joy is absent, "Jesus calls us actively and continually to walk with Him—even when we can sense neither His presence nor His blessing ..."[2] Even though you cannot see Him, you believe in Him and this brings joy!

We see from other passages that joy can be a mindset as well as an emotion. James admonishes us to "Consider it all joy, my brethren, when you encounter various trials, knowing that the testing of faith produces endurance ..." (James 1:2-3). These are not emotional terms; these are accounting terms. You take a trial and instead of putting it in the debit column of sorrow, you put it in the credit column of joy. You can by faith count up this trial to be a joy, not because you enjoy the pain, but because you believe God will use the pain to make you "perfect and complete lacking in nothing" (James

1:4) . You count the trial to be a joy as an act of your will in obedience to James 1:2. You have the Holy Spirit to give you the power to believe and obey this clear command of scripture. He can help you to thank God for the trial—telling Him, by faith, that you believe He will use it for good and His glory. The deep good feelings of joy follow the act of obedience. The deeper the depression, the longer it takes for the feelings to catch up.

I'm sure the apostles didn't always have the happy feelings of joy as they poured out their lives for Christ and finally died as martyrs. But they did have the mindset of joy. They had the rock solid joy of hearts that were focused on Christ. Let's just look at Paul's life. Paul had joy despite his circumstances because he had *Christ's perspective* on his circumstances! When other preachers tried to cause Paul distress in his imprisonment by preaching out of envy and strife, Paul retorted, "What then? Only that in every way, whether in pretense or in truth, Christ is proclaimed; and in this I rejoice. Yes, and I will rejoice" (Phil. 1:18). That joy consisted in loving Christ and believing that He was more precious than life itself or freedom or reputation. He could have been down in the doldrums because he was under house arrest chained to two Roman guards, but his letter to the Philippians is full of joy! You remember how that church got started—out of a prison ministry. He got thrown in jail for casting out a demon from a slave girl. He and Silas sang praises to God at midnight, God opened the doors and released their stocks, and instead of fleeing they stayed and led the jailer to Christ.

Are there circumstances that have discouraged you to the point where you've lost your joy? Life is hard. People let us down. We let ourselves down. Stock markets fail. Our bodies break down and wear out. There is suffering because we belong to Christ. We need not be reminded that we live in a fallen and broken world. There will always be suffering. We can't be ruled by our emotions which would take us down into doubt, fear, anxiety, and bitterness. Rather we can rule over our emotions by setting our minds on Christ—the one who rules over our circumstances. We can trust God to help us obey His command to rejoice even in suffering.

We find through reading the letter to the Philippians that Paul's circumstances didn't rob him of joy because he looked on them as a platform for the Gospel and for drawing closer to Christ. Joy has nothing to do with temporal circumstances or our subjective feelings. As we look to Jesus, He alone can become our source of joy. Joy is found in a person. Paul's key to joy was in making *Christ his all in all*! Christ is his goal—knowing Him! Paul tells us that there is only one thing that can possess our hearts and bring joy! What is it? Jesus Christ! He had something worth living for and dying for! He says, my chief concern is that "Christ will ..., be exalted in my body, whether by life or by death. For to me, to live is Christ, and to die is gain" (Phil. 1:20-21). Could this have been the secret to Paul's joy which was steady regardless of what was going on or how much he possessed or lacked? That the knowing and loving of Christ was everything to him—in life or in death—and in that was found his greatest joy? Absolutely! That is because in freedom or in jail, in satisfaction or in hunger, in life or in death, his joy was not based on his situation or his heart but on Christ.

You and I can know consistent, abiding joy despite our circumstances even in depression because our joy doesn't need to depend on what is going on right now in our lives or what we are feeling. We cannot rely on our own understanding (Prov. 3:5-6). In fact things may not be going well. You might be facing the loss of a ministry, a job, or a home. You may have a body in pain and mind that is not functioning. Yes, even in these circumstances (that we went through) there can be an inner seed of joy.

Joy comes from rejoicing not in our circumstances but in the Lord! Paul gives us this command, "Finally, my brethren, rejoice in the Lord" (Phil. 3:1). Then he goes on to explain how we can do it. We are going to study Philippians 3:1-14 to see how we can have joy that stands like a mountain in a storm. The winds can assail, the rain can pummel, the snow can fall, but the mountain will stand. Rock solid joy is not only possible for you, it is commanded!

Christ Is Your Treasure

But whatever things were gain to me, those things I have counted as loss for the sake of Christ. More than that I count all things to be loss in view of the surpassing value of knowing Christ Jesus my Lord, for whom I have suffered the loss of all things, and count them but rubbish in order that I may gain Christ, and may be found in Him, not having a righteousness of my own derived from the Law but that which is through faith in Christ, the righteousness which comes from God on the basis of faith, that I may know Him, and the power of His resurrection and the fellowship of His sufferings, being conformed to His death; in order that I may attain to the resurrection from the dead. (Phil. 3:7-11)

When Paul reminds them to rejoice, he is picking up the theme of joy from the previous chapter where he told them that it was his joy to be poured out as a drink offering for their faith. He then told them about Timothy and Epaphroditis who also knew how to find joy in laying down their lives for others. Paul wants the whole church to have this same kind of joy that comes from a different value system. They will not find joy if they follow false teachers who preach salvation through their own abilities and attainments. They must follow Paul who learned from his dramatic conversion that he had to have a new treasure.

First he lists for us the treasures that he used to hope in before he met Christ. He was one of the most highborn, well-respected, highly trained, zealous religious leaders of his day. He says, "If anyone else has a mind to put confidence in the flesh, I far more" (Phil. 3:3-7). And then he says, "But whatever things were gain to me, those things I have counted as loss for the sake of Christ" (v. 7).

Before Paul met Christ on the Damascus road, no one could have accused him of violation of the Law or neglect of the necessary sacrifices for sin or of lack of zeal for God. But when he met Christ he learned that his heart was actually sinful and self-righteous. He was a proud and lost legalist. He had to come to realize that all of the outward religiosity was of no use. When he saw Christ in all of His glory, he was never the same again. He treasured Christ which means he loved and followed Him; he proclaimed Him and suffered for Him!

Have you seen Christ? Do you glory in Him? If Christ is your treasure, all those things that you hold dear—your heritage, your religiosity, your credentials, accomplishments, reputation, or material things—are valueless compared to knowing Christ. What's more, you will consider them but rubbish. And, if you were counting on any one of those things to earn you favor from God, you now must see them as vile self-righteousness. If you are depending on them for joy, they will rob you blind. Could it be you've lost your joy because something else other than Christ has grabbed hold of your heart? If so, then it is time to trade in those trinkets for the real treasure. Listen to Augustine who wrote so beautifully of this great exchange:

> How sweet all at once it was for me to be rid of those fruit-less joys which I had once feared to lose…! You drove them from me, *you* who are the true, the *sovereign joy*. You drove them from me and took their place, you who are sweeter than all pleasure, though not to flesh and blood, you who outshine all light, yet are hidden deeper than any secret in our hearts, you who surpass all honor, though not in the eyes of men who see all honor in themselves…. O Lord my God, my Light, my Wealth, and my Salvation (emphasis mine).[3]

Sometimes God removes our distractions, our things we think we need for joy, so we can come to see their worthlessness and His supreme value. When we see that He alone is our source of joy, we can experience the same triumph of "sovereign joy" that Augustine and the apostles enjoyed.

My depression stripped away many of the things that I held important in life. But my wife and I came to treasure Christ as we have never treasured Him before. I found that if I have nothing left but Him, He is enough! Just give me Jesus! I understood His grace at a deeper level, valued His love more, and had to fight for my relationship with Him more strongly through that time than ever before in my life. A treasure like that is worth the fight.

Knowing Christ is Your Goal

If Christ is your treasure, then your goal in life changes. Your goal used to be to acquire accomplishments and accolades for yourself. Now you realize that Christ has done it all and you just want to know your hero and be associated with him. You are like the ship's captain who had a goal of transporting his goods home from a far off land. Then he sees an enemy ship laden with a rich horde of gold. He immediately changes course, dumps his meager cargo so he can overtake the prize ship and bring home the gold.

The gold for Paul was "the surpassing value of *knowing* Christ Jesus my Lord" (emphasis mine). To "know" Christ is not simply to have intellectual knowledge about Him; Paul used the Greek verb that means to know "experientially" or "personally." It is equivalent to shared life with Christ. It also corresponds to a Hebrew word that speaks of a husband "knowing" his wife so that she conceives a child. This is not head knowledge about someone. It is delightful intimacy.

Ken and Joni Tada speak of this aspect of knowing Christ in their book. They had just attended the funeral of Corrie ten Boom (a survivor of a Nazi concentration camp). The pastor related, how "before Corrie's passing she had specifically instructed him not to speak about her, but rather about the love of Jesus." Joni thought:

It had been the same way every time she had visited with Corrie: Jesus was always at the center of her thoughts and words. She rarely spoke of "the Christian walk" or "the Christian experience." She didn't speak of Christ as though He were some creed, doctrine, or even lifestyle. She spoke about a Person. Someone she loved more than anyone or anything else in all the world.
She spoke then to her husband Ken:
"Corrie's life reminds me of that Scripture in Corinthians where Paul says he didn't come to them with eloquence or all this wisdom or beautiful words. Remember? He said, 'I resolved to know nothing while I was with you except Jesus Christ and Him crucified.'"[4]

This is what we strive for—just to know Him. Paul had known Christ for thirty years and yet he said, "I want to know Christ." When you love someone, you want to know them more and more. In Christ are hidden all the treasures of wisdom and knowledge (Col. 2:3). We can spend all eternity exploring the riches in Christ and never exhaust them. Look for people to emulate who center their lives on Jesus, people whose confidence and constant boast is in Christ alone. You can read the story of Corrie ten Boom in her book *The Hiding Place*. Follow the faith of people like Paul and Corrie and you will have joy that can withstand suffering as harsh and as murderous as a concentration camp. Your goal is to gain Christ. All the comforts that are sacrificed in that pursuit are nothing but rubbish.

Christ Is Your Righteousness

Paul goes on to say that he wants to be "... found in Him, not having a righteousness of my own derived from the Law but that which is through faith in Christ, the righteousness which comes from God on the basis of faith."

Your goal is not only to gain Christ and know Him and own Him as your own, you want to be immersed in Him. You want to be found *in Him*. Your identity should be wrapped up in Christ. When we realize that all our righteous deeds are like filthy rags to God (Isa. 64:6), we want to be found in Christ. We don't want God to look at us with His holy eyes without the covering of Christ's righteousness. We don't want to be like the wedding guest who came in his own garments and was cast out into outer darkness (Matt. 22:11-14). We want to be found in Christ. Then when God looks at us, He sees His beloved Son in whom He is well-pleased. What greater joy could there be than having God's smile of approval. Just think about it, dear sufferer! "He made Him who knew no sin to be sin on our behalf, that we might become the righteousness of God in Him" (2 Cor. 5:21). That should result in an awed sense of thankfulness! We have become the righteousness of God in Him! We are positionally free from sin and condemnation at all times. No other religion gives the verdict of "not guilty" without performance that leads to it. They all require performance leading to the verdict. But in the Gospel,

God justifies us on the basis of Jesus' performance for us and we are declared righteous! What peace, what unshakable joy!

Christ Is Your Source of Resurrection Power

When Christ is your treasure, your goal and your righteousness, then your suffering doesn't bring defeat; it gives you an opportunity to experience power that is not your own. As you lay down your life, you will see God raise you up. Paul bursts forth with this exclamation, "That I may know Him in the power of His resurrection" (Phil 3:10a). What greater power is there in the world? By rising from the dead, Christ showed His power over our greatest enemy. He defeated death which had reigned since Adam. Jesus declared, "I am the resurrection and the life; he who believes in me will live even if he dies and everyone who lives and believes in Me will never die" (John 11:25, 26). Jesus proved that death for the believer is only a doorway into eternal life. Jesus was the first fruits to show that all those who sleep will also be raised. He overcame the grave. What a source of power! What a source of *joy!*

Just think of the transformation the resurrection made in the disciples. They were timid and frightened souls at the time of the crucifixion but within a few weeks' time they became fearless preachers of the Gospel! They realized the power of His resurrection. Seeing Christ gave them incredible courage and conviction. They knew beyond a doubt that He had truly arisen. Their Lord had conquered death! What could man do to them?

That is why Paul said that he could face any opposition including wild beasts at Ephesus (1 Cor. 15:32) (whether literal wild animals or a fierce crowd) because of the hope of the resurrection! He wrote "O Death where is your victory? O Death, where is your sting" (v. 55)? Paul's joy in serving and risking his life for Jesus was because of the reality of the resurrection. Christ had conquered sin and death by His resurrection.

Paul closed that magnificent chapter on the resurrection with these words, "Therefore my beloved brethren, be steadfast, immovable, always abounding in the work of the Lord, knowing that your labor is not in vain in the Lord" (1 Cor. 15:58). The power of the resurrection is available to you today. If God can raise Jesus from the dead, He can help you to throw off any sin, no matter the hold it has had on your life. He can help you to put on obedience. He can give you the power to thank God for your trials and to continue to faithfully serve Christ by faith. If you don't have to fear death, you can overcome all your fears as you share in the power of His resurrection.

Friend, do you believe in the resurrection of Christ? I mean, *really* believe it? Are you *living* like it's so? In what dark place have you forgotten the resurrection of Christ from the dead? You can share in His resurrection power. Let this reality grip your heart! We need to ask God for His power for everything we do. Jesus said "Without me you can do nothing" (John 15:5). But through His resurrection power we can do everything He calls us to do! We access His power through our dependence on Him, our oneness with Him.

Christ Is Your Leader and Companion in Suffering

Knowing Christ experientially can also be a painful thing. What is resurrection? It is life after death. If we are going to share in Christ's resurrection, we must *first* share in His sufferings, in His death. Paul continues, "that I may know Him, and the power of His resurrection *and* the fellowship of His sufferings, being conformed to his death in order that I may attain to the resurrection from the dead" (Phil. 3:10).

It is easy to see how we would want to share in His resurrection power. But why would anyone want to share in the fellowship of his sufferings? First, it is because these sufferings show us that we are followers of Christ. Jesus said, "If anyone wishes to come after Me, let him deny himself, and take up his cross daily, and follow Me. For whoever wishes to save his life shall lose it, but whoever loses his life for My sake, he is the one who will save it. For what is a man profited if he gains the whole world and loses or forfeits himself (Luke 9:23-25)? Death to self also shows us that we are truly in Christ. "If anyone is in Christ, he is a new creature; the old things passed away; behold, new things have come" (2 Cor. 5:17). The old has *passed away*. The person I used to be had to die. Paul puts it this way in Galatians 2:20: "I have been crucified with Christ: and it is no longer I who live, but Christ lives in me; and the life which I now

178

live in the flesh I live by faith in the Son of God, who loved me and gave Himself up for me."

How do we first show the world that we are Jesus' followers? We obey Christ by getting baptized. This isn't about getting wet. It is performed to show that we identify with Christ in His death, burial, and resurrection. We are buried in a watery grave and lifted up again to show that we "are conformed to his death" in order that we might attain to His resurrection from the dead. The Christian life is one of death to self, it is one of suffering. But not fruitless suffering, suffering that leads to glory! Christ's suffering led to our redemption! Paul's suffering led to the good news being preached throughout the world!

Did Paul gain?! Oh yes!—far more than he lost. He learned what it means to be crucified with Christ and to die to self. He learned submission to God's will—and to allow Christ's life to be lived through him! In fact, these gains were so thrilling that Paul considered all other things nothing but garbage in comparison!

No wonder he had joy. He no longer had to wonder if he had done enough to earn God's approval. He knew he was in Christ, covered with His righteousness. His life did not depend on the cheap things of the world but on the eternal values found in experiencing Christ. Are you willing to suffer with Christ in order to experience the new life and inexpressible joy that comes from knowing Him in deeper ways?

It is a dying to self that helps us understand what Jesus went through for us in a deeper way. He only loved and ministered to people but He was condemned and put to death as a felon. He underwent separation from His Father so that we would never have to be totally alone. He suffered untold agony and bowed His head in death so that we could uplift ours in glory.

Dietrich Bonhoeffer said on bearing suffering:

In denying Christ Peter said, "I do not know the man" (Matt 26:74). Those who follow Christ must say that to themselves. Self-denial means knowing only Christ; no longer knowing oneself. It means no longer seeing oneself, only Him who is going ahead, no longer seeing the way which is too difficult for us. Self-denial says only; "He is going ahead; hold fast to

Him." ... "When we know only Him, then we also no longer know the pain of our own cross. Then we see only Him." ... "The cross is neither misfortune nor harsh fate. Instead, it is that suffering which comes from our allegiance to Jesus Christ alone."[5]

Is your suffering helping you to know Christ more deeply — through learning what it means to die to self and submit to His will, to take up your cross daily and follow Him? You see, that's what it's for! And *then* your suffering can turn out to be a source of joy! Or, you can just waste it in feeling sorry for yourself and never know the joy that comes from experiencing Christ in deeper levels — the "fellowship of His sufferings."

What kind of suffering qualifies as a sharing in "His sufferings"? Any suffering of a Christian becomes the "suffering of Christ" when it brings about death to self and submission to God's will. When Jesus died on the cross for our sins He prayed, "Not my will but Yours be done." He is our example. God's perfect will accomplished our salvation, and God has a perfect will in our suffering.

I remember when my ninety-year-old father-in-law was an invalid in our home. I wondered why God had chosen to preserve his life through brain surgery only to have him lie here and suffer for months on end. This active, godly man was now uselessly lying in bed being fed through a feeding tube, unable to do anything for Christ. Then I read this passage and realized that he *was* doing something for Christ. He was suffering for Christ. He was enduring to the end. He was being conformed to Christ's death so that he might attain to the resurrection from the dead. He would receive the crown of life which the Lord had promised to those who love him.

Jesus understands what we're going through. He was here! And what is so amazing is that Jesus said in that same conversation with His disciples about dying to self, "If anyone serves Me, the Father will honor him" (John 12:26). Can you imagine being honored by the Father for dying to self and living for His glory? He is the one who chose us, redeemed us, justified us, gifted us by His Spirit, and works in us the will and the power to use those gifts for Him and His glory. He keeps us and will glorify us in heaven, and then He's going to reward us! What a giving God we serve!

Is it worth it to suffer? Yes, it's worth it now as we gain assurance of our salvation and oneness with Christ. It's worth it as we see the gospel advance through our sufferings. It's worth it even if we see no earthly good but we experience the joy of knowing Christ Jesus our Lord in a deeper way. And it's worth it for the future rewards which we are accumulating. This "momentary, light affliction is producing for us an eternal weight of glory far beyond all comparison" (2 Cor. 4:17). There's joy coming on the other side when we see our Savior and all sufferings cease.

This is life-transforming. As you willingly die to self and find the joy of being freed from the tyranny of self, as you embrace your trials in order to know Jesus in a more intimate way, your trials become stepping stones to joy!

Christ Is Your Upward Call

> Not that I have already obtained it, or have already become perfect, but I press on in order that I may lay hold of that for which also I was laid hold of by Christ Jesus. Brethren, I do not regard myself as having laid hold of it yet, but one thing I do; forgetting what lies behind and reaching forward to what lies ahead, I press on toward the goal for the prize of the upward call of God in Christ Jesus. (Phil. 3:12-14)

Now that I am in Christ, I don't just sit and wait for resurrection day. God is continually calling me upward—upward into holiness, upward into Christ-likeness, upward into glory. The goal is that when Jesus returns He "will transform the body of our humble state into conformity with the body of His glory, by the exertion of the power that He has even to subject all things to Himself" (Phil. 3:21). But until that day of final transformation, I get to participate by responding to God's upward call.

I respond to that call by living in Christ Jesus and "forgetting what lies behind" (v. 13). Before your depression, you may have been a spiritual giant. But that doesn't help you now. Don't worry, it is not forgotten by God. All the good that you have done has been seen by Him and even a cup of cold water given in His name will be rewarded. But you must forget about it now. You must refuse to rely on past good deeds and achievements. It is he who endures to the end who will receive the crown of life (Rev. 2:10). You must press on.

Before your depression you may have been a spiritual failure. Forget about it. If you have repented for those sins, then you must refuse to dwell on them. We can learn from the past but we need not be crippled by it. God has forgiven your sins and buried them in the deepest part of the sea (Mic. 7:19). He has removed them as far as the east is from the west (Ps. 103:12). God says, "Their sins and iniquities I will remember no more" (Heb. 10:17). So why should you remember them? Don't dig them up and let them weigh you down. Every sin is covered! Hallelujah! To be distracted by the past debilitates one's efforts in the present.

If you are depressed because of the wrongs done to you in the past, forget what is behind and press on. You must forgive others as you have been forgiven (Eph. 4:31, 32). You must not let any root of bitterness grow up which will defile many (Heb. 12:15). The past is in the hands of our loving Savior. You must go on! You must make this day and this minute count for His glory!

Paul tells us, "I press on so that I may lay hold of that for which also I was laid hold of by Christ Jesus." "Press on" like an Olympiad on the first lap, second lap, third lap, then lunging for the finish line. Don't give up in your quest for spiritual growth. Jesus died to make you His possession. When He bore God's wrath on the cross, He descended into the pit of hell so that he could lay His hands on you and pull you out and make you His holy bride. When you strive for holiness, you and Jesus have the same goal and you are sure of victory.

One of the ways to press on to know Him better is through the time you spend in His Word and prayer. I've made it my practice to have a quiet time with the Lord each morning—a time to seek Him and to seek to know Him better. It is a time set aside in my day to meet with my Lord. It is to hear from Him and to give Him the worship, devotion, and fellowship that He deserves and desires from us.

During my depression I kept this up even though I was dry as a bone. I came with the heart of the psalmist who said, "As the deer pants for the water brooks, so my soul pants for You, O God. My soul thirsts for God, for the living God" (Ps. 42:1, 2a). I was panting in thirst as I came but I still felt that same thirst after reading. I cannot say in my depression that reading His Word raised my spirits. I did not feel any better after seeking Him. The truth is that in my feelings, nothing changed. In fact, many times I felt more convicted or guilty knowing that the truth I had read should lighten my burden or bring cause for shouts of praise and yet my heart was hollow and empty of feelings. However, I knew that there was no other fountain. Only in God's presence could this thirst in my inner soul be quenched so I must stay at the oasis and keep drinking. For me, it was almost a year before I felt the joy of satisfaction again. For others it may be shorter or longer. But there is no other cure. If you desert the fountain of living waters, you will die in the wilderness. If you keep drinking, you will eventually be satisfied.

What if you don't desire the Word of God? John Piper proposes these questions:

What if when you read it (the Bible) you don't see anything that gives you joy? Or when your joy is weak and disintegrates before the allurements of the world? What do you do if you are not satisfied in the God of the Bible, but prefer the pleasures of the world? Did Paul or the psalmists or the celebrated saints of history ever struggle with this? Yes, they did. And we should take heart. We all struggle with seasons of lukewarmness and spiritual numbness of heart. There are times in the lives of the most godly people when spiritual hunger becomes weak, and darkness threatens to consume the light, and everything but the vaguely remembered taste of joy evaporates.[6]

Piper says that the key to joy is to get into the Word of God and prayer. "The key to joy in God is God's omnipotent, transforming grace, bought by his Son, applied by his Spirit, wakened by the Word, and laid hold of by faith through prayer."[7] So my fellow sufferer, you and I must persevere to seek Him no matter what our feelings tell us.

Conclusion

So, is joy absent and unattainable during depression? Absolutely not! If we have Jesus, we have joy. We've seen from Peter that joy is knowing and loving Christ for who He is and trusting Him for what He will do. We've seen from Paul that joy is in the Lord. Joy comes from a mind set on Christ and all the benefits that He provides. Even our trials can be added to the benefit column as we trust God to bring beauty from ashes. As you make Christ your treasure, as you make knowing Him your goal, your losses are of no account; your sufferings only bring you into closer fellowship with Him and give you the opportunity of experiencing His resurrection power. As you immerse yourself in Christ you trade in your futile efforts for His accomplishment and find God's unfading smile warming your face as you forget the past and press on toward the upward call of God in Christ Jesus. This then is your key to joy! John Piper says it so well:

> The fight for joy in Christ is not a fight to soften the cushion of Western comforts. It is a fight for strength to live a life of self-sacrificing love. It is a fight to join Jesus on the Calvary road and stay there with Him, no matter what. How was He sustained on that road? Hebrews 12:2 answers, "For the joy that was set before Him (He) endured the cross." The key to endurance in the cause of self-sacrificing love is not heroic willpower, but deep, unshakable confidence the joy we have tasted in fellowship with Christ will not disappoint us in death.[8]

The feelings of joy may be lying dormant under the heavy winter snow of depression but if Christ is your life, springtime will come with resurrection glory. Ask Christ to be your life—to saturate your soul with His glories as you behold Him in His Word until His beauty captures your heart and gives you joy.

Response

Because joy is deeper than anything we suffer, even depression, we need to fight for it by reminding ourselves of Christ's love for us and our position in Him. Are we loving Him for what He has done and trusting Him for what He will do? Joy is wrapped up in Him! As God grows us in faith, we will be able to endure suffering with joy, knowing that He is using our trials for our good and for His glory.

- If you are covered by Christ's righteousness, in what ways do you find yourself trying to establish your own righteousness instead of accepting His which was provided for you on the cross? Examine your heart for any ways you are seeking to establish your own righteousness? (For example—do I always have to be right, never able to admit I'm wrong? Am I trying to build my own record of accomplishments for my identity instead of resting in my identity in Christ?)
- Can you respond by giving God thanks, by faith, for each of the various trials that you face (James 1:2-5)? (See contributing factors you listed after chapter 4.) The author of Hebrews tells us that "without faith it is impossible to please God ..." (Heb. 11:6). No prayer expresses our faith more completely than the prayer of faith that says *Thank you Lord for this trial/depression* especially when you are still unable to see any good that may come from it. That truly expresses your faith!
  - o If so, write out a thank you for the privilege of knowing Christ in a deeper way through your suffering. Ask Him to help you grow in trusting Him—that He is *love* and He is *good*, that He will only do what's best for you, and that He's powerful enough to bring life from "empty tombs" as He did when He raised Christ from the dead.
  - o Ask God for wisdom in each trial and faith to go on trusting Him (James 1:2-8). Be specific in asking for the wisdom you need in each aspect of the trial.
  - o Seek to list at least three ways God could use each trial for good! Form a prayer asking God to use the trial in that

way as he sees fit. Write these prayers out in your journal and pray them back to God consistently.

- Read through Philippians 3:1-14. Write it out in your own words.
  - o Make a list of your treasures that you are willing to count as loss in order that you might gain Christ.
  - o Tell Christ that you are willing to suffer with Him in order to attain to the resurrection from the dead. List the benefits that you have through His resurrection power.
  - o Forgetting what lies behind, make a plan for how you will press on to know and love Christ more daily through his Word and prayer and ask a friend to hold you accountable.

A Story of Hope Deferred and Beauty out of Ashes

*I*t is appropriate that depression should be called a "dark valley." One day I looked around, so to speak, and realized I was no longer *up there* where the light was shining and all was clearly illuminated. Things *up there* were never by any means perfect or easy—in fact, in the three-year period immediately prior to my depression, God had carried my wife and me through a good number of extremely difficult and painful times of frustration, disappointment, and loss; but we made it through and knew God had carried us. Yet, in spite of these trials, I could still essentially see where I was and where I was headed; I felt God was with me, and I had a generally positive and optimistic view of my life and future.

I was already weak from the combined stress of all the moves, family crises, financial problems, and personal and professional concerns of the previous years. Then in a very short time, I was struck by the loss of true intimacy with two of my dearest, most beloved friends; friends with whom I could be totally transparent. This loss was doubly heavy upon my heart because they were believers and I not only loved them dearly, I cared for their walk with Christ as well. I feel I can point to this as an early main contributor to my depression.

It might seem silly, but another element that contributed was the death of our cat. We got her at the beginning of the preceding difficult three-year period, and she somehow was a kind of reminder of God's faithfulness during that time, so her death caught me off guard and affected both me and my wife in a deep way we didn't anticipate.

Another factor was that, even though I had always viewed teaching as my "calling," I had become disillusioned with my university position and moved to pursue a different direction which initially seemed promising. I ended up in a very easy, reasonably paying hourly job I liked, but it was largely monotonous and increasingly unfulfilling. Seven months later, excited by an unexpected opportunity to inherit a new home, we moved again. At first the future seemed bright, but our life quickly became much worse. As a short-term job solution, I took a warehouse job. It was exhausting physical labor, a demeaning environment, and on an opposite shift from my wife. We rarely saw each other, and I was not able to regularly attend church. As the months passed, no teaching positions at the university level opened up, anywhere in the vicinity. I was only able to interview for two public school positions, both of which seemed promising, but ultimately fell through. I was crushed. By God's grace, I was hired at our neighborhood grocery store to stock the frozen food section; it was a better schedule and work environment, was not difficult, and it provided enough money to supply our needs.

In both of these cities we never really found a church home. The churches in which we attempted to serve did not have a need for what we saw as our main gifts. We attended, served, and participated as best we could, yet even then we never seemed to be able to make real friends, something which had never been difficult in the past.

Then in the midst of these things, I found out that I was going to be a daddy. It was wonderful news, yet the weight of pressure I felt was abruptly magnified. Like a valley, my decline into depression had felt so gradual that for the most part I didn't even notice the descent; I simply found myself there. It was a time of darkness.

My new job was not physically taxing, but I was constantly exhausted. Though I continued to go to work and execute basic daily functions, I was declining quickly; my wife saw it early but I refused. First, I "self-medicated" in a variety of ways: reading, sleeping, eating and drinking, "reward" eating and drinking (having to go out to eat often or buy special food and drink) wasting time online (no pornography)—all legitimate pleasures but not done for enjoyment and usually not enjoyed when done. Second, I began avoiding open, intimate communication with my wife (and anyone) as well as ignoring many of her genuine efforts to help and her suggestions to call someone to talk about it (if I wouldn't talk to her) and later when she suggested I consider counseling.

Third, I let myself feel all alone. The two very dear friends of many years were no longer in my life in the intimate way I would have liked them to be to talk about all this, and I didn't let myself realize I had others whom I could have called and spoken to—not many, but I was not alone. I did not turn to close Christian friends in other cities; I allowed myself to falsely think them far away and uninterested.

Fourth, I was experiencing growing hypochondria of the severe and irrational sort in that I constantly feared something terminal, often with genuine-seeming symptoms. Over the course of about three years it manifested itself until it was a regular struggle in my life. As a result, I was beginning to fear I had somehow "let God down" and that He would allow me to die. This is the cheapest lie of the devil and I knew it. Thus I was constantly battling against such wrong thinking as best I could, yet I would have real symptoms which I later learned were the result of stress. When I went to the doctor, my health was fine, but the mental stress fed the worry that fed the symptoms, and I was regularly losing the battle of telling myself that it was just in my mind. It also manifested itself in related fears that God would let me die in an accident. I developed a fear of flying, for example, despite having flown possibly hundreds of times before I feared that God would "take away" my wife, leaving me alone.

Fifth, I became angry in a variety of ways. Internally I questioned why God would let this go on so long and leave me in a situation that seemed so easily "solved." Why was He seemingly ignoring my prayers? God was caring for me and providing for us; I could see this, why did He seem to be disinterested in the condition of my heart? Outwardly, I was becoming argumentative, quite harsh (even severe) in my manner of disagreement, as well as overly defensive when encouraged to hope or cynical when encouraged to trust in God. In my opinion, I felt that I was already doing my utmost to trust Him. Since I am very familiar with the Bible, I wondered what counsel from there I could be given that I would not already be familiar with, or with what could I be encouraged that I hadn't already considered.

Most importantly, I became spiritually dry. I read my Bible less, but when I did read it I was so distracted I often wouldn't remember what I had read. I knew what it said and was rehearsing those things consistently in my mind to find whatever I could hold onto which I could grasp in order to persevere, but it was almost like my brain wasn't letting new information in. I prayed also, but must admit that it was difficult when I did pray because, honestly, it often seemed like God was the problem—indeed that He was the primary antagonist. It was as though He had shut out the requests that really mattered to me. I would pray that He would simply give me Himself, that He would enliven my walk with Him, not to change my circumstances but grant me a solid walk with Him (which was how my trials had been lived through before)—but then nothing would seem to change.

Finally, I felt like a failure as a man, I felt emasculated. I wanted to provide for my family. I had gone to college for fourteen years, I had a Ph. D, and I had significant experience and achievement in my field. Why was God not providing me an opportunity to do what He had seemingly called me to do and attested to with miraculous provision every step of the way (until now)? If He wanted me to make a career change, He wasn't opening any doors in that direction. It seemed bleak everywhere I looked.

What happened was that I closed up like a hedgehog and only opened when and to the degree I was comfortable, even then mostly only to my wife. For two years I fought internally with God and with circumstances (while believing unequivocally in His truth and faithfulness) by personally, emotionally, and spiritually hardening into a ball that must, *must* wait it out. In retrospect, I was making myself instead into a bomb that would have exploded if God had not been merciful and simply "opened me up."

It is difficult to describe exactly how God continued to lead me while I was in the valley. He never left me. That was the problem in a way. I knew He was there. He was meeting our needs. He was carrying me—kicking and screaming—through the difficulties. He did not leave me entirely unfruitful in my calling. He did not let me lose all hope. He gave me my wife who steadfastly stuck by me and prayed and hoped and encouraged me, so I could very clearly see Him in her as well; just her presence was comforting. He had led me through a multitude of difficulties in my (at that time) twenty-two-year walk with Him before, and I trusted in spite of myself that He would eventually lead me through this. He promised never to forsake me, and I knew He wouldn't, but I did fare worse and worse the more He delayed, the point of which I could not understand, and the end of which I could not see. He never permitted me to let go of Jeremiah 29:11-13, my "motto" verses that God has a plan for me and a future; when I seek Him with all my heart I will find Him. I did read a very few Christian books during that time that gave me a bit of comfort on a personal level, just to hear that I wasn't alone in struggling, but they weren't about depression because it was only reluctantly that I admitted I was depressed. Then very shortly afterward things began to noticeably change.

A glimmer of hope: another professorial job opened at a Christian university. After a long, arduous interview process, I did receive the position, and I began to brighten. It was not primarily getting the job that God used to begin to lead me out of depression, but that I finally felt heard and affirmed by Him. Upon moving for this new job, He provided us a church home with solid biblical teaching where we were openly encouraged to use our gifts, and He quickly sparked intimate relationships with fellow believers. In the coming months, the brightening continued and still continues.

I am still working out what God taught me and is teaching me by having permitted this. I discerned early on a truth I've encountered again and again in my Christian walk: this was one of those times when God blocked my path. He did not send the depression—I would say in all honesty that, in many particulars, I chose it, but He did block my path. It got to the point where I was certain this obstruction was intentional on His part. Lamentations 3:9 says "He has blocked my ways with hewn stone; He has made my paths crooked." The word that always struck me in that verse was the word "hewn:" that God is so intent on blocking my way that He has troubled Himself to personally carve out the stones specifically suited and intended to halt my progress.

He taught me that my job is not who I am, but also that my lifework for which He gifted me and temporally provided for its development is bound up in who I am and in how I express myself as His child. It is not something I can cast aside. He taught me that my frustration with my career before was typical and to some extent a given; there is no perfect job.

Though the Lord has blessed me with dramatic change, I still struggle as He continues to lead me all the way out of the valley. I must confess that I am tempted to feel like a prisoner suddenly freed who keeps expecting to be thrown back into jail. I regularly combat thoughts that God has not truly given me deliverance but is going to take it away again all of a sudden. I still struggle with the hypochondria I mentioned above (though lessened), as well as with feelings that He will permit something bad to happen to my wife or my son. I still struggle with temptations to "self-medicate" in various ways. I am working to restore lost levels of intimacy with my wife and am opening up with honest communication within my church family. I am still rebuilding my relationship with God and my willingness to trust Him and His provision. I am eager for Him to restore more of my feelings toward Him and my passion for His kingdom and righteousness. There is a spiritual "atrophy" that has taken place and those "muscles" need to be flexed and enlivened once again. This is still ongoing.

The most important things I would recommend to someone facing depression are these; they were things I can see now that I largely failed to do:

1. Remember. The Bible is teeming with exhortations to remember what God has done. I do not feel I faced this trial well as a believer, but what God never let me lose sight of was the fact that He had carried me through so many other things. If He had carried me before so many times, including past times when I didn't think He was or

would, He will carry me this time as well! Couch yourself in His promises to be faithful and to sustain you. Remind yourself of them often.

2. Stay in His Word no matter how dry your spiritual walk seems, no matter how closed God's ears seem to your cries, no matter how far God and hope seem to be. You may feel that way and worse, nevertheless His Word is absolutely true! It is always reliable. You might not think He is feeding your soul in a particularly dry and dark time, and you might not think it will make a difference whether you read that day or not, but He is and it does. Just because it seems unsavory to your afflicted heart does not make it false. A damaged tongue may not be able to taste for a time, but that does not make the food tasteless or non-nutritive.

3. Find believers who will love you through it. Nothing is worse than feeling alone and unheard when you're struggling with this kind of darkness. Immerse yourself in contact with people with whom you can suffer openly and who will listen. Talk to them often, even when you sound like a broken record and say the same things repeatedly, even when you think to yourself *what's the use of talking about it or getting together with someone?* Do not pretend to be strong or to have it all together. By no means go through this alone.

A Professor in a Christian University

Privileges

O Lord God,
Teach me to know that grace precedes, accompanies, and follows
    My salvation,
    That it sustains the redeemed soul,
    That not one link of its chain can ever break.
From Calvary's cross wave upon wave of grace reaches me,
    Deals with my sin,
    Washes me clean,
    Renews my heart,
    Strengthens my will,
    Draws out my affections,
    Kindles a flame in my soul,
    Rules throughout my inner man,
    Consecrates my every thought, word, work,
    Teaches me thy immeasurable love.
How great are my privileges in Christ Jesus!
Without him I stand far off, a stranger, an outcast;
    In him I draw near and touch his kingly scepter.
Without him I dare not lift up my guilty eyes;
    In him I gaze upon my Father-God and friend.
Without him I hide my lips in trembling shame;
    In him I open my mouth in petition and praise.
Without him all is wrath and consuming fire;
    In him is all love, and the repose of my soul.
Without him is gaping hell below me, and eternal anguish;
    In him its gates are barred to me by his precious blood.
Without him darkness spreads its horrors in front;
    In him an eternity of glory is my boundless horizon.
Without him all within me is terror and dismay,
    In him every accusation is charmed into joy and peace.
Without him all things external call for my condemnation;
    In him they minister to my comfort,
    And are to be enjoyed with thanksgiving.
Praise be to thee for grace,
    And for the unspeakable gift of Jesus.

—⚜ CHAPTER 10 ⚜—

How does the Caregiver Cope? Comfort for the Caregiver

Written by my wife, Mary

Blessed by the God and Father of our Lord Jesus Christ, the
Father of mercies and God of all comfort; who comforts us
in all our affliction so that we may be able to comfort those
who are in any affliction with the comfort with which we
ourselves are comforted by God. (2 Cor. 1:3)

O ften when our friends are in a long-term difficult situation we
ask them, "How are you coping?" Or in other words, "Are
you surviving? Are you keeping your head above water? Are you
managing?" This is a legitimate question to ask a caregiver who is
dealing with the constant strain of living with a depressed person. It
would be so easy for him or her to give up and be sucked under by
the constant undertow of hopelessness. But I want to show you from
God's Word that we caregivers can cope; and we can do more than
just cope, we can rejoice, we can rescue, we can glorify God!

We can be so full of the comfort of God, that it overflows to
everyone around us and brings deliverance. For when we are weak,
He is strong! But I am getting ahead of myself. In this chapter I will
share with you the comfort that I received so that I could become
a channel of God's comfort to my husband. I take my precedent
from the apostle Paul who shared his weaknesses and his comfort
in a similar fashion. Let's dig into his comforting words to find

encouragement in this fight for hope. I want to take you through this passage as we go along.

Blessed by the God and Father of our Lord Jesus Christ, the Father of mercies and God of all *comfort*; who *comforts* us in all our affliction so that we may be able to *comfort* those who are in any affliction with the *comfort* with which we ourselves are *comforted* by God. For just as the sufferings of Christ are ours in abundance, so also our *comfort* is abundant through Christ. But if we are afflicted, it is for your *comfort* and salvation; or if we are *comforted* it is for your *comfort*, which is effective in the patient enduring of the same sufferings which we also suffer; and our hope for you is firmly grounded, knowing that as you are sharers of our sufferings, so also you are sharers of our *comfort*, For we do not want you to be unaware, brethren, of our affliction which came to us in Asia, that we were burdened excessively, beyond our strength, so that we despaired even of life; indeed, we had the sentence of death within ourselves in order that we should not trust in ourselves, but in God who raises the dead; who delivered us from so great a peril of death, and will deliver us. He on whom we have set our hope. And He will deliver us, you also joining in helping us through your prayers, that thanks may be given by many persons on our behalf for the favor bestowed upon us through the prayers of many (emphasis mine). (2 Cor. 1:3-11)

Our Sentence of Death

Indeed, we had the sentence of death within ourselves in order that we should not trust in ourselves, but in God who raises the dead.
(2 Cor. 1:9)

Paul knew about suffering. In this passage he calls it affliction, suffering, an excessive burden, beyond our strength, despairing of life, the sentence of death within ourselves. We don't know exactly what situation he was referring to. But we could take our pick from the list that he gives us later in the book (imprisoned, beaten times without number, stoned, shipwrecked, spending a night and a day in the deep, apart from such external things, the daily pressure upon him of concern for all the churches (2 Cor. 11:23-30). There were many times he feared for his life and this seems to have been the worst. The fact that we do not know exactly what his situation was gives us room to fill in the blank spaces with our own most difficult test. Let me recap for you the "sentence of death" that my husband and I faced from my perspective and see if you can relate.

It's an interesting coincidence that the number forty shows up a number of times in scripture related to testing— forty days and nights of rain for Noah, forty years of testing before entering the Promised Land, Jesus had forty days in the wilderness being tempted by Satan. One thing is sure; God was testing us in our fortieth year of marriage!

We were in the winter of adversity! The one who wrote "I see that grace grows best in winter" did so while imprisoned for his faith in Scotland in 1637, having lost his wife and his two children along with his pulpit and pastoral work for Jesus Christ.1 That man was Samuel Rutherford, a fearless Scottish minister and theologian who so feasted on the love of Christ that he could also write, "My prison is a palace to me and Christ's banqueting house."2 This was our time to see if we would, like him, experience Christ's comfort as altogether sweet and enough to sustain us.

My man, who had always been a tower of strength to me, was reduced to the lowest of states. The shepherd and expert counselor now lay flat on his back, needing shepherding and counsel. For four years he had loved his new role as a college professor equipping graduate students to equip others in biblical counseling. But suddenly our very active, productive life ground to a halt.

Our trip to Russia to deliver my book for pastors wives (translated into Russian) to my heroes there was a dream of a lifetime. But it was also exhausting with the rigorous travel and speaking schedule. Bob's back began to bother him and got increasingly worse, and you know the rest of the story of his physical condition. Worse than the physical maladies was the depression (the dark night of the soul) that left him with the inability to experience all the expressions of grace that we have known all our lives. There are no words to describe the agony of soul that he was in!

I was shocked when it finally dawned on me, *Bob is in depression! I can't believe it! This can't be! Not my husband—full of fun, athletic, resilient, always hopeful no matter what, full of faith in God and taking His Word at face value, comforting anyone in the midst of their adversity, my pastor for thirty-five years and spiritual leader, the one who has counseled others through depression! How can it be?*

We had been on many adventures in two pastorates, weathered many storms of our own and of those in our two churches, but this one I had never expected to go through!

I was also in pain with a bad hip causing a severe limp and needing surgery. After postponing the hip replacement twice, we determined it had to be done. It seemed like a good time because Bob's sister had come from the east coast to help us through the time of his severe depression and would be there to help me as well.

So that is what I did—had my hip replaced. I thought we would just recover side-by-side. But his concern for me exacerbated his depression. It was oh so terrible! My hip surgery went well, all praise to God! I can't say it was a piece of cake, but through the rigorous rehab I knew healing was coming and a new pain-free ability to walk. That was wonderful but Bob's depression had taken a turn for the worse.

The surgeon wanted a second surgery on his back but we opted for physical therapy. Slowly, slowly, his back was helped over a period of months during which he was continuing to suffer and experience deep depression. Here we were stripped of our health, beautiful home (having moved into a tiny apartment), jobs, ministries, and Bob's ability to think and feel normally.

One of the hardest things for me was his passivity. He had been one of the most passionate men I have ever known. He enjoyed his work and ministry and seemed to never tire of it. Now he had no passion or energy for anything. I hardly knew him.

We didn't know exactly what had caused this depression. We didn't know if he would ever return to the man he had been before. We didn't know if we would ever be able to enjoy hosting our boisterous grandchildren or discipling college students. Life had come to a grinding halt. How long would we have to sit in our little apartment and stare out at the parking lot watching the world go by? It was like a sentence of death.

The Caregiver's Source of Comfort

"Blessed be the *God and Father of our Lord Jesus Christ*, the *Father of mercies* and *God of all comfort;* who comforts us in all our affliction...." (2 Cor. 2:1)

When you are like Paul, facing a dead-end with no way of escape, you need God's comfort. You don't need soft squishy comfort like a nicely padded coffin so you can lie down and die in peace. You need someone to come alongside you and give you courage and boldness to get up and carry on. This is exactly what God does for Paul. Ten times in this passage Paul exults in the comfort of God — his paraclete, His encourager. He praises God as the Father of mercies and God of all comfort. Mercies flow from God's very nature. Because He is a Father, mercies flow to His children. Mercies are not deserved or earned. On the contrary, they are kindnesses bestowed on the sinful and undeserving. They are available to the most frail and depressed and their caretakers. *All* comfort comes from God. Those without God have no real hope. Psychology doesn't have the answers. Only the omniscient and all-powerful God can bring good out of evil and strength out of weakness. God can give *all* comfort in *all* situations. There is no trial too big for God. And the comfort God gives enables the Christian not only *to endure* but even to *rejoice* in weakness and boast in trials.

Listen to God's reply to Paul when that suffering apostle was begging for his thorn in the flesh to be removed. "And He said to me, 'My grace is sufficient for you, for power is perfected in weakness.'" Paul obediently replied, "Most gladly, therefore, I will rather boast about my weaknesses, that the power of Christ may dwell in me. Therefore I am well content with weaknesses, with insults, with distresses, with persecutions, with difficulties, for Christ's sake; for when I am weak, then I am strong" (2 Cor. 12:9-10).

As the caregiver, you don't have to be the "strong one." You just have to be the dependent one. You have to know that God is your source of comfort, courage, strength, and hope. He is the One "who comforts us in all our affliction so that we may be able to comfort those who are in any affliction with the comfort with which we ourselves are comforted by God. For just as the sufferings of Christ are ours in abundance, so also our comfort is abundant through Christ" (2 Cor. 1:4, 5). I can testify that God showed up in precious ways to minister to me personally. His Word became my meat and drink, my comfort, my encouragement. If the caregiver does not experience God's comfort, she will have nothing to give to the one dependent on her.

Make time to meet with God daily. His comfort is *abundant* through Christ. It is even more than we need. Remember the counsel Jesus' brother gave us, "But if any of you lacks wisdom, let him ask of God who gives to all men generously and without reproach, and it will be given to him" (James 1:5). Our Father is generous and He will make us adequate for this task to which He has called us.

Another way to go to the Father of Mercies and find His comfort is through reading books which are full of Scripture and wise counsel. I read books and articles on depression because I wanted to be the best support possible for Bob. That is the reason for this book—to reassure you that there are those who have been there who understand and want to lend support. It was hard for me to find anyone to talk to who had gone through it.

I have since found out that many have experienced depression but are afraid to share what's happened to them even with those with whom they are the closest. If that is you, take courage and be willing to share with those whom you trust in the Body of Christ. You may be surprised by how your sister or brother in Christ will seek to understand and feel blessed and honored by your openness. We need to learn from each other and we can do that through books or face-to-face relationships. Books can be such a blessing as we learn from the comfort that others have received from the God of all comfort. I laid next to Bob on the bed while he read to me hour after hour, book after book for the two months that he was bedridden and the months following.

These books were strengthening my faith tremendously even while Bob's faith was nonexistent. His pit was so dark that he despaired even of his salvation! But my faith could keep his smoldering wick from going out as I encouraged him to focus on the gospel through these books we read together —*Because He Loves Me*, *Comforts from the Cross*, *The Cross-Centered Life*, *The Cup and the Glory*, *When God Weeps*, *Trusting God When Life Hurts*, *A Shelter in the Time of Storm*, *The Reason for God* and so many others. He also read *The Chronicles of Narnia* for diversion. Stories have a way of transporting us away from our pain into another world. It is especially helpful if a Christian author is depicting the redemptive story through his sanctified imagination. In this way we can see spiritual realities with a whole new vividness. Who hasn't seen our great Savior in the great lion Aslan who dies and comes alive to walk with the children?

I'm here to tell you that God's comfort gave us hope, sustained us and brought us through! His Word was our anchor. Our family and the Body of Christ were our lifeline as they ministered to us in many practical, wonderful ways that I will never forget! Our marriage was strengthened as we were closer than we have ever been before through it all. All praise to Him! Look at me boasting! You too can have God's power to go through even the stubborn darkness of depression! You can even be filled with joy and peace and abound in hope by the power of the Holy Spirit" (Rom. 15:13). Go to the Father of mercies to find the comfort you need to help you show your sufferer that his prison can become a sanctuary.

The Recipient's Need for Comfort

"But if we are afflicted, it is for your *comfort* and salvation ..."
(2 Cor. 1:6).

Paul considered it a privilege to be afflicted in order to bring comfort to those he loved. If the one we love needs comfort, we are willing to make whatever sacrifices are necessary even if it becomes a full-time job. I had to care for my husband 24/7, except for when I was recovering from my surgery. [*Bob editing here: She even ministered to me when she was recovering as she quoted scripture, maintained such an encouraging spirit in the Lord, and took her own pain and rehab in such a Spirit-filled manner!*] I stepped back from teaching part-time at the college and from my other ministries to care for him. I hardly left his side for many months. I waited. I did the next right thing. It seemed like all I could do was to be there and lovingly seek to comfort him and assure him of God's promises.

I had been there to support him in his calling as a pastor, united in carrying each other's burdens and sharing each other's joys. You can read about our journey through years of ministry in my book *One with a Shepherd: The Tears and Triumphs of a Ministry Marriage*.[3] Those years were very busy as we served our flock and raised our children. Our sphere of fruitfulness was broad. Now I was learning that I could please God just as much by only serving one man—the man I had promised to love in sickness and in health.

Our oneness was borne out of a deep love and affection for one another—a deep knowing. He was part of me. He had humbly laid down his life to provide for me and lead me for so many years. Now I was called upon to literally lay down my life for him on a moment-by-moment basis through the strength that God was giving me. I didn't consider it a sacrifice. It was a privilege to be afflicted in order to bring comfort to my beloved.

Reassurances of My Love

How did I bring him comfort? I reassured him of my love. Paul told the Corinthian church to do this with a man who was in danger of being overwhelmed with excessive sorrow, "Wherefore I urge you to reaffirm your love for him" (2 Cor. 2:8). How much easier this is with your own spouse. This is my beloved, my friend (Song of Sol. 5:16). I let him know that I wasn't giving up and we would walk through this together. Since he had no feelings whatsoever, even of God's presence, it was especially important for me to reassure him of my assurance that he belonged to Christ. Christ's love would never let him go and neither would mine. "Many waters cannot quench the flame of love; neither can the floods drown it." (Song of Sol. 8:7 LB). The best way for me to express my love was to just be there. He didn't always need great insights to help him overcome. He needed someone to sit with him and be quiet and battle through with him. Remember Job's counselors? They showed their greatest wisdom in the first seven days and nights when no one spoke a word because they saw that his pain was very great (Job 2:13).

Our physical intimacy was severely diminished. I mention this because it is something to deal with as the spouse of someone in deep depression. I looked on it as something that would pass. I missed my husband's passion for me but asked God for His grace to express my affection in ways to which he could respond. There was an understanding there, borne over years of faithful physical intimacy, which carried us through. I knew that if he were not in this terrible depression, his passion for me would not be diminished.

Physical Protection and Care

I comforted him with my constant presence. I knew that it was important to be with him in order to keep him safe as he had shared with me his suicidal thoughts that plagued him constantly. Although he battled those self-destructive lies with godly arguments and a well-informed conscience, he still needed a vigilant eye to keep him from a moment of weakness. I knew that God had given me to my husband as a helper, and it was a privilege to serve him by seeking to meet his physical needs for safety, preparing him nourishing meals, and seeing that he got to the doctor and biblical counselor to receive the help he needed.

A Positive Attitude and Environment

I comforted Bob by seeking to keep a positive attitude in the home. We didn't watch the news for months. The world was passing us by. But I wanted to keep the tone of our lives as positive as possible by keeping the conversation and other influences to things that would encourage rather than discourage. I even cautioned people about this.

When he was able to walk after the surgery we took walks together hand-in-hand to get into the sunshine, seeking to dispel the gloom. We played games together in the evenings as had been our custom. We tried watching comedies, but they only made the sadness worse as they were meaningless and trivial. It seemed we needed to make the most of this time. We made up a missionary prayer journal and daily lifted up the many missionaries that we have come to know over the years.

I kept flowers in the apartment and music playing. This was an encouragement to my own heart to fill the long periods of silence. Comfort your loved one with the comfort you receive whether from God's common grace gifts or his special revelation.

The Recipient's Need for Salvation

"But if we are afflicted, it is for your comfort and *salvation ...*" (2 Cor. 1:6).

We all need encouragement to persevere through sanctification to our final salvation. "But the one who endures to the end, he shall be saved" (Matt. 24:13). Depression can be a steep incline on the narrow path to glory and you just need to encourage your sufferer to persevere. Or it can be an indicator that the one you love has wandered from the path or is not on the right path at all. It can come as a direct result of sin as in the case of Cain who was bitter at God because of his own jealousy. God asked him, "Why are you angry? And why has your countenance fallen? If you do well, will not your countenance be lifted up" (Gen. 4:6, 7)? If you see that there is unrepentant sin in your loved one, you need to confront him when the time is right. This may be the solution to his depression, "Confess your sins to one another and pray for one another that you may be healed" (James 5:16). We need to courageously refuse to cover over our spouse's sin if it needs to be brought out in the open in order to deal with it. "He who conceals his transgressions will not prosper, but he who confesses and forsakes them will find compassion" (Prov. 28:13). With repentance and restitution you can help him to rebuild his life. The Gospel gives the Law to the proud and grace to the humble.

This depression may also be the affliction that God is going to use to draw your loved one to Himself for the first time. He may want to use you to be a minister of reconciliation as you suffer with him. "For how do you know; O wife, whether you will save your husband? Or how do you know, O husband, whether you will save your wife" (1 Cor. 7:16)? If they are saved from an eternity of torment into an eternity of bliss, no earthly suffering could be too great to endure if it was to that end.

Not Trusting Ourselves

Indeed, we had the sentence of death within ourselves *in orderthat we should not trust in ourselves*, but in God who raises the dead....
(2 Cor. 1:9)

This is a great theme of the entire book of 2 Corinthians. God does not want us to trust in ourselves but in Him. "But we have this treasure in earthen vessels, that the surpassing greatness of the power may be of God and not from ourselves" (2 Cor. 4:7). Understanding the frailty of your own vessel, it is important to take breaks and request help from others as you lean on God to supply all of your needs. I asked men from our church to come over for a couple of hours once or twice a week so I could get out. They came with the knowledge that they weren't going to have much if any conversation, but they understood. They wanted to be there for us and this was comforting.

Our two children and their families, as well as our extended family made sacrifices to lend support. Tiffany, our daughter-in-law organized visits from Bob's brother and sister. They traveled across the country to be with us. Our daughter Michelle came all the way from South Africa to our home in California. Her church family there provided meals and care for her four children so that she could come and sit with her dad for a week. She didn't know the full extent of her father's condition until she arrived because I had no privacy to email or phone her without alarming my husband any more. She felt distant and cut off until she came and fellowshipped with us in our suffering. We are called to "rejoice with those who rejoice, and weep with those who weep" (Rom. 12:15). Don't suffer alone! Just her presence boosted Bob's spirits so much that we decided to go ahead with my operation.

Our son Dan and his family were nearby. What a comfort it was to have their loving support at such a time! It was humbling for us as parents to be on the receiving end, but we knew that it was important to accept and learn what God was doing in our lives through it.

Our church family supported us in many ways including meals, visits, phone calls, cleaning our apartment when I was unable, counseling, and praying constantly. For all of this we will be eternally grateful. We also received cards and notes from our brothers and sisters in Christ who said that they could see what God was doing in our lives and were encouraged by it. Do that if you see how God is using the suffering in someone's life. It will encourage them.

Here is a sampling of the many notes that brought us comfort:

My Dear Doctor,
There are many lessons you have taught me that I continue to learn. Your faithfulness to God and His Word demonstrate such a dependence on Him and hope that it is contagious. I pray that even now that hope would continue to give you peace, for the object is now closer than it has been at any other point in your life. Are you "manifesting satisfaction," sir? Are your circumstances drawing you closer to your Savior? Because if they are, and if you are, then somehow I can, too. The same God will infuse us both with the strength He provides. Your example is a blessing and a challenge. Your God loves you, cares for you, understands you, protects and provides for you and your wife, and will be your strength and shield. My family and I are praying for you and yours.

Observing and following,
M.J. (a student)

"Brethren, join in following my example, and observe those who walk according to the pattern you have in us" (Phil. 3:17).

We love you Bob! Think about this scripture and what the metaphor means for you: "'I love You, O Lord, my strength.' The Lord is my rock and my fortress and my deliverer, my God, my rock, in whom I take refuge; my shield and the horn of my salvation, my stronghold" (Ps. 18:1-3).

Your Brother, E.B. (a colleague)

We also received phone calls from God's people both locally and far away. Bob's colleagues in biblical counseling from around the country as well as fellow pastors and church members from the community where he had served for twenty-five years called to let him know of their concern and prayers. Laura Hendrickson, a non-practicing psychiatrist, biblical counselor, and friend made her counsel available to us night or day. These calls were extremely encouraging to me, the caregiver! In the loneliness of carrying the burden, it is so good to know that others care and are praying for you and giving advice out of their experiences!

Don't trust yourself. Invite counsel. My husband had trained hundreds of counselors, but he was humble enough to know that now he needed one, not to figure out some hidden solution but to speak the same truths. When he couldn't see and he couldn't feel, they could see and feel for him. They could remind him of God's promises and hold him accountable to submit to God's purposes in His life. They were sharing our burden and so fulfilling the law of Christ (Gal. 6:2). Don't be afraid to seek help.

Trusting in God who Raises the Dead

Indeed, we had the sentence of death within ourselves in order that we should not trust in ourselves, *but in God who raises the dead....*
(2 Cor. 1:9)

It may seem that deliverance from the current state of depression is impossible. Is it as impossible as raising the dead? You need to remind yourself and your charge that the same God who gave Isaac back to Abraham after the knife was lifted can also deliver him at just the right time. The same God who raised Lazarus from the grave when he was stinking can restore him when he is at his worst. The same God who brought our Lord Jesus up from the grave after all hell had spent its fury can give him new life. Don't trust in yourself; trust in the God who can raise the dead!

Dr. Edward Welch, in his insightful book on depression, which was such a source of direction for us counseled:

What depressed people need—what we all need—are daily *reminders of spiritual reality (emphasis mine)*. As the truth of Christ is impressed on our hearts, we must offer that to others, and they to us. The target is always Christ and Him crucified. The words are not magic, but they are food for the soul. Don't get derailed. What you need is not something new. You simply need to persevere in applying old truths to present situations.[4]

When you're living with depression, you need good news! Amidst the worst of circumstances we have the best news in the universe: Christ crucified and Christ alive! Fix your eyes on Christ. We lived in Romans, especially chapter eight which begins with the fact that there is "now no condemnation for those who are in Christ Jesus" (Rom. 8:1). The chapter ends with the fact that there is no separation from the love of God in Christ Jesus (Rom. 8:39). Everything in between is encouraging—He is for us and will work it together for good although we can't understand why this is happening (Rom. 8:28).

We sought to saturate our minds with the promises from God's Word. I had to further emphasize these to my husband who was lacking any assurance. I wrote them on 3x5 cards and posted them all around our apartment—actual verses and phrases based on them: "Jesus Loves Me!—perfectly, sacrificially, eternally, extravagantly," "God's forgiven a debt I could never pay!" "I'm His!" "God is faithful!" and "Jesus went to hell for me to make me His perfect bride!" "Jesus' blood gives me victory over my accuser!" and "I'm forgiven!"

The gospel passages that Bob mentioned in chapter two, which included the first three chapters of Ephesians, were especially precious to us as well and we immersed ourselves in them. Thus we were reminded that the Gospel is all of God and not dependent on us: our works or our feelings.

Keep reminding the downcast soul of the facts of the gospel. It's incomprehensible even when we have the full exercise of our faculties that God the Father, Son, and Holy Spirit—the entire Godhead—loves us fully. Tell him: "The Father chose you, from eternity past and adopted you so that you would be holy (Eph. 1:4, 5). You are chosen to be part of Christ's bride and no matter how you feel, you're His! The Father poured out His wrath on His own Son (in your place) so that He could lavish you with His grace and love (Eph. 1:5-8)! Sweetheart, the Son, Jesus Christ would take on flesh, bare your sin in His own body on the cross, to redeem you through His blood (Eph. 1:7)! The Spirit has sealed you in Christ when you first believed which makes you secure in your salvation (Eph. 1:13)! Because of that, you have resurrection power (Eph. 1:19)! Just think of it—the triune God is for *you*!" The Holy Spirit will direct you as to when to speak and when to be silent.

I spoke those same words to my own heart many times. Like Samuel Rutherford, I sought to feast on the love of Christ every day. I preached the Gospel to myself and to my doubting husband day after day. (See Appendix 1 for a tool for doing this.) In spite of his unresponsiveness, it was good for him to hear these words of truth from the God who raises the dead and brings life out of dead seeds. In God's time these gospel truths will bear fruit. John Piper reminds us:

> There is no wasted work in loving those without light. You cannot persuade a depressed person that he has not been utterly rejected by God if he is persuaded that he has been. But you can stand by him. And you can keep soaking him, as Newton did for Cowper, in the 'benevolence, mercy, goodness, and sympathy' of Jesus, and 'the sufficiency of the atonement,' and 'the fullness and completeness of Christ's justification.'... In God's time these truths may yet be given the power to awaken hope and beget a spirit of adoption. Or, even in the absence of evidence that peace is given, they may be used in some mysterious way to sustain the mustard seed of faith that is so small it cannot be seen.[5]

Show your trust for the God who raises the dead by praising Him together. As was our practice before, but now with more time together, we sought to include praise to our Lord every day. We added to our journal things that we could praise him for every day. Yes, God's blood-bought children can sing to Him no matter what!

Through our tears, we can thank God for our trials by faith as we're admonished by James to do (James 1:2). We can be thankful for what God is up to in our suffering.

We praised God with Psalms and other songs written by suffering Christians who have experienced God. I put on praise music, and we tried to sing along. Sometimes we'd start the day with "Count It All Joy" sung by Majesty, our college's singing group. The Holy Spirit enables us to pour out our hearts before the Lord in psalms and hymns and spiritual songs, which bring Him glory. The words to some of these hymns came to us in the night watches when we couldn't sleep. We've sung most of them our whole lives but the truths were dawning on us with even more meaning.

My dear husband and I chose a hymn to read every night before trying to sleep. A favorite hymn was "How Sweet the Name" by John Newton focusing our hearts on that Name that calms our hearts with His love. (See Appendix 4.)

We also read daily a prayer from *Valley of Vision*. These Puritan prayers, saturated with truth and faith, helped when we couldn't form our own words. We've included some of our favorite ones for you to enjoy as well. The last thing we did before turning out the light each night was to quote the twenty-third Psalm together: "The Lord is my shepherd, I shall not want..." We were thinking *Lord, You're a constant when everything else is taken from us—our Good Shepherd who laid down your life for us.* "He restores my soul." *Yes, Lord, restore my soul!* "He is with me even in the valley of the shadow of death." *Praise you Lord! It feels like we are there right now and You are with us!* "Surely goodness and loving-kindness will follow me all the days of my life, and I will dwell in the house of the Lord forever." *This pain won't last forever, but your goodness and loving-kindness will. Help us to sleep now as we look forward to real rest in heaven.* We prayed and then waited for sleep to come.

Help Through Prayer

And He will deliver us, you also joining in helping us through *your prayers*, that thanks may be given by many persons on our behalf for the favor bestowed upon us *through the prayers of many*. (2 Cor. 1:10, 11)

I wept in private when I saw my strong husband laid so low. I ached for him. There was nothing I could do for him to bring healing. The doctors were powerless. I felt helpless and dependent on God alone—not a bad place to be! In reality this is the best place to be but that was hard to see at the time. It is the place that drives us to prayer. I pled with God for the release of this darkness! What a comfort to know that the Holy Spirit was praying for us with groaning too deep for words (Rom 8:26).

We as caregivers need to enlist the prayers of others to hold us up in these times. Shortly after Joni Eareckson Tada's cancer surgery, her husband Ken was out in the garage on an errand and he just "happened" to hear his wife praying on her radio broadcast not only for those who suffer but also for their caregivers. It touched his heart greatly as it did mine when I read it. This is her prayer:

Dear Father in heaven, as I think of the cross Your Son endured for me, I thank You that the cross You have called us to bear will never, never be heavier than You have designed. Our cross is exactly the right size and weight for each of us, Your willing children. And daily as we pick up this cross and follow You, we bless You for more than matching the burden with grace upon grace upon grace.... And if at times our hardships seem too heavy a thing to daily endure, if these struggles are too much for our caregivers, too much for our husbands or wives or children to bear, then remind us that You are there right beside us, shouldering the worst of the weight of the cross. Never let us forget that You are with us through it all, whether it is we who are always sitting down in a stand-up world, or whether it is our caregivers who are always tending to our needs. And...please, Lord Jesus, expand our vision, that we can appreciate the influence our trust in You is having on people, others who watch and learn, even from a distance. For that brings You glory! And brings rich and wonderful meaning to our days. In Jesus' name.[6]

For a caregiver, it does *seem* too heavy a thing to endure, but we can pray for His abundant grace realizing that He is with us all the way and He promises to never give us more than we can bear (1 Cor. 10:13). But like any good coach who wants to build endurance in his players, He gives us more than we *think* we can bear. He does this to equip us to win the prize—knowing Jesus!

As we pray and enlist the prayers of others, God gets more glory. We all admit that we have no resources, no recourse, and no solution. He must act if there is to be any deliverance, and He delights to act on behalf of His people. And because they have asked, they will rejoice when He answers. They will not just see it as a change in circumstances but as an intervention of the All-mighty Father of mercies. Thus more people will thank Him for His favors which He generously bestows.

Deliverance!

… who *delivered* us from so great a peril of death, and will *deliver*
us. He on whom we have set our hope. And He will
yet *deliver* us...." (2 Cor. 1:10)

The apostle Paul was confident that the God who delivered him in the past would continue to deliver him in his present circumstances and in what might lie ahead. We can also speak with that same confidence. What eventually happened? After six months the depression started to lift. Gradually Bob's body was responding to the medicine and physical therapy. His spirit was being renewed in answer to prayer and through meditation on God's Word and saturation with wise counsel. After having been out for the fall semester, he was able to go back to teaching in January for the spring semester, all praise to God! I was also able to go back to teaching part time in the counseling department.

The depression eventually lifted completely. God delivered us! He was able to get off of all medication. His joy in the Lord has once again become his confidence. He was able to finish up the semester strong in the Lord and was able to preach again at our former church and give them an account of God's faithfulness through it all.

Subsequently he has spoken to other churches, camps, and conferences and many hearts have been strengthened.

Bob continues to teach a full load and I'm back to part time. He has manageable discomfort with his back but is continuing to do the physical therapy that is needed. He is again my strong leader and support in every way. We now have a beautiful place to call home in a lovely subdivision built around waterways where we walk together often. It's great to see the joy he gets from playing with his grandchildren again and enjoying good humor and lots of laughter. Of course we don't know if the depression will ever return, but we don't fear it because we have set our hope not on our circumstances or on our own strength but on God who delivered us and will deliver us. We also guard against the return of depression by doing the best we can to care for our bodies and our souls staying close to the Shepherd.

Now we can see looking back that God delivered us at just the right time, after He had taught us what He wanted us to learn through walking through the dark valley with Him. God could have kept Paul from "so great a peril of death." But instead He showed His great power and sufficiency by rescuing him from a cliff-hanger. Similarly, since our trial my husband and I are both stronger in our faith and confidence in God's goodness and grace to carry us when we can't go on. I can testify by experience that the One who did not spare His own Son, but delivered Him over for us all, will freely give *you* all you need to get through your trial as He did us (Rom. 8:32). We know that He will give you the grace not only to endure the suffering He is taking you through but to embrace it for His glory. He alone is worthy!

As I look back, I see that one of His goals was to teach me more love and compassion through the gospel; to work the fruit of the Spirit into my life. As I continually focused on God's amazing love for me as shown on the cross, in response, I was called upon to love my husband. Did I grow in that area? You bet! My love for my husband was flowing out of God's love for me. I also have way more compassion for those going through suffering than I ever did! Adversity teaches us how desperately love is needed to sustain us and just what kind of selfless love is needed. It all comes from Him who loved us first (1 John 4:8-9).

He wanted to teach me to have joy through the gospel despite the discouraging circumstances. Adversity drives us to our Savior—the fountainhead of all joy. I experienced a deep and abiding joy within through meditating on the gospel—all praise to His grace!

He wanted to teach me about peace through the gospel. Adversity drives us to cast our cares on Him, and His peace garrisons our hearts. I had a peace that goes beyond understanding all because Jesus' work on the cross had accomplished it.

He wanted to teach me about patience through the gospel—to wait on Him. And oh, how I needed this! I wanted Bob to snap out of it: to begin talking again and feeling the mercies of God and having the old desires for me again! Adversity produces perseverance or steadfastness as we go through it with *His* strength. We leave the mysteries to our loving Father.

I still have a long way to go in the sanctification process but thankfully I can see some growth through what we went through, all praise to His grace! I can testify that grace does grow best in winter! This winter of suffering that you and I go through will turn into spring. This dark night will break forth into light when we see Him face to face. Remember that "weeping may last for the night but a shout of joy comes in the morning" (Ps. 30:5).

Deliverance is coming. We need not be reminded that we live in a fallen and broken world because of man's sin in the Garden. We are so conscious of the consequences. In these bodies we're groaning in ourselves and all of creation is groaning until Christ comes to set us free (Rom. 8:22). What a hope we have, that there is coming a day when we will no longer be subject to sin, pain, and suffering! Until then, in hope we persevere; we walk by faith in the One who will set us free from our body's slavery to corruption, into "freedom of the glory of the children of God" when He comes again or takes us home to be with Himself (Rom. 8:20-25). In the meantime we find comfort in the Father of mercies and God of all comfort. We place our hope in Him who can raise the dead! He will deliver us!

214

Response

As a caregiver I hope you will read the entirety of this book, not just this chapter. Bob's lessons learned were mine as well. We share this story with you to encourage you in God's faithfulness. It can be overwhelming to try to implement everything shared but if you choose things that resonate with you, you will be rewarded. Here are some suggestions:

- Keep a journal of your time with God—what He's teaching you from His Word, your struggles, and prayers. Pour out your heart to Him. Use chapter 8 as a template for your expressions of grief taken from the Psalms. Journal your praises as well for who God is, answers to prayer, and what He's teaching you.
- Make up reminders of God's promises for you and your charge to focus on and post them around the house.
- Keep worship songs playing at appropriate times throughout the day to keep your hearts focused on Christ.
- Choose some gospel-centered books to read to keep the main thing the main thing through it all. (If possible read them aloud to the sufferer. See Appendix 6 for an Annotated Bibliography)
- Enlist the help of your family and church body in practical ways such as giving you respite time off as I did or just times to fellowship with someone with a sympathetic ear.
- Get ready to share how God saw you through.

Solo Deo Gloria

Now to Him who is able to keep you from stumbling, and
to make you stand in the presence of His glory blameless with
great joy,
to the only God our Savior, through Jesus Christ our Lord,
be glory, majesty, dominion and authority,
before all time and now and forever. Amen.
Jude 1:24-25

APPENDIX 1

The Gospel Assignment

ow does the Gospel intersect your life right now? Each day preach or rehearse the Gospel to yourself this way:

- Record each truth in your journal.
- Under each truth, write out the verses in your journal.
- Read these seven truths and the verses aloud, if possible, *each day.*
- Pray the prayer of thanksgiving *each day.*

Seven Gospel Truths

1. I am saved. "For whoever will call upon the name of the Lord will be saved" (Rom. 10:13). All I must do is "repent and believe in the gospel" (Mark 1:15). It is true "that if you confess with your mouth Jesus as Lord, and believe in your heart that God raised Him from the dead, you shall be saved" (Rom. 10:9). "And Peter said to them, 'Repent, and let each of you be baptized in the name of Jesus Christ for the forgiveness of your sins; and you shall receive the gift of the Holy Spirit'" (Acts 2:38). As soon as I repented from my sins and believed in the gospel, my sins were forgiven and I received the Holy Spirit. I can look back to my baptism and remember how I made my faith public and it was affirmed by the body of Christ. This is real.

2. I have Christ's perfect record put to my account.

"He made Him who knew no sin to be sin on our behalf, so that we might become the righteousness of God in Him" (2 Cor. 5:21).

3. No longer is there punishment due to me.

"Therefore there is now no condemnation for those who are in Christ Jesus. For the law of the Spirit of life in Christ Jesus has set you free from the law of sin and of death. For what the Law could not do, weak as it was through the flesh, God did: sending His own Son in the likeness of sinful flesh and as an offering for sin, He condemned sin in the flesh, so that the requirement of the Law might be fulfilled in us, who do not walk according to the flesh but according to the Spirit" (Rom. 8:1-4).

4. I can rest in the grace of God and my standing before Him regardless of my performance. My position is based solely on the work of Jesus and I have nothing to boast about. This is the antidote to my pride. I deserve only God's wrath but have received His grace.

"For by grace you have been saved through faith; and that not of yourselves, it is the gift of God" (Eph. 2:8).

5. Jesus bore my wrath on the cross. This promotes in me a spirit of thankfulness and a hatefulness of my sin as I think about the great lengths God took to rescue me.

"Much more then, having now been justified by His blood, we shall be saved from the wrath of God through Him" (Rom. 5:9).

6. I am God the Father's child and a joint heir with Jesus, part of His bride, one with Him as a recipient of His magnificent never-ending love!

"See how great a love the Father has bestowed on us, that we would be called children of God; and such we are. For this reason the world does not know us, because it did not know Him" (1 John 3:1).

"But in all these things we overwhelmingly conquer through Him who loved us. For I am convinced that neither death, nor life, nor angels, nor principalities, nor things present, nor things to come, nor powers, nor height, nor depth, nor any other created thing, will be able to separate us from the love of God, which is in Christ Jesus our Lord" (Rom 8:37-39).

7. As I recognize and dwell on the Gospel, it motivates me to fight against my sin and fervently obey God out of love for my God and Savior.

"If you love Me, you will keep My commandments" (John 14:15).

"What shall we say then? Are we to continue in sin so that grace may increase? May it never be! How shall we who died to sin still live in it" (Rom 6:1-2)?

"I have been crucified with Christ; and it is no longer I who live, but Christ lives in me; and the life which I now live in the flesh I live by faith in the Son of God, who loved me and gave Himself up for me" (Gal 2:20).

A Prayer of Thanksgiving and Commitment:

Dear Father,
Thank you for Jesus who paid the price for my sins once and for all. Thank you that His perfect record has been credited to my account. I am grateful there is no longer any punishment due me. Thank you, Father, for giving Jesus to take my punishment for me. You give me grace I don't deserve. I can do nothing to deserve what you have given to me. There is nothing I can do that is worth boasting about. I acknowledge Jesus bore my wrath on the cross. I am saved, I am a child of God; nothing can take that from me. I obey because I love you. I choose to trust you and to believe that I can have victory over my sin through obedience to Your Word in the power of the Holy Spirit. Thank you, Father, for loving me. Amen.

APPENDIX 2

Discovering Wonderful Things
Study Guide

~

"DISCOVERING WONDERFUL THINGS" Psalm 119:18
Before you begin to study...Pray for understanding! (Proverbs 1:23)
PASSAGE _Philippians 4:6-7_____ DATE: _____

OBSERVATION	INTERPRETATION	APPLICATION	PRAYER
What does this passage say? Write out the text. Read the text out loud slowly in different translations. Memorize it.	What does this passage mean? (Define words, see cross-references and examine the context). Write out the interpretation. Is there a doctrine (teaching) to know? What declarations of the Gospel are included in this text? How does God's work in the Gospel motivate you to obedience? What are the imperatives in this text?— Is there a reproof (a sin to avoid)? Is there a correction (a command to obey)? Is there instruction in righteousness (practical steps in how to put off the old nature and put on the new nature, Eph. 4:17-32)? 2 Tim. 3:16.	How does this passage apply to me? How does this passage show us God's love and grace given to us in the Gospel? Be specific. Write out the Gospel declarations related to this passage. These may be found in the greater context of the passage. How should this change my life? What specific things can I do to apply this truth to my life? Write down what you are going to do, with whom and for whom and when you will start.	Write out a personal prayer praising God for what the passage affirms about God's work on your behalf and asking God to accomplish in your life what the passage demands.

4:6-7 Be anxious for nothing, but in everything by prayer and supplication with thanksgiving let your requests be made known to God. And the peace of God, which surpasses all comprehension, will guard your hearts and your minds in Christ Jesus. (NASB) Observations: • We are commanded: "don't be anxious" • About "anything" • "But" instead of this, do this "In everything" no exceptions Pray With supplication and with thanksgiving • We are commanded to make our requests to God. • The peace of God: Surpasses understanding Guards hearts and minds	• Supplication: action of asking or begging for something earnestly or humbly • Peace: freedom from disturbance; quiet, tranquility. • Guard: Greek military term meaning "to watch over" • Paul was imprisoned while writing this book, and calls us not to be anxious while his own circumstances may have seemed bleak. The fact that the Bible states "don't be anxious" means that anxiety is a sin, and not a natural reaction to stressful times. • We are called *not* to be anxious about *any*thing. • God wants us to let our requests be made known to Him. He knows what we will request, but He still wants us to communicate these requests to Him. • Make requests known to God in the context of thanksgiving. Being thankful is included here in the context of being anxious and having worries, not in the context of blessings.	Throughout the process of applying to graduate school, I feel that I was a lot less anxious. Now, I worry about simple things like finding an apartment, even though I know I will find one. I also worry about things outside of my control, like my brother's girlfriend. When I'm tempted to worry, I will recall this verse from memory and meditate on it as I ask God to help me. My anxiety reflects a lack of trust in God's sovereignty, wisdom, love, goodness, and power. I'll remind myself of these attributes even when a worry doesn't enter my head. I'll recall this verse even when not tempted to worry so that I'm reminding myself to trust God, delight in Him, and meditate on his Word at all times, not just stressful times. It's a truth to enjoy in all circumstances as I rest in the peace God offers. This passage made me realize that I don't thank God enough. Supplication is much more common in my prayers than thanksgiving. I'd like for my prayers to reflect humble gratitude and contentment, and not just requests, I will turn my attention to all the things I can thank God for as I make my requests known to Him.	Father, help me not to be anxious or worry about anything but rather help me to pray about everything big or small. Help me to commit everything to you in prayer with specific requests and help me to do that with thanksgiving. Help me to remember that if I will pray specifically with thanksgiving then you will guard my heart and my mind with the peace that I have in Christ Jesus. **Fruit in your life! What happened in my life because I applied this truth?** I had a worry creep into my thoughts, and recalled this verse, which took my mind off worrying and turned my attention to God. Meditating on this passage was a successful remedy for my anxiety in that moment.

APPENDIX 3

Praying the Psalms of Lament

Psalm 6

Prayer for Mercy in Time of Trouble.
For the choir director; with stringed instruments,
upon an eight-string lyre.
A Psalm of David.

Read this Psalm over twice aloud allowing it to express your heart. Based on this model prayer for help in trouble you can pray to your merciful God and Savior in the midst of your depression:

(1) Vent Your Lament

In prayer make your cries of desperation to God—tell Him exactly how you feel or don't feel right now. (Write them out.)
First use David's prayer:

"O Lord, do not rebuke me in Your anger, nor chasten me in Your wrath. Be gracious to me, O Lord, for I am pining away. Heal me, O Lord, for my bones are dismayed and my soul is greatly dismayed. But You, O Lord—how long" (v. 1-3)? "I am weary with my sighing; every night I make my bed swim, I dissolve my couch with my tears. My eye has wasted away with grief; it has become old because of all my adversaries" (v. 6-7).

(Paraphrase David's cry in your own words in your journal.)
Lord, ...

(2) Express Your Trust

Express your trust in and dependence on your God and tell Him that He is your only hope. Lay out your complaint or trouble before God. Tell Him that you are helpless without His intervention. Express your trust in Him because He knows all about it and has ordained this trial for your good.

First use David's words:
"All my enemies will be ashamed and greatly dismayed; they shall turn back, they will suddenly be ashamed" (v. 10). (This is what God will do!)

Pray and express your dependence on your God and tell Him that He is your only hope. Tell Him on what basis you come to Him—only through the shed blood of your Savior Jesus Christ and on the basis of His mercy and grace.
Write your prayer

(3) Cry for Deliverance

Pray and lay out your petitions before your God. State if there is a motivation given for God to answer.

First use David's prayer:
"Return, O Lord, rescue my soul; save me because of Your lovingkindness" (v. 4). "For there is no mention of You in death; in Sheol who will give You thanks (v. 5)?

(Write out your petitions, be bold.)

Lord, I ask ... in the powerful name of the *resurrected* Jesus. Amen.

(4) Vow to Praise Again

Pray and give thanks to your God for what He will do. (How could God use this trial for good in your life and bring Him glory?)

First use David's prayer:
"The Lord has heard the voice of my weeping. The Lord has heard my supplication. The Lord receives my prayer"(vv. 8b-9).
Lord, I praise You for ...

Psalm 130
Hope in the Lord's Forgiving Love
A Song of Ascents.

Read this psalm over twice aloud asking God to allow it to express your heart to Him.

Based on this model prayer for help in trouble you can pray to your merciful God and Savior in the midst of your depression:

(1) Vent Your Lament

In prayer make your cries of desperation to God—tell Him exactly how you feel or don't feel right now. (Write them out.)

First use David's prayer:
"Out of the depths I have cried to You, O Lord.... If You, Lord, should mark iniquities, O Lord, who could stand" (vv. 1, 3)?

(Paraphrase David's cry in your own words in your journal.)
Lord, ...

(2) Express Your Trust

Pray specifically about what is going on in your life. Express your trust in and dependence on your God and tell Him that He is your only hope. Pray specifically about what is going on in your life. Lay out your complaint or trouble before God. Tell Him that you are helpless without His intervention. Express your trust in Him because He knows all about it and has ordained this trial for your good.

First use David's words:
"But there is forgiveness with You, that you may be feared. I wait for the Lord, my soul does wait, and in His word do I hope. My soul waits for the Lord—more than the watchmen for the morning; indeed, more than the watchmen for the morning" (v. 4-6).

Pray and express your dependence on your God and tell Him that He is your only hope. Tell Him on what basis you come to Him—only through the shed blood of your Savior Jesus Christ and on the basis of His mercy and grace.
Write your prayer

(3) Cry for Deliverance

Pray and lay out your petitions before your God.

First use David's prayer:
"Lord hear my voice! Let Your ears be attentive to the voice of my supplications" (v. 2).

(Write out your petitions, be bold.)

(4) Vow to Praise Again

Pray and give thanks to your God for what He will do. (How could God use this trial for good in your life and bring Him glory?)

First use David's prayer:

"Hope in the Lord; for with the Lord there is lovingkindness, and with Him is abundant redemption. And He will redeem Israel from all his iniquities" (vv. 7-8).

Lord, I praise You for ...

APPENDIX 4

Hymns for the Soul in Depression

There is a Fountain Filled with Blood
Written by William Cowper after he attempted to take
his own life while in depression. (1772.)

There is a fountain filled with blood drawn from
Emmanuel's veins;
And sinners plunged beneath that flood lose all their guilty stains.
Lose all their guilty stains, lose all their guilty stains;
And sinners plunged beneath that flood lose all their guilty stains.

The dying thief rejoiced to see that fountain in his day;
And there have I, though vile as he, washed all my sins away.
Washed all my sins away, washed all my sins away;
And there have I, though vile as he, washed all my sins away.

Dear dying Lamb, Thy precious blood shall never lose its power
Till all the ransomed church of God be saved, to sin no more.
Be saved, to sin no more, be saved, to sin no more;
Till all the ransomed church of God be saved, to sin no more.

E'er since, by faith, I saw the stream Thy flowing wounds supply,
Redeeming love has been my theme, and shall be till I die.
And shall be till I die, and shall be till I die;

Redeeming love has been my theme, and shall be till I die.

Then in a nobler, sweeter song, I'll sing Thy power to save,
When this poor lisping, stammering tongue lies silent in the grave.
Lies silent in the grave, lies silent in the grave;
When this poor lisping, stammering tongue lies silent in the grave.

Lord, I believe Thou hast prepared, unworthy though I be,
For me a blood bought free reward, a golden harp for me!
'Tis strung and tuned for endless years, and formed by power divine,
To sound in God the Father's ears no other name but Thine.

How Sweet the Name
Words by John Newton—former slave trader and pastor to
William Cowper (1725-1807) [From 1 Peter 2:7]

How sweet the name of Jesus sounds
In a believer's ear!
It soothes his sorrows, heals his wounds,
And drives away his fear.

It makes the wounded spirit whole,
And calms the troubled breast;
'Tis manna to the hungry soul,
And to the weary rest.

Dear Name! the Rock on which I build,
My Shield and Hiding place,
My never failing Treasury, filled
With boundless stores of grace.

Jesus! My Shepherd, Husband, Friend,
My Prophet, Priest, and King;
My Lord, my Life, My Way, my End,
Accept the praise I bring.

Weak is the effort of my heart,
And cold my warmest thought;
But when I see Thee as Thou art,
I'll praise Thee as I ought.

Till then I would Thy love proclaim
With ev'ry fleeting breath;
And may the music of Thy name
Refresh my soul in death.

Lamb of God!
Words by James G Deck (1802-1884) [From Rev 5:12]
A hymn to focus the depressed on the grace of God's Lamb!

Lamb of God! Our souls adore Thee,
While upon Thy face we gaze;
There the Father's love and glory
Shine in all their brightest rays;
Thine Almighty power and wisdom
All creations' work proclaim;
Heav'n and earth alike confess Thee
As the ever great "I AM."

When we see Thee, as the victim,
Bound to the accursed tree,
For our guilt and folly stricken,
All our judgment borne by Thee,
Lord, we own, with hearts adoring,
Thou hast loved us unto blood,
Glory, glory, everlasting Be to Thee,
Thou Lamb of God.

Lamb of God! Thou soon in glory
Wilt to this sad earth return;
All Thy foes shall quake before Thee,
All that now despise Thee mourn;

229

Then Thy saints all gather'd to Thee,
With Thee in Thy kingdom reign;
Thine the praise and Thine the glory,
Lamb of God, for sinners slain!

He Giveth More Grace
Words by Annie J. Flint
Public Domain

Based on James 4:6, "God is opposed to the proud,
but gives grace to the humble."

He giveth more grace as our burdens grow greater,
He sendeth more strength as our labors increase;
To added afflictions He addeth His mercy,
To multiplied trials He multiplies peace.

When we have exhausted our store of endurance,
When our strength has failed ere the day is half done,
When we reach the end of our hoarded resources
Our Father's full giving is only begun.

Fear not that thy need shall exceed His provision,
Our God ever yearns His resources to share;
Lean hard on the arm everlasting, availing;
The Father both thee and thy load will upbear.

His love has no limits, His grace has no measure,
His power no boundary known unto men;
For out of His infinite riches in Jesus
He giveth, and giveth, and giveth again.

APPENDIX 5

How to Become a Christian

This is the most important information that I can communicate to you. It's the best news in the universe because it determines where you will spend eternity. Our bodies and minds fail and disappoint us, but one day we will die and where we go after death is most important. So let me tell you what the Bible says about this life and death matter.

The Bible is our source book as it is God's revelation to man in which He tells us what is important to know—the truth about both Him and us. First off, we need to know that God is good and created everything perfect including mankind (Gen. 1). Then man fell into sin, earning God's wrath as a consequence because of God's justice. We all have sinned and fall short of the glory of God (Rom. 3:23). God says that the wages of our sin is death—separation from Him forever (Rom. 6:23a).

Though we did not deserve it, by the grace of God, Jesus, who was both God and man, came to earth to pay for those sins in our place (Rom. 5:8; John 3:16). It had to be that way because only God could appease that wrath, and only a man could stand in our place (Col. 1:19-20). There is only one God and one mediator between God and man—Jesus Christ who gave himself to ransom us through His death on the cross (1 Tim. 2:5-6).

Jesus conquered the grave, opening the way to God through His resurrection. He said that He was the resurrection and the life and that the one who believes on Him will live, even though he die (John

11:25). The Bible says that it is God's great mercy that gives us the new birth into a living hope through the resurrection of Jesus from the dead (1 Pet. 1:3; John 3:1-21; 1 Cor. 15).

We must come to Him in faith (not by works) and receive the gift of God which is eternal life in Jesus Christ (Rom. 6:23b; Eph. 2:8-9). We respond to His grace through faith and repentance. We declare with all sincerity that "Jesus is Lord," and believe in our heart that God raised Him from the dead (Rom. 10:9).

We count the cost and decide to give ourselves as a living sacrifice to God as our reasonable service on a daily basis seeking to put off our sin and obey His Word (Rom. 12:1). We consider everything as loss because of the surpassing worth of knowing Jesus as Lord (Phil. 3:8-9). He is our supreme Treasure!

And the work of salvation is complete! We stand clean before God through Jesus' atoning sacrifice. We have peace with God (Rom. 5:1). There is now no condemnation—the best news you can ever have (Rom. 8:1)! God has placed your sin on His righteous Son as He paid its penalty and gave you His righteousness (2 Cor. 5:17-21). You have been created to now live for His honor and glory through loving Him first and letting His love flow through you to others (1 Cor. 10:31). You are a part of His Body, the Church and should join with a local church that proclaims this gospel and teaches clearly from God's Word.

APPENDIX 6

Annotated Bibliography

- Adams, Jay E., *How to Handle Trouble*, Presbyterian and Reformed Publishing Co., 1982.
  - An excellent study of Romans 8:28 in relationship to trials. It clearly brings out the truth that God is in your problem and He is in it for good.
- Antioch Bible Church. http://www.antiochbiblechurch.org.za/multimedia-category/seminar/ Sermons, Bob Somerville, Depression Seminar 1 & 2.
- Bridges, Jerry, *The Transforming Power of the Gospel*, NavPress, 2012.
  - A basic book applying the Gospel to our life experience by one skilled in guiding us through the scriptures.
- Bridges, Jerry, *Trusting God*, NavPress, 1990.
  - How to trust a sovereign and loving God especially when you are going through the deep hurts of life and when we don't have all the answers. The study guide is also very helpful.
- Carson, D.A. *How Long, O Lord? Reflections on Suffering and Evil*, Baker Academic, 2006.
  - This astute scholar of God's Word helps us grapple with the challenges brought about by suffering by applying permanent truths to bolster faith in God's goodness and sovereignty.
- Duncan, Ligon, *Does Grace Grow Best in Winter?* P&R Publishing, 2009.

- o A Biblical explanation of how God grows His grace best in the difficulties of life.
- ➢ Elliott, Elisabeth, *A Path Through Suffering*, Servant Publication, Ann Arbor Michigan 48107, 1990.
  - o Discovering the relationship between God's mercy and our pain. Once again this book is written by someone who has been there.
- ➢ Fitzpatrick, Elyse M., *Because He Loves Me*, Wheaton, Crossway Books, 2008.
  - o Leading us to love Christ because He has first loved us. Tremendous motivation for loving God and glorifying Him with our lives in response.
- ➢ Fitzpatrick, Elyse M., *Comforts from the Cross*, Crossway Books, 2009.
  - o Thirty one excellent daily devotions giving you great comfort in what Christ has accomplished for us, leading your heart to worship God for His love and grace.
- ➢ Fitzpatrick, Elyse M. & Johnson, Dennis E., *Counsel from the Cross: Connecting Broken People to the Love of Christ*, Crossway Books, 2009.
  - o Teaching us how to counsel from the basis of Christ's work for us on the cross.
- ➢ Fitzpatrick, Elyse, & Hendrickson, Laura, *Will Medicine Stop the Pain? Finding God's healing for depression, anxiety, & other troubling emotions*. Moody Publishers, 2006.
  - o Helpful in understanding the inner and outer causes and medical and biblical cures of these maladies by two who are thoroughly equipped to tackle the subject. A must read.
- ➢ Guthrie, Nancy, *Holding On to Hope: A Pathway through Suffering to the Heart of God*, Tyndale, 2002.
  - o The title says it all. Excellent Biblical encouragement and great examples.
- ➢ Harris, Greg, *The Cup and the Glory: Lessons on Suffering and the Glory of God*, Kress Christian Publications, 2006.
  - o A study of 1 Peter 5:5-11 and other texts relating to the growth that comes through suffering and again from the perspective of one who has suffered deeply.

➢ Maheney, C. J. *Living The Cross Centered Life*, Sisters, Multnomah Publishers 2006.
  o An exposition of the cross and what it means to keep the work of Christ at the center of your life.
➢ Miller, Paul, *A Praying Life*, NavPress, 2009.
  o Leads you into the joy of a praying life from the most practical and daring aspect of trusting God with everything. Advice from an individual that has practiced this truth.
➢ Miller, Paul, *When Love Walked Among Us*, NavPress, 2001.
  o Teaches you how to love others from the example of the love of Christ.
➢ Myers, Ruth & Warren, *31 Days of Praise: Enjoying God Anew*, Multnomah Press, 1994.
  o A delightful book teaching the marvelous blessing of praising God in every aspect of life; every day for a month. Mary and I have read it over and over.
➢ Piper, John, *Seeing and Savoring Jesus Christ*. Crossway, 2001.
  o The title says it and the book truly enables you to see and savor the work of Christ.
➢ Piper, John, *When I Don't Desire God: How to Fight for Joy*, Crossway Books, 2004.
  o This is great practical pastoral advice on how to fight for joy that is the by-product of delighting in God's worthiness.
➢ Piper, John, *When the Darkness Will Not Lift*, Wheaton, IL: Crossway Books, 2006.
  o A powerful summary of what to do when you are depressed and the depression will not lift. Read it along with Ed Welch's Depression: A Stubborn Darkness.
➢ Tada, Joni Eareckson Tada, *A Place of Healing: Wrestling with the Mysteries of Suffering, Pain and God's Sovereignty*, David C. Cook Publishing, 2010.
  o This is a personal book on dealing with the questions about suffering that gives great hope from one who is there herself.
➢ Tada, Joni Eareckson, *Diamonds in the Dust, 366 Sparkling Devotions*, Zondervan Publishing House, 1993.

- o Devotional studies for those going through suffering written by someone who has been there and experienced all manner of suffering victoriously in Christ.
- ➤ Tada, Joni Eareckson, *One Step Further*, Zondervan, 2001.
  - o Deals with the very practical theological issues of suffering from an individual who has been there.
- ➤ Tada, Joni Eareckson, *Secret Strength*, Multnomah Press, 1988.
  - o More devotional studies for those going through suffering written by someone who has been there and experienced all manner of suffering victoriously in Christ.
- ➤ Tada, Joni Eareckson and Steve Estes, *When God Weeps: Why Our Sufferings Matter to the Almighty*, Grand Rapids, Zondervan Publishing House, 1997.
  - o This book will cause you to weep and grow as you struggle with the deep questions of suffering and God's love and care for us.
- ➤ Tada, Ken & Eareckson, Joni, *Joni & Ken: An Untold Love Story*, Zondervan, 2013.
  - o We highly recommend this book on marriage that puts our suffering in perspective and demonstrates how God's grace is sufficient for anything we might go through.
- ➤ Tripp, Paul, *A Shelter in the Time of Storm: Meditations on God and Trouble*, Crossway Books, 2009.
  - o Sweet meditations to strengthen the soul in times of suffering.
- ➤ Welch, Edward T., *Depression: Looking Up from the Stubborn Darkness*, New Growth Press, 2011.
  - o A clear study of the stubborn darkness of depression from a Biblical perspective giving clear insight and practical help with a gentle spirit of helpfulness.

APPENDIX 7

Resources for Biblical Counseling

In most cases the pastor of a Bible teaching church would counsel regarding most issues that you face including depression. However, if you, your pastor or church leaders would like to study more in depth about biblical counseling or need to seek out another biblical counselor in your area (there is wisdom in many counselors Prov. 15:22) I've provided the following resources that I highly recommend.

- Association of Certified Biblical Counselors (ACBC) www. BiblicalCounseling.com; info@biblicalcounseling.com Certifies biblical counselors for doctrine and skill in counseling. It is a resource for finding counselors in your area who will counsel from God's Word. They also offer counselor training, resources and conferences.
- Biblical Counseling Coalition (BCC) http://wwwbiblical-counselingcoalition.org Brings together resources, including a blog, written by those who hold to the sufficiency of scripture in counseling from across the United States and around the world.
- Biblical Counseling and Discipleship Association of Southern California (BCDA SoCal) http://wwwbcdasocal.org Provides counselor training and resources.
- Christian Counseling and Educational Foundation (CCEF) Offers counseling in the Philadelphia, PA area and provides

counselor training and resources including The Journal of Biblical Counseling.

- International Association of Biblical Counselors (IABC) http://wwwiabc.net Certifies biblical counselors, provides training resources and conferences.
- Institute for Biblical Counseling and Discipleship (IBCD) http://wwwibcd.org Offers counseling in the San Diego, CA area and provides counselor training, resources and conferences.
- Biblical Counseling Center http://www.biblicalcounseling-center.org Trains counselors, has resources and does counseling in the Chicago area.
- Faith Biblical Counseling Center, Lafayette, IN. http://www.faithlafayette.org/counseling Offers counseling in the Lafayette, IN area and provides counselor training, resources and conferences.
- Lowcountry Biblical Counseling Center www.lcbcc.org Offers counseling in the Charleston, SC area and provides counselor training and resources.
- Wordtruth   http://www.wordtruth.net Provides helpful articles on a variety of counseling issues.
- The Institute for Nouthetic Studies http://www.nouthetic.org Provides counselor training and resources. Founded by Dr. Jay Adams.
- The Master's College http://www.masters.edu provides training in biblical counseling that leads to a master's degree in Biblical Counseling (MABC).

NOTES

INTRODUCTION

1. C. S. Lewis, *The Inspirational Writings of C.S. Lewis, Book 1, Surprised by Joy* (N.Y., N.Y.: Inspirational Press, 1994) 3.

Chapter 1 The Story of My Depression

Arthur Bennett, editor, *The Valley of Vision: A Collection of Puritan Prayers & Devotions* (Carlisle: PA: Banner of Truth Trust, 2007), 0.

1. Wes Burgess, *The Depression Answer Book* (Naperville, IL, SourceBooks, 2009), 3.
2. Scelfo, Julie, *Men and Depression: Facing the Darkness.* Newsweek, February 25, 2007, www.thedailybeast.com/.../02/.../men-depression-facing-darkness, (accessed July 5, 2012).
3. Jonathan Edwards, *The Life of David Brainerd: Missionary to the Indians; With an Abridgment of His Diary and Journal.* (London: F. Westley, 1820), 31.
4. Ibid, 174.
5. C.H. Spurgeon, *Lectures to My Students* (Grand Rapids: Zondervan, 1954), 154-165. Charles H. Spurgeon, or "The Minister's Fainting Fits," in *Lectures to My Students* (Lynchburg, VA: The Old Time Gospel Hour, n.d.), 167-179.

Chapter 2 Where's the Hope?

Arthur Bennett, editor, *The Valley of Vision: A Collection of Puritan Prayers & Devotions* (Carlisle: PA, Banner of Truth Trust, 2007), 157.

1. John Piper, *When I Don't Desire God How to Fight for Joy*, (Wheaton, IL: Crossway Books, 2004), 135.
2. Ibid.
3. Jerry Bridges, *Growing Your Faith*, (Colorado Springs, CO: NavPress, 2004), 39.
4. William Cowper, 1774 *God Moves in a Mysterious Way*

Chapter 3 Lessons from the Life of Elijah

Arthur Bennett, editor, *The Valley of Vision: A Collection of Puritan Prayers & Devotions* (Carlisle, PA: Banner of Truth Trust, 2007), 110.

1. John Piper, *When the Darkness will not Lift* (Wheaton, IL: Crossway Books, 2006), 210.

Chapter 4 If I'm a Christian, Why Am I Depressed?

Arthur Bennett, editor, *The Valley of Vision: A Collection of Puritan Prayers & Devotions* (Carlisle: PA: Banner of Truth Trust, 2007), 42.

1. Ligon Duncan, *Does Grace Grow Best in Winter?* (Phillipsburg: N.J.: P&R Publishing, 2009), 29-30.
2. D.A. Carson, *How Long, O Lord: Reflections on Suffering and Evil* (Grand Rapids, MI: Baker Academic, 2006), 141.
3. John Bunyan, *The Pilgrim's Progress: From This World to That Which Is to Come*, edited by C.J. Lovik, illustrated by Mike Wimmer, (Wheaton, Ill: Crossway, 2009), 163.
4. Ibid., 163-64.
5. Joni Eareckson Tada, *A Place of Healing: Wrestling with the Mysteries of Suffering, Pain and God's Sovereignty* (Colorado Springs: CO: David C. Cook Publishing, 2010*)*, 174.

Chapter 5 How Do I Handle My Guilt?

Arthur Bennett, editor, *The Valley of Vision: A Collection of Puritan Prayers & Devotions* (Carlisle, PA: Banner of Truth Trust, 2007), 84.
1. John Piper, *When the Darkness will not Lift* (Wheaton, IL: Crossway Books, 2006), 21.

Chapter 6 What's Going on with My Body and Mind?

Arthur Bennett, editor, *The Valley of Vision: A Collection of Puritan Prayers & Devotions* (Carlisle: PA: Banner of Truth Trust, 2007), 75.
1. John Piper, *When the Darkness Will not Lift* (Wheaton, IL: Crossway Books, 2006) 25-26.
2. Edward T. Welch, *Blame It on the Brain* (Phillipsburg, N.J.: P&R, 1989), 212.
3. Ibid.
4. Wes Burgess, *The Depression Answer Book* (Naperville, IL: SourceBooks, 2009)150.
5. John Piper, *When I Don't Desire God: How to Fight for Joy*, (Wheaton, IL: Crossway Books, 2004), 20.

Chapter 7 How Do I Deal with My Fear, Worry, and Anxiety?

Arthur Bennett, editor, *The Valley of Vision: A Collection of Puritan Prayers & Devotions* (Carlisle, PA: Banner of Truth Trust, 2007), 196.
1. Jerry Bridges, *Trusting God Even When Life Hurts* (Colorado Springs: CO: NavPress, 26.
2. Ibid.
3. Ken & Joni Eareckson Tada, *Joni & Ken: An Untold Love Story* (Grand Rapids, MI: Zondervan, 2013), 25- 26.

Chapter 8 How Do I Express My Grief to God?

Arthur Bennett, editor, *The Valley of Vision: A Collection of Puritan Prayers & Devotions* (Carlisle, PA: Banner of Truth Trust, 2007), 171.
1. Ronald B. Allen, *And I Will Praise Him: A Guide to Worship in the Psalms* (Grand Rapids, MI: Kregel Publications, 1999), 19.
2. *D.A. Carson, Scandalous The Cross and Resurrection of Jesus* ((Wheaton, IL: Crossway Books, 2010), 33.
3. D.A. Carson, *How Long, O Lord: Reflections on Suffering and Evil* (Grand Rapids, MI: Baker Academic, 2006), 141.
4. James Montgomery Boice, *Psalms Vol. 1,* (Grand Rapids, MI: Baker 2005), 107.

Chapter 9 Is Joy Out of the Question?

Arthur Bennett, editor, *The Valley of Vision: A Collection of Puritan Prayers & Devotions* (Carlisle, PA: Banner of Truth Trust, 2007), 162.
1. John Piper, "True Christianity: Inexpressible Joy in the Invisible Christ" (sermon, Bethlehem Baptist Church, Minneapolis, MN, November 14, 1993), http://www.desiringgod.org/resource-library/sermons/true-christianity-inexpressible-joy-in-the-invisible-christ (accessed September 10, 2012).
2. Greg Harris, *The Cup and the Glory: Lessons on Suffering and the Glory of God*, (The Woodlands, TX: Kress Christian Publications, 2006), 45.
3. John Piper, *When I Don't Desire God How to Fight for Joy*, (Wheaton, IL: Crossway Books, 2004), 16.
4. Ken & Joni Eareckson Tada, *Joni & Ken: An Untold Love Story* (Grand Rapids, MI: Zondervan, 2013), 80-81.
5. Nancy Guthrie, Holding On to Hope: A Pathway through Suffering to the Heart of God (Wheaton, IL: Tyndale Publishing, 2002) quoted from Dietrich Bonhoeffer Works, Vol 4 (Fortress Press, 2001) reprinted from the German

edition published in 1937 and then The Cost of Discipleship, (N.Y., N.Y.: Macmillan Co, 1949), 79.

6. John Piper, *When I Don't Desire God How to Fight for Joy*, (Wheaton, IL: Crossway Books, 2004), 137.
7. Ibid., 138.
8. Ibid., 20-21.

Chapter 10 How Does the Caregiver Cope?

Arthur Bennett, editor, *The Valley of Vision: A Collection of Puritan Prayers & Devotions* (Carlisle, PA: Banner of Truth Trust, 2007), 158.

1. Alexander Whyte, "Lady Culross," Letter Written to her from Samuel Rutherford, http://www. Fire and Ice: Puritan and Reformed Writings (accessed June 23, 2013).
2. "Captive Faith," Letter LXXX [80] from *The Letters of Samuel Rutherford,* FOR MARION MACKNAUGHT (accessed June 23, 2013).
3. Mary Somerville, *One with a Shepherd: The Tears and Triumphs of a Ministry Marriage* (The Woodlands, TX: Kress Christian Publications, 2005).
4. Edward T. Welch, *Depression: Looking Up from the Stubborn Darkness* (New Growth Press, 2011) 225.
5. John Piper, *When the Darkness will not Lift* (Wheaton, IL: Crossway Books, 2006), 74.
6. Ken & Joni Eareckson Tada, *Joni & Ken: An Untold Love Story* (Grand Rapids, MI: Zondervan, 2013), 30.

CPSIA information can be obtained at www.ICGtesting.com
Printed in the USA
LVOW10s1156040115

421444LV00022B/337/P

9 781498 407779